THE CLEVER COOK

THE CLEVER COOK

DIANE HOLUIGUE

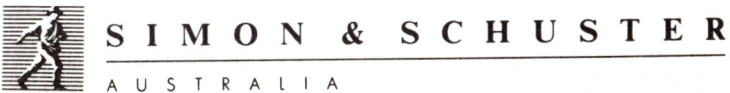

SIMON & SCHUSTER

AUSTRALIA

Note: The metric to imperial conversions in this book are in proportion, but are approximate only. Please use either metric weights and measures or imperial weights and measures, not a combination of the two.

THE CLEVER COOK

First published in Australia in 1994 by Nationwide News
This new and fully revised edition published in Australia in 1995 by
Simon & Schuster Australia
20 Barcoo Street, East Roseville NSW 2069

Viacom International
Sydney New York London Toronto Tokyo Singapore

Text copyright © 1994, 1995 Diane Holuigue
Illustrations copyright © 1995 Penny Lovelock

National Library of Australia
Cataloguing in Publication data

Holuigue, Diane.
        The clever cook.

        Includes index.
        ISBN 0 7318 0537 2.

        1. Quick and easy cookery. 2. Cookery. I. Title.

        641.5

Cover designed by Megan Smith
Designed and typeset by Joy Eckermann
Illustrations by Penny Lovelock
Printed by Australian Print Group

CONTENTS

INTRODUCTION

The modern-day cook is informed and inquisitive. In the 25 years I have run The French Kitchen (my cooking school based in Melbourne, Australia), interest in good food has sky-rocketed. The Anglo-Saxon 'short-order cook' who prepared only roasts, three veg and grilled steaks has given way to a sophisticated food-lover embracing a whole world of different cuisines, new ideas and new produce.

In any cosmopolitan city we are now exposed to an enormous variety of eating habits — Chinese, Italian, Eastern European, French and South-East Asian. Some 85 per cent of households now own a wok. At school we learn to make satays, stir-fries and French onion soup between lessons on scone-making and pavlova, and we eat out at excellent restaurants representing all these styles.

The variety of produce available has burgeoned enormously, and we can now afford to idolise the fresh — we have it in constant, wondrous supply. Seemingly daily, new vegetables, new seafoods and different cuts of meat appear to appease the demands of the Vietnamese community, the Calabrian, or food buffs reading up on Californian cuisine. In addition, what we don't grow in the south, we manage to grown in the north, bequeathing us a peculiarly unique problem — an innocent lack of respect for the seasons quite unbecoming to the aspiring gourmet.

This plethora, and the fact that it is all so affordable, allows us to turn our hand to a fabulous variety of meals. Our lifestyle, however, is far from that of a French or Vietnamese mother who spends the day totally absorbed in marketing and preparing food for the family.

So the newest — and perhaps the most essential — ingredient in the modern cook's kitchen is, to use a good old-fashioned word, *nous*. Brains, intelligence . . . call it what you will. The modern cook needs to be a clever cook. He or she knows it is not enough to arm oneself with recipes. Recipes are for cooking for an occasion. They are for inspiration, for reference, and for preparing the shopping list. But if a cook wants to use the latest product found yesterday in the market, or try to copy a dish that excited elsewhere, or simply use up the products in the fridge that are now a somewhat mixed bag of left-overs from last week's shopping — if only one could figure a way to put them all together — then searching in a recipe book is not going to solve the problem.

A clever cook can instantly spot the cooking technique that lies behind the dish tasted last night at that new little bistro. A clever cook has spent time smelling, tasting and touching — and knows the flavour, texture and unique properties of every ingredient and how each reacts in cooking. A clever cook easily reads the possibilities held by those left-overs in the fridge, and knows which ones have an affinity for each other. A clever cook instantly takes into account the amount of time there is to prepare dinner, and knows that a chicken casserole requires 1–1$^{1}/_{2}$ hours cooking plus time to joint the chicken, whereas a roast takes 50 minutes and, if chicken breasts, a pan-fry would take only 10 minutes.

And a clever cook will certainly know that if there are some well-chosen garnish vegetables or herbs in the crisper, a variety of stocks in the freezer, alcohols or vinegars in the pantry, or cream in the fridge, then there is no need to serve those chicken breasts the same way each night — a simple sauce can be stirred up from the sediment on the base of the pan or the roasting dish.

This book is designed to help you become that clever cook.

What good is a cook who can only follow recipes? The clever cook grasps an idea in one recipe and applies it to many. Having twigged to a basic technique, it is possible to soar — easily — to great culinary heights. You only need to generalise that technique and use your imagination as a springboard to develop a whole hoard of related recipes. Faced with wonderful fresh produce in the market, you will buy without hesitation, and, using experience and those little grey cells, produce a meal without the slightest difficulty.

This, then, is an ideas book — written for people who already love to cook and for those who aspire to become better cooks. It provides some essential facts to ensure the reader starts from a solid methodology, but is laced with ideas to stimulate and to broaden your culinary horizons. It urges you to take your fate into your own hands in the kitchen and to cook with confidence — to spread your wings, take flight and develop your own personal style.

Happy cooking!

FABULOUS FAST FOOD
FROM THE HOME SHELF

Some people think fast food is what you buy from the takeaway shop down the street. I think of fast food as food I can make quickly. I'll pit my fast food against anyone's — and guarantee it's a lot more tasty and can never be nicknamed 'junk food'.

Fast food in the home depends, above all, on having the right ingredients on hand. The trick is to make that shopping trip at the beginning of the week count, and to fill the pantry, freezer and fridge with 'tools' to help you whip up something quickly when cooking time is down to a minimum.

In my house, back-up support comes from fresh herbs in the garden, a few staple vegetables in the fridge, and beef, chicken and fish stock made in large batches every so often and stored in 300 ml (10 fl oz) plastic cartons in the freezer. I also have an amazing array of bottles and jars and cans of the better class of preserved products found in the supermarket.

There is a lot of good, helpful canned food on the market; you simply need to know which ones are worthwhile and how to make them even better. I can't be forced to eat canned asparagus, for example. There's not a brand that can possibly replace the real thing. But I am a great fan of canned tomatoes. I would rather heat canned tomatoes, squash them with a potato masher and add bottled chopped chilli, than open a can of not-so-great Bolognese sauce to put on my spaghetti.

Pasta is one of the great all-time speedy dishes. It can be whipped up at any time with ingredients from the fridge. Try blanching a few chopped pieces of green vegetables, throwing them in a frying pan with a little butter to bring out the colour, stirring in some cream and then tossing this mixture through drained, cooked spaghetti or fettuccine. Serve with grated Parmesan, also from the fridge. If the available vegetables are red rather than green, aim for crispness and finish with oil. For example, capsicum (bell pepper), parsley, fresh herbs, capers (buy only the tiny ones in jars, or keep a packet of salted ones and rinse them as needed) and sun-dried tomatoes from a jar make up the pasta on page 49. Chopped bacon and eggs make a classic carbonara — but I don't want to take up all this space on pastas. The fact is, though, it's great fast food — from the home cupboard.

Canned tomatoes also make a great soup, diluted with water or water and canned tomato juice, and heavily laced just before serving with loads of freshly chopped chives, parsley and spring onions (scallions). There's also a good little product in bottles called *passata di pommodoro* —Italian-style crushed tomatoes. They make a good start for a Neapolitan sauce for pasta, and can also be watered down and seasoned with plenty of black pepper and chopped basil or spring onions (scallions) for soup. Before we leave the topic of tomatoes, however, remember to buy a bottle of sun-dried tomatoes in olive oil — try a few of them cut and scattered over a couple of sliced fresh tomatoes with black pepper, shredded basil and a drizzle of virgin olive oil for a great starter. If you've got some mozzarella or bocconcini to slice as well, it will be even better.

Still on the subject of speedy preparation — make sure you take advantage of the new salad mixes that the greengrocer now sells by the tongful, and have on hand different flavoured oils and vinegars. Used as a nest, *mesclun* (mixed baby salad leaves) makes a wonderful base for shredded poultry or smoked trout, as well as for fried chicken fillet, seared scallops, prawns (shrimps) and other warm foods.

Any green peppercorns in the pantry? A tablespoon of green peppercorns and their brine from the can will dress any number of dishes. In three minutes you can steam or fry a piece of fish, in five minutes you can fry a steak, veal or a fat-free pork escalope. When cooked (in butter, not oil, if you're adding cream), remove it from the pan, add the green peppercorns and a bit of cream, stir up all the sediment from the base of the pan to form a sauce, and spoon over the chosen food. Pink peppercorns can be used in a similar way, but with a completely different effect — less peppery and more vinegary. Compare the two.

There's an Italian bottled product on the market called *pasta d'oliva*. It's a black olive paste, or spread. There are several brands available in better delicatessens. It keeps well, and I always have it on hand, as I do a jar of black olives. I can make a fish meal in five to six minutes using these products.

I take a fillet of fish — actually, you can choose one long fillet and cut it later at table, or several chunky pieces of about 130 g ($4^{1}/_{2}$ oz) each. I use ling or blue eye for preference. Simply wrap it in foil with a bit of parsley and some roughly chopped chives. Onto this chop slivers of black olives. Sometimes I even open a jar of artichoke hearts and slice some of these over the fish too. Grind black pepper all over, drizzle with virgin olive oil, seal the foil and cook the fish in the oven at 200°C (400°F) for about six minutes (depending on the thickness of the fillet). When I serve the fish, I place a little *quennelle* of black olive paste on the side, spooned directly from the bottle and formed between two teaspoons to make an attractive shape. Not even a pan to wash!

I make a great five-minute oyster soup with 24 bottled oysters (the cheap ones the oystermongers sell when they break them opening the shells, not those sold in vinegar). For this you need to have fish stock on hand, and I do again urge you to use a rainy day to ensure a supply of stocks in the freezer. You can make my soup by pouring 300 ml (10 fl oz) of fish stock into a pot and bringing it to the boil with a julienne of carrot and green beans and the oyster water, seasoning with pepper (no salt, oysters are salty), and then tipping in the oysters just as you turn off the heat. If you are serving the soup to guests, you should be able to top it with parsley and cream without having to go further than the fridge.

If I haven't bought the oysters, I use a can of oyster soup, dilute it with fish stock instead of water, add a can of oysters and their brine, and finish in the same way. The potential is always right there in the cupboard.

While we're on seafood, sauté some prawns (shrimps) and add bottled Chinese chilli sauce or oyster sauce — Hoisin if you prefer a sweet sauce. Three minutes is all it takes, frying in 3 tablespoons of oil then coating well with the sauce. Chopped chives or spring onions (scallions) dress the dish further if you have these on hand.

The secret of all the above 'fast food' is a well-stocked pantry, fridge and garden. Rest assured these need not be particularly unusual products to get a good effect. I sometimes buy a veal kidney, chop it up and sauté it in a little oil, and, as it fries (2–3 minutes maximum so it doesn't go rubbery), I add a dash of tomato sauce (ketchup) from the bottle, a dash of Worcester sauce and a little water. Served with mashed potatoes it pleases my family much more than all the simmered French-style kidney dishes I have ever made.

Elsewhere in this book we will touch on the many different flavours of oil on the market (page 37), but don't forget the vinegars, too, or the alcohols. I pan-fry duck breasts (they're not just chic — they take less time to fry than a steak), deglaze the pan with blackcurrant vinegar and add a couple of tablespoons of bottled black or red currants with a bit of their juice, stirring up the sediment on the base of the pan as I go. I do the same with Cassis liqueur along with the currants on other occasions, and I'm known to change the meat to venison or a chicken fillet.

Ducks love figs, and they combine divinely. Pan-fry the duck fillets and deglaze with Stone's green ginger wine and a bit of beef stock (even stock can now be bought in little cartons, but try to make reserves on a slow day and keep it in the freezer). While you're stirring up the sediment and boiling it down to a sauce, heat some fresh figs in a small saucepan and serve alongside the fanned-out duck slices sitting on (it's more attractive than under) the spooned-out sauce.

Packet couscous is another great standby when you're in a hurry. You simply pour on boiling water and a couple of tablespoons of oil. Some brands need to be steamed for a few minutes, but others are instant — check on the packet. It is great as a soft, not-too-filling accompaniment to anything you may have put rice with. By adding many of those left-over vegetables in the fridge, you can make up a dish akin to fried rice. Here, too, I'm inclined to add chopped chilli, another great standby in a bottle. On page 143 you'll find further ideas for this marvellous grain.

Great tastes, minimum fuss. All with a little help from some friends in the pantry, faster than most 'fast food', and much more appetising. I promise!

THE CLEVER COOK'S TOOLS

Below is your guide to being well stocked and ready to prepare a great meal — out of thin air. Over and above the obvious staples, here are some basics to have on hand always:

Freezer
- Stocks, clearly marked, frozen in ice cream or cream cartons in convenient quantities
- *Demi-glace* (page 225) frozen in 250 ml (8 fl oz) containers. Can be gouged out by the spoonful to improve a gravy or pan-fried dish
- Crêpes, separated by plastic wrap
- Tomato paste, stored in a plastic container
- Puréed raspberries and mangoes, unsweetened or with 10 per cent sugar
- Vanilla icecream
- Green prawns (shrimp), school 'baby' prawns and scallops, loose-frozen
- Bunches of dill and French tarragon (two herbs that can be sliced while still frozen)
- Compound butters (page 134)
- Peanuts, almond meal, sliced and slivered almonds, pecans, walnuts, macadamias, pine nuts and hazelnuts

Refrigerator
- Cream
- Olives, black and green
- Bottled black olive paste or Tapenade
- Gruyère (Swiss) and Parmesan cheese, plus a variety for the table
- Sliced ham/tongue and smoked chicken (to julienne for pan-fries, or shred for composed salads)
- Pink peppercorns
- Bottled sun-dried tomatoes in olive oil
- Jars of Thai red and yellow curry pastes
- Bottled chilli paste, sambal oelek or harissa (page 147), which keeps for several months as long as oil is above the solid levels.
- Smooth apricot jam and redcurrant jelly
- Preserved shredded or sliced ginger (from Japanese supermarkets)
- 'Napoleon' gravy — left-over gravy from a roast refrigerated to reinforce the next one. Remove the grease (which has shut out the oxygen and preserved it) prior to re-using

- Home-made mayonnaise (page 158)
- Cold bottle of sugar syrup at 30 Baumé (ratio: 1 cup sugar to 1 cup water), for poaching fruit, and, with puréed fruit, can be the basis of a granita or sorbet that can be made in 20 minutes
- Fresh vegetables. Apart from a variety for the week, always have on hand carrots, leeks, celery, onions, spring onions (scallions), fresh ginger, parsley, chives and *mesclun* (mixed baby salad leaves)

Pantry
- Sultanas (golden raisins) and dried muscatels
- Two blocks of dark cooking chocolate
- Dried French tarragon — it's better than the Russian in the garden. (Most other herbs should be used only fresh.)
- Cloves, mace, coriander seeds, cumin, cinnamon, fennel and dill seed, dry ginger, juniper berries, star anise — good spices; a few dried herbs, such as thyme and tarragon, as a safeguard
- Couscous
- Preserved lemon (page 147)
- Julienne of lemon, lime and orange peel cooked in heavy sugar syrup, bottled in the syrup and on hand for garnishes
- Variety of interesting oils and vinegars
- Thai fish sauce (nam pla)
- Soy sauce
- Range of dried pastas
- Cans of coconut milk, Roma (plum) tomatoes, tomato paste, artichoke bottoms and bases, quail eggs, tiny first-quality champignons, green peppercorns, canned oysters (fresh and smoked), red salmon, hearts of palm, water chestnuts
- Canned oyster soup, beef consommé and/or stocks
- Brandy, vermouth, Madeira, kirsch, brown rum, Grand Marnier or Cointreau, Crème de Cassis or Framboise, red and white wine, and very dry cider
- Lots of seasonal fresh fruit

Garden
- Parsley, chives, sage, rosemary, basil, chervil, oregano, mint, sorrel for sauces, and nasturtiums for salads

APPETISERS

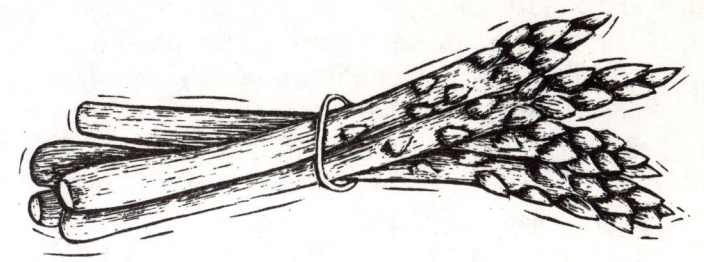

JUST FOR STARTERS

Appetisers are openers. They are designed to lead you into a meal . . . gently, but with impact. They make a statement about the type of occasion, about the style of food to follow, about the season, and about you. Will it be a formal occasion — best crockery, best tablecloth, formal food? Will it be outdoors — around the pool, a picnic in the park or on the beach? Will it be an informal Sunday night around a fire, or a casual get-together with friends? Will your guests be sitting upright in their best clothes, or relaxed in their jeans seated around a large trestle? Will they serve themselves or be served, use knives and forks or take from a platter with paper napkins?

Planning a menu should be half the fun, and above all it should reflect the atmosphere you want to set. Having chosen the type of occasion, most people tend to choose the main course first, closely followed by the dessert. For the most part, these things come together nicely, although beware the cook who puts together all their favourite recipes only to find that each one has cream in it, is the same colour, or uses a different type of nut or some other ingredient that will unbalance the meal.

The appetiser comes last in most people's thoughts. But last is not a bad thing. If you choose the appetiser last, you have such a range to select from that you can easily put balance back into the meal and correct any faults you have inadvertently built in. It goes something like this . . .

Too much cream in the rest of the menu? Choose something light and crunchy to start with. Much too bland? Pick something a little more provocative and controversial; a shock to the palate. Lacking colour? Balance out with a large plate of *antipasti,* or a salad of lots of little mixed greens with fish or seafood on top, or perhaps some goat cheese and red capsicum (bell pepper) bruschetta (Italian-style fried bread first rubbed with garlic) to pass around before you start. No vegetables? Then choose a vegetable starter. Dishes like halved eggplant (aubergine), zucchini (courgette) or cucumber can be baked with ratatouille or ham and rice stuffings. Try a couple of prawns (shrimp) with sliced honey melon and rockmelon (cantaloupe), and a dob of mango chutney, or the Italian classic, fig and melon with prosciutto. I often serve a tartlet per person filled with a pan-fried mix of summer vegetables of all colours (yellow and green zucchini (courgette), lobes of green and red capsicum (bell pepper), baby corn, snow peas (mangetout), slices of thin Japanese eggplant (aubergine), etc.) cooked quickly and served with blackened butter. Blackened butter may sound frightening, but it is a classic idea. Cook the butter to a deep hazelnut colour then throw a little vinegar in, which sizzles and creates a tangy sauce. I then pile the vegetables into the pre-cooked tartlets — the higher the mound, the better — and spoon the black butter over them. It's delicious, crisp, and a dramatic way to start a meal that may otherwise be low in vegetable content or colour.

In the social context, the beginning of a meal is the most awkward time of the evening. Having drinks with the guests, seating them at the table, 'breaking the ice' and getting the evening flowing are the responsibilities that take priority. The clever cook knows that something easily heated like soup or, better still, something prepared in advance and served cold or cool, are the dream starters. Because the dish is an introduction, keep it light, fresh and, if possible, colourful, so that it greets the eye and starts the dinner off with a stylish punch. If possible, use the products of the season; your guests will know you're not just pulling out your 'tried and trues'.

The Carpaccio of Atlantic Salmon is for the more formal occasion, the Chicken Liver Terrine suits the buffet or the outdoor trestles, and there is a variety of salads which can appear casual or formal depending on the prettiness or the prestige of the combined ingredients. An inventively topped pizza is a bit of fun, modern and chic in style, and may serve, like the bruschetta mentioned above, to pass around at drinks parties. Some pastas which do well as starters, but can also act as one-course meals are included. And don't forget that there are dishes in the soup, fish and seafood chapters that can also be served as appetisers.

All the following dishes are tasty, have 'this year's' feel, and will start your meal with pizazz.

CARPACCIO OF FRESH SALMON

Serves 6

400 g (12 oz) piece of Atlantic or Pacific salmon fillet
(cut from the central, or thickest, section)
3 tablespoons very finely chopped
red, green and yellow capsicum (bell pepper)
1 tablespoon very finely chopped cucumber or
raw zucchini (courgette)

1 tablespoon lemon juice
4–5 tablespoons best quality extra virgin olive oil
cracked or coarsely ground black pepper

Cut the salmon lengthways into as many thin slices as possible. Lay each slice in turn between leaves of baking parchment and lightly tap with a meat mallet or rolling pin until each slice extends, without mashing or making holes. Transfer 2 or 3 slices per person (depending on the size of the finished slices) to dinner plates. Scatter the salmon slices with the finely chopped vegetables (when chopped this size, they are known as a *brunoise*), drizzle with the lemon juice and olive oil, then season to taste with black pepper.

Variation

Substitute tuna or swordfish for the salmon. I have also seen a version with very lightly seared then roasted (but still pink) veal, which approaches the original dish done with raw beef at Harry's Bar in Venice. Veal must be cut very thinly, but preferably not bashed with the mallet — neither should beef be, even if served raw. Try freezing the piece of meat first as an aid to slicing thinly. If you're a fan of edible flowers, you may prefer a 'confetti' of chopped colourful flowers to the vegetable *brunoise*.

GATEAU OF SMOKED SALMON

Serves 8

400 g (12 oz) smoked salmon offcuts
300 ml (10 fl oz) cream
freshly ground black pepper
8–10 large, top-quality slices smoked salmon

The cucumber coulis

1/2 medium cucumber, peeled, seeded and diced
1–2 tablespoons olive oil
1 tablespoon white wine vinegar
salt and pepper

The garnish

red salmon eggs (salmon roe)
watercress or mustard and cress
triangles of toast

Equipment: 16 cm (6 1/2 in) cake ring or springform tin without a base

Place the salmon offcuts in a food processor and work to a purée, adding cream after the mix has broken down. Pepper the mixture and set aside.

Place the cake ring on a flat wooden board. Cover the base and walls with a large piece of plastic wrap, then carefully line the base of the mould with overlapping smoked salmon slices, in such a way as to line the walls as well. Use the thinner end of the salmon towards the centre of the mould; the wider edge then covers the larger diameter of the outer part of the ring.

Pour the puréed mixture into the salmon-lined mould and spread evenly. Fold any overlapping slices inwards. Allow to set in the refrigerator for at least 2 hours before removing it from the mould.

The cucumber coulis: Place the diced cucumber in the food processor and work to a purée with the olive oil and vinegar. Season with salt and pepper.

To serve: Unmould the gâteau by inverting it onto a serving plate and peeling away the plastic wrap. Decorate the top with the salmon roe, perhaps in little teaspoonsful designating each serve — a little like rosettes on a cake. Cut into wedges, and serve with the cucumber coulis and a sprig of watercress. Pass around a breadbasket full of triangles of fresh toast with which to eat it.

CHICKEN LIVER TERRINE

A rough, country-style pâté, great to have on hand in the fridge as a speedy starter or picnic fare. Best made three days in advance, it is traditionally served sliced on crusty bread with continental gherkins.

Makes 12–14 slices

500 g (1 lb) chicken livers
4 teaspoons salt
freshly ground black pepper
$^1/_2$ teaspoon nutmeg
100 ml ($3^1/_2$ fl oz) brandy
600 g ($1^1/_4$ lb) pork neck
350 g (11 oz) speck (brined pork fat) plus *enough in sheets to line the mould (optional)*
2 eggs
50 ml ($1^1/_2$ fl oz) milk
24 pistachio nuts, peeled
fresh thyme leaves

Equipment: 1.5 L ($2^1/_2$ pt) pâté mould (terrine) or loaf tin; bain-marie filled with hot water

To prepare the terrine: The day before, pick over the chicken livers; discard the nerves and any sign of bile. Sprinkle with a little of the salt, pepper and nutmeg and drizzle with the brandy. Cover the dish with plastic wrap and refrigerate overnight.

The next day, mince the pork neck and speck together. Separately, mince one-third of the chicken livers and mix with the first mince. Add the remaining salt, pepper and nutmeg, then the eggs and milk. Blend well. Cut the rest of the livers lengthways into pieces, and fold into the mixture along with the pistachio nuts and the brandy from the maceration.

Line the mould with the sheets of speck. (If you cannot get sheet speck, it is possible to make the pâté without it, but then it is served sliced from the mould rather than turned out). Sprinkle the base of the mould with fresh thyme leaves, then place the mixture in the mould.

To cook the terrine: Place the terrine in a bain-marie of hot water. Cook in the oven at 250°C (500°F) for 45 minutes, then reduce heat to 100°C (210°F) and continue cooking for a further 1 hour 20 minutes. Remove from the bain-marie to cool; refrigerate for at least 24 hours before cutting.

ASPARAGUS MIMOSA

Serves 6

1.5 kg (3 lb) asparagus, peeled and ends trimmed
2 hard-boiled eggs, whites and yolks sliced separately
1 bunch fresh dill, finely chopped

The sauce
75 ml (2¹/₂ fl oz) egg mayonnaise
150 ml (5 fl oz) cream, whipped until firm
salt and pepper
remainder of the hard-boiled eggs
2 tablespoons chopped dill

Place a rack in a wide saucepan of boiling, salted water. Lay the asparagus on the rack with the tips all pointing in the same direction. Depending on the thickness of the stems, it should cook until tender, but still be a vibrant green, in about 4 minutes. (All undercooked asparagus is tough, and overcooked asparagus loses colour.) Lift the rack out of the saucepan and quickly plunge the asparagus into cold water. (This prevents it from cooking any further and preserves its colour.) When cool, drain on a tea towel, then set aside to cool further.

When ready, place the asparagus, tips aligned, on small serving plates. Decorate by layering the stalk end (not the tips) with a line of sliced egg white, then sliced yolks, then finely chopped dill, placed side by side. This should not be done more than an hour before eating, as the dish dries out easily.

The sauce: Place the mayonnaise in a bowl and fold in the whipped cream. Season with salt and pepper and finish with the remaining egg and the dill.

ONION AND GOAT CHEESE TARTLETS

<u>Serves 6</u>

350 g (11 oz) unsweetened shortcrust pastry (or puff pastry, if preferred)
70 g (2¹/₂ oz) butter
8 onions, sliced into rings
salt and pepper
3 heaped tablespoons thick (double) cream
8-10 sun-dried tomatoes, chopped
1 tablespoon dwarf capers, rinsed and drained
6 round slices goat cheese, 6–8 mm (¹/₄ in) thick

The garnish

small salad of witlof (endive) and walnut dressed in extra virgin olive oil
and sherry vinegar vinaigrette
a little extra virgin olive oil
chopped dill or shredded basil

Equipment: 6 tarlet moulds, 10–12 cm (4–5 in) in diameter

Line the tart moulds with pastry and the centre of the pastry with foil. Par-bake in the oven at 200°C (400° F) for about 10 minutes.

Meanwhile, melt the butter in a wide saucepan and sauté the onion rings without browning. Place a sheet of buttered paper butter-side down on top of the onions, then cover with the saucepan lid. Reduce the heat and cook until tender, turning from time to time to avoid scorching. When ready (about 15 minutes), transfer the onions to a bowl. Season with salt and pepper, then blend in the cream and add the sun-dried tomatoes and capers.

Fill the par-baked tartlet shells with the onion mixture, then return to the hot oven until cooked through, about 15–18 minutes.

To serve: When ready to serve, place a disc of cheese in the centre of each tartlet and return to the oven for just enough time to warm the cheese. The sides of the cheese should just begin to soften and wilt, but there should be no real cooking.

Meanwhile, place a small circle of witlof salad in the centre of each of six small serving plates. Place the warm tartlet in the centre of each salad, and drizzle with extra virgin olive oil. Decorate with the dill or basil.

FRESH CHERRY TOMATO
AND GOAT CHEESE TARTLETS

A recipe from Greg Brown of Brown's Bakeries, Melbourne, Australia.

<u>Serves 8</u>

The basil oil
1 bunch basil, stalks removed and set aside, leaves finely chopped
peanut oil

The tartlets
250 g (8 oz) fresh goat cheese
3–4 punnets cherry tomatoes
(about 10–12 per tartlet)
150 g (5 oz) baby spinach leaves, or 1 bunch spinach,
stalks removed and deveined
oil, for sautéing
salt and pepper
8 pre-baked tartlet shells of 12 cm (5 in) diameter,
made from your preferred pastry (pages 191, 194)

The basil oil: (can be prepared in advance). You can use freshly chopped basil and a little fresh olive oil over the tartlets, but if you can spare the time a couple of days in advance, prepare some basil oil. This is a useful herbal oil that will keep for up to 2 or 3 months, and can be put to any number of uses.

To make basil oil, pluck the stalks from the rinsed bunch of basil, then place them in a saucepan and cover with peanut oil. Bring to the boil, then turn off the heat and leave to infuse overnight.

The next day, strain the oil and discard the stalks. Pour the oil into a bowl and stir in the finely chopped basil leaves. You may add more peanut oil if it is too highly flavoured. Transfer the mixture to a sealed jar.

The tartlets: Use a melon baller to cut rounds of goat cheese the same size as the cherry tomatoes. You can peel the tomatoes if you wish, but it is not essential.

Sauté the spinach gently in a little oil; season with salt and pepper. Set aside to cool. Place a thin layer of spinach in the base of the tartlet shells. Arrange the tomatoes in a spiral pattern in the shell, interspersed with 5 or 6 balls of goat cheese. Just before serving, spoon a little basil oil (and some of the leaves from the oil) over the top of the tartlets. Decorate with a fresh basil leaf.

WHICH CAME FIRST . . . ?

We eat it so often and cook with it so regularly that the egg is a part of the kitchen inventory that we take for granted. Here's a little basic knowledge to keep the gremlins out of your egg cookery.

An egg's composition is 30 per cent yolk, 60 per cent white (albumen) and 10 per cent shell. The yolk is about half water, with 16 per cent protein and 32 per cent fat. It is rich in vitamins A and D and in iron, but unfortunately one yolk contains 240 mg of cholesterol (300 mg is the recommended daily intake!). The white is nearly all water, with 11 per cent protein, no fat, and some riboflavin. The good news is that the white does not contain cholesterol. I've been experimenting for my low-cholesterol cooking classes, and nearly all my cake recipes, including sponges, make up just as well with the weight in whites rather than whole eggs.

Whether eggs come from young birds or from old, whether they're brown eggs or white, battery or free-range, there is no difference in their nutritional value, although farm eggs have firmer shells. Major nutritional differences depend much more on the diet of the hen and on the freshness of the eggs you buy.

HOW FRESH IS FRESH? A WORD ON STORAGE

Eggs remain of first quality for about 12 days in a warm room, but for three weeks in a refrigerator. Their actual life is much greater — about five weeks in the refrigerator, where they should be kept in their carton, for the porous shell absorbs odours. The fresher the egg, the thicker the white. A blood spot is not an indication of a fertilised egg, but of a ruptured blood vessel in the yolk. Only about 1 per cent of eggs have a blood spot; simply remove it and use the egg normally.

Eggs are usually graded by weight, and the choice of size is yours as the consumer, but, for the record, in cookery books recipes require a 60 g (2 oz) egg for pastry making — pâtissiers expect the egg to weigh 50–55 g ($1^1/_2$ –$1^3/_4$ oz) after removing the shell.

THE EGG AS AN INGREDIENT

Aside from the simple use of an egg cooked for its own enjoyment, the egg plays five major roles as an ingredient in recipes:

1. **It aerates**: When whisked, an egg traps millions of tiny air bubbles between its molecules. The egg white can reproduce its volume up to six times.

2. **It binds**: An egg, being rather sticky, holds together ingredients that would otherwise crumble, such as croquettes, rissoles, forcemeat, stuffings and pâtés. Its binding effect is essential when

coating fish or other ingredients with breadcrumbs to be fried. When heat is applied, the egg sets and its binding effect is strengthened.

3. **It thickens**: A beaten egg can be used instead of flour to thicken soups, sauces, stews and custards. As the egg is heated it coagulates and holds the liquid in suspension. Never overheat it, as curds result (see 'Making custards' on page 25)

4. **It emulsifies**: A yolk can hold oil or butter in suspension (i.e. exceedingly small fat globules are suspended in the beaten yolk), and this fact is the basis of sauces such as mayonnaise or hollandaise. An acid is added to these sauces to flavour and preserve them, and to keep the emulsion from separating.

5. **It glazes**: The shiny texture of egg gives a gloss to pastry and to icing, for example. You can make an egg wash go further by adding milk or water. The richer glazes use only yolks without the whites.

THE EGG IN ACTION

How to beat or whisk egg whites successfully

For use in a cake, soufflé or mousse, egg whites are best whipped at room temperature. It's also best to use thinner whites — the whites of farm-fresh eggs don't whip! Use whites that you have separated and stored in the refrigerator; they will keep for up to 10 days or a fortnight.

The method of incorporating air into the egg whites (beating) can change the texture of the foam you produce, and thus the molecular structure of the protein strands. These strands can actually break, resulting in overbeaten or 'furry looking' whites that are grainy, with no cohesion between the particles.

In terms of texture, too much air at the beginning will result in wide airholes rather than a firm texture (beer froth rather than snow), so start beating the whites on a slow speed if using an electric mixer, increasing speed as you go. The best and creamiest whites result from hand whisking with a balloon whisk in a copper bowl (or a bowl with a well-rounded base). A hand-held rotary whisk is the next best thing.

When whisking egg whites, remember that any grease or fat, including particles of egg yolk or grease on the utensils, will prevent whites from rising; so too will any water (so be careful when thawing frozen egg whites). Use a metal spoon when folding aerated whites into a mixture because wooden implements retain grease more readily.

Creaming egg yolks and sugar

When sugar is left in contact with egg yolk without stirring, the sugar is said to 'burn' (crystalise) the yolk. Egg yolks and sugar must never be left together, but creamed as soon as they are in contact. Use either a wooden spoon or a rotary or electric mixer, and they will rise to twice their volume and become whiter, lighter and fluffy. This is common procedure for cake and soufflé baking.

Making custards

When making a custard, the egg acts as an enriching ingredient (owing to its fat content) and as a thickener (owing to its action as a binding ingredient). A custard will naturally be thicker the more yolks used per litre (1³/₄ pt) of milk. When making a classic *crème anglaise* (custard with no flour), the usual proportions are three, four or five yolks to the half litre (16 fl oz), depending on whether it is for a custard base (*bavarois*), or for a pouring or spooning custard.

Thickening results as the egg begins to coagulate when heated, but at around 84°C (183°F) the yolks actually firm, and a scrambled texture (curds) results. When this happens, the custard is said to have 'turned'. A simple cooking thermometer can be used as a guide, but it somewhat inhibits your stirring the custard at the edge of the saucepan. Usually recipes suggest that you simply stir the custard thoroughly and dip a spoon in it from time to time. When the custard coats the spoon well, you stop. The thickening effect is very visible, but beware bringing the custard too near the boil. Obviously, the thickness depends both on the heat and the number of egg yolks per litre, but practice leads to being a good judge before long.

Eggs as a soup binding

Known in French cuisine as a 'liaison', egg yolks are often combined with cream and a knob of butter to bind or thicken and enrich soups and sauces. The yolks and cream are combined off the heat, the butter added, and then a little soup or sauce is blended with this mixture in a bowl before being added to the rest of the soup or sauce. Stir well, but never pass the crucial temperature of 84°C (183°F), for if the soup or sauce reheats to the boil, the egg will curdle, giving the soup or sauce a grainy texture, and ceasing to act as a binding agent.

FREEZING EGGS

Whole eggs cannot be frozen in their shells. Hard-boiled eggs will become tough if frozen. But raw eggs that have had their shells removed can be frozen if necessary. Raw whites freeze well, provided they are sealed properly, for water escaping into whites will prevent them whipping into a snow. Freezing yolks or whole eggs is more tricky, for when frozen, the gelatine property of the yolk causes it to thicken or gel. To help retard this process, add either ¹/₈ teaspoon salt or 1¹/₂ teaspoons sugar to each 4 yolks or 2 whole eggs. Label containers with the number of yolks or eggs, and differentiate between those for use in savoury or sweet dishes.

EGG-FLIP!

People either seem to be marvellous omelette-makers or have absolutely no idea how to start. And since this tricky little meal-in-a-moment is, for the most part, real family cuisine, very few cookbooks set out to enlighten the cook in such ordinary matters.

Good omelette-making is in the flick of the wrist or the sleight of the hand, so to speak. But when you're trying to describe it, it seems to take a multitude of words for a simple two-minute technique. I hope this doesn't mean burning your first effort while you're bending over these instructions, but I can't be more concise without being less precise. Read this through thoroughly once and try to envisage the operation before you put the recipe into action. First, a few fundamentals:

- An omelette pan has a deep, rounded edge and traditionally is made of black pressed steel. Pressed steel must be seasoned because it is not rust-proof and because an omelette must be able to slip around in the pan. A non-stick pan will help with this, but rarely makes an omelette with good colour and eye-appeal.

  To season the pan, wash and dry it, then heat it while a third full of oil. Let it cool, then heat the oil a second time. Pour out the oil and wipe the pan clean, but make sure the pan still has a slight greasy coating. After each use, wash and dry the pan quickly (never scour it), and wipe it over with oil each time before putting it away.
- A 20–22 cm (8–9 in) pan is ideal for a three-egg omelette; a 26–28 cm (10–11 in) pan for a five- or six-egg omelette.
- Milk is anathema to an omelette — it renders an omelette heavy and leathery. If you wish to make the eggs go a little further, try adding a tablespoon of water, soda water or beer.
- The best omelettes follow the Chinese and French methods, which are designed to obtain a firm outside and a moist inside. To do this, the mixture is scrambled for about 80 per cent of the cooking time. This is to even up the texture throughout, otherwise the outside becomes leathery while waiting for the inside to cook.

  The trick is to know when to stop scrambling, then to flatten the egg mixture out over the pan for a moment to let it bind together and cook into one piece in the base of the pan. Then it is pushed to the farthest edge of the pan from the handle, both edges folded in towards the centre. The final moment of cooking is done with the omelette perched in the curved edge of the pan wall, to give it its traditional shape when upturned onto the serving plate.

- An omelette may be served plain, but if used as a luncheon or light supper dish, it is most likely to have a flavouring. Ingredients that can be chopped and are unlikely to stick to the pan, such as fresh herbs, are most often served dispersed throughout the egg, but the more bulky fillings, such as chopped vegetables, precooked seafood or chicken, ham and grated cheese, are placed in the centre to warm between the folds of the omelette.

PRAWN OMELETTE

To serve 1: use a 20 cm (8 in) pan and 3 eggs. To serve 2: use a 26 cm (10 in) pan and 5 eggs, and follow the ingredients in square brackets.

3 [5] eggs
1 [2] tablespoon water
salt and pepper
pinch of cayenne pepper
1 tablespoon chopped dill or chives
25 g (1 oz) [35 g / 1¹/₂ oz] butter
3 [5] tiger prawns (shrimps), diced, or 15 [22] school prawns
— cooked, shelled and deveined

Break the eggs into a bowl. Season with salt, pepper and cayenne, and add the dill or chives. Set aside, without stirring, until ready to cook.

Heat the omelette pan well, especially if cooking on an electric hob, as you must, above all, make sure to heat the edge of the pan opposite the handle, where the all-important final browning of the omelette will take place.

When hot, replace the pan flat on the stove, then add the butter. Swirl the butter around the pan, then, as it is melting, quickly whisk the eggs with a fork and pour them into the sizzling butter.

Whisk the eggs in the pan as if you were setting out to make scrambled eggs. Continue this brisk, whisking motion until the eggs are 80 per cent cooked (about 20 seconds), then spread the omelette out to fill the base of the pan. Cook to a nice golden brown, ensuring the middle remains undercooked (about 15 seconds).

Place the cooked prawn pieces in the centre of the omelette. Fold the one third of the omelette nearest the handle back over the prawns. Knock the handle of the pan, tilting the pan away from you and encouraging the omelette to slide over to the edge furthest away from the handle. In a well-seasoned pan, the omelette should slip easily; if not, it can be encouraged with a fork. When the edge of the omelette protrudes over the lip of the pan, fold this far-side third of the omelette back over the centre and the prawn filling. Finish the cooking with the omelette nestling in the curve of the pan.

Unmould the omelette by inverting it onto the serving plate. It is these last two steps that give the omelette its characteristic shape. Serve immediately.

PIPERADE

The traditional omelette of the Basque country. Its technique is markedly different from the classic omelette on the preceding page. It is fried on both sides like an Italian frittata.

<u>Serves 2</u>

6 large eggs
salt and pepper
2 tablespoons water
parsley, chopped
3 tablespoons olive oil
¹/₂ green capsicum (bell pepper), roasted, peeled and sliced lengthways
¹/₂ red capsicum (bell pepper), roasted, peeled and sliced lengthways
1 large tomato, peeled, seeded and cubed
2 cloves garlic, finely chopped
2 small shallots, finely chopped
5 slices prosciutto, torn into pieces
Equipment: 20–22cm (8–9 in) well-seasoned omelette pan

Place the eggs in a bowl with salt and pepper to taste; add the water and parsley. Heat the oil in the pan and quickly stir-fry the capsicum, tomato, garlic, shallots and prosciutto. Whisk the eggs with a fork and pour them over the mixture in the pan. Scramble the eggs with a fork for 30 seconds, then stop forking through to let the eggs set and the underneath colour. Slide the omelette out onto a plate, then upturn it back into the pan and cook the other side for about 1 minute. Serve immediately.

Variations

To make a frittata, use the same technique with any vegetable combination (use at least three different vegetables, but no more than five). Tomatoes, onions, eggplant (aubergine), zucchini (courgette), capsicum (bell pepper) and spinach are common; silver beet (Swiss chard) is one of my favourites.

Remember to fry the vegetables until they wilt and give up their moisture before adding the eggs. Some would say that you should use a smaller pan for this volume of vegetable, and an extra egg, so that the frittata will be higher when unmoulded. Frittata can be eaten hot or cold, cut into wedges.

SHIRRED EGGS WITH SALMON CAVIAR

Serves 4

triangles of toast (crusts removed) or toasted brioche
7 large eggs
2 tablespoons water
25 g (1 oz) butter
salt and pepper
2 tablespoons cream
4 tablespoons salmon caviar

Make the triangles of toast (or better still, toasted brioche) first; keep warm. Set out the plates ready on the bench, for you need to concentrate on the eggs to ensure they don't overcook.

Break the eggs into a bowl; set aside the shells. Add the water, but do not stir. Melt the butter in a saucepan. Spill in the eggs and water, then stir gently — don't overwork or they won't form round, lovely-shaped clumpings. Season with salt and pepper. Just before the mixture sets, stir in the cream.

Transfer a quarter of the mixture to each plate, then arrange a broken eggshell at the apex of each plate to simulate the egg spilling out from the shell. Spoon the caviar around the opposite end from the shell, then place three triangles of toast or toasted brioche attractively on the edge. Serve immediately.

RISOTTI

Classic Italian risotti are starters in their homeland, but also serve as excellent one-course meals, followed simply by salad and cheese. There are many variations (see below), made by changing the main garnishing ingredient, and hence the stock liquid required to flavour it. Changing them is simple, but success depends on your understanding of the true texture of risotto. Two Italian terms sum this up. The rice should be *al dente* (i.e. with a small 'bite' left in its texture), and the whole dish should be *al onde* (i.e. 'on the wave'), or wet enough to move with a rolling action when you shake the pot. This texture comes from the style (and starch content) of the rice it was developed with — the Arborio rice of the Po Valley in Italy, now widely available throughout the world. You cannot make risotto correctly with any other type of rice.

RISOTTO WITH PRAWNS

Serves 6

200 g (7 oz) peeled green prawns (shrimp)
1.5 L (2¹/₂ pt) water or fish stock
75 ml (2¹/₂ fl oz) olive oil
1 very small onion, chopped
2 cloves garlic, finely chopped
500 g (1 lb) Italian Arborio rice
250 ml (8 fl oz) dry white wine
1 tablespoon tomato paste
saffron
salt and pepper
3 tablespoons Italian parsley, chopped
Parmesan cheese, grated

Chop large prawns into pieces; if small, keep them whole. Heat the water or stock until boiling. In a large pot, heat the oil and fry the onion until softened, then add the garlic. Add the rice and stir well, then ladle in 2 cups or so of the water or stock, plus the wine, tomato paste and saffron to add colour. Stir until the liquid is absorbed, then ladle in another 1 cup of boiling water or stock. Continue until the rice is cooked, but still firm (*al dente*). Italian risotto is served fairly wet (*al onde*). Add green prawns for the last 5 minutes. Season with salt and pepper, and stir in the parsley. If adding canned shrimp, do so only when cooking is finished.
   Serve with grated Parmesan cheese.

Note: This recipe is made with fresh green (uncooked) prawns. If your area sells only cooked ones, stir them in at the last moment so as not to double cook, since they would become rubbery. In this case, make a little shrimp-flavoured essence by boiling the heads and carcasses, and add with the liquid to reinforce the flavour. Canned shrimp are acceptable, but again, stir in only at the last minute so they do not mash.

Variations

A variety of risotti can be made with what may be found in the refrigerator, such as shredded chicken, chopped capsicum (bell pepper), asparagus tips, or sliced or cubed mushrooms. (10 g (¹/₃ oz) dried porcini or ceps mushrooms, rehydrated, give a very pungent flavour mixed with a few fresh.)

Although risotti can be made with water, using a fish, chicken or vegetable stock, chosen to match the flavouring ingredients, naturally gives a richer, better result.

RISOTTO NERO

Literally, 'black risotto' after the colour of the squid ink used in the recipe. A southern Italian classic, with a touch of chilli.

Serves 6

3 medium squid or cuttlefish, bought whole, not in tubes
4 tablespoons olive oil
1 small onion, chopped
¹/₂ stalk celery, sliced
2 small cloves garlic, finely chopped
2 Roma (plum) tomatoes, peeled and chopped
400 g (12 oz) Italian Arborio rice
1.5–2 L (2¹/₂ –3¹/₂ pt) fish or seafood stock
200 ml (7 fl oz) dry white wine
2–3 tablespoons ink from the squid
(also available commercially frozen in jars)
1 red chilli, shredded
salt and pepper
dash of Tabasco sauce (optional)
50 g (1¹/₂ oz) unsalted butter
grated Parmesan cheese (optional)

Remove the 'celluloid' (sometimes known as the 'feather') and the 'beak' from the squid. (For cuttlefish, remove cuttle and beak.) Cut the tentacles free, and pierce the ink bags carefully to save the ink. Rinse the tube and slice into rings; set aside with the tentacles, cut into short lengths.

In a large saucepan, heat the oil and sweat the onion and celery for 2 minutes, then add the garlic, tomatoes and rice. In a separate saucepan, bring the fish or seafood stock to the boil (chicken or vegetable stock is the next best thing; water is less successful). Stir the rice until well greased, then add the white wine, squid ink and 2 cups of the boiling stock.

Continue adding the stock by the cupful, stirring the rice until each addition is absorbed before adding the following one. When the rice is nearing the end of cooking (after 12–15 minutes), add shredded chilli and the squid. Season with salt and pepper, and perhaps also a drop of Tabasco sauce. Remove from the stove when the rice is tender, but still *al dente*, and stir in the butter until it melts.

Serve immediately, with or without grated Parmesan cheese.

SUPER SALADS

When I was young a salad was a monstrosity — a slice of lettuce with coleslaw tucked into it, a slice of beetroot, a couple of asparagus spears (usually canned), a square of cheddar cheese and, for no reason at all, a slice of orange, complete with peel. On the side, condensed milk mayonnaise. Oh, the horrors of my youth!

Currently, salads are some of the most interesting dishes on the restaurant menu. All the best chefs show their style with two or three varietal salads of their own, and the range is enormously varied, variable and interesting. There are cold salads based on the myriad of mixed greens and baby vegetables now available; there are hot-on-cold salads served up with any and all types of meat that take the chef's fancy. Pieces of barbecued or roasted meats, from strips of chicken to pheasant or quail, beef fillet marinated in Thai spices, prosciutto and even air-dried kangaroo meat can be found lying on beds of salad greens, crunchy green blanched vegetables or freshly steamed baby vegetables.

The dressings vary in ways we would once never have imagined — vinaigrettes made from extra virgin olive, peanut, grape seed, safflower and any number of other oils are combined with vinegars made from red and white wines, sherry and Champagne, and flavoured with everything from raspberries and blackcurrants to chilli or green peppercorns. Better chefs use puréed fruits through the dressing to give an added dimension to both flavour and texture. To dress up the plate, garnishes now include black olives, fetta and goat cheeses, sun-dried tomatoes, dwarf capers, julienne of pickled ginger or chilli, snow peas (mangetout), peas, snap peas, snake beans, small fruits like raspberries or redcurrants, and prawns (shrimp), yabbies (crawfish or écrevisses) and Moreton Bay bugs (slipper or hammer-headed lobsters).

The salad is in its heyday, and the combinations are both eye-appealing and delicious. Here are some examples . . . the clever cook will doubtless find many, many more.

- Peeled, cooked yabbies (crawfish or écrevisses) or prawns (shrimp), or both combined, make a lovely salad when mixed with blanched asparagus tips, blanched fresh green peas and blanched sugar or snow peas (throw them all into the same pot of water in the order of their cooking time, rinse under cold water then drain well). Toss together in a bowl with a few torn salad leaves, and dress with a classical gravelax dressing (in a blender, combine 3 tablespoons French mustard and a dash of powdered mustard with 2 tablespoons sugar, 2 tablespoons white wine, 3 tablespoons chopped dill and 8 tablespoons light olive or peanut oil; keeps in a jar for weeks). To make it decorative, I serve this salad in a square grid of large asparagus spears, and at Christmas, add a few tiny bunches of fresh redcurrants for colour.

- Blanched or seared scallops mix well with chopped (unpeeled) Granny Smith apples and can be dressed simply in a light olive oil and vinegar dressing or even a light mayonnaise, thinned down with yoghurt if you want it tasting more tart and less creamy. Serve a little pile of these on a plate, dotted with a few raspberries or fresh lychees as the season comes in. For contrasting green on the plate, try a border of rocket or lamb's tongue lettuce (*mâche*); both flavours complement this salad well.

- Cold fish has not been everyone's favourite salad ingredient, but try using left-overs cut into chunky pieces and tossed with chopped cashew or macadamia nuts, small slices of celery, and a few capers. Add tomato if you like; being a fish lover I add some chopped anchovy, then bind it all together with a light mayonnaise.

- There is nothing so slimming, nor so beautiful, as a sliced tomato salad when summer tomatoes are at their finest. Slice thinly, intersperse with little chunks of bocconcini or mozzarella as the Italians do if you wish, drizzle with rich extra virgin olive oil, and finish with shredded basil. If you prefer it richer, drizzle with basil oil (page 22) instead; if you want a modern touch, top with a little shredded sun-dried tomato or garnish with lampshade or cherry tomatoes.

- A more modern version of this salad comes with access to a goat cheese *crottin*, the name given to the small whole goat cheeses you can now find on the shelves in numerous degrees of maturation. Take a fresh or semi-matured cheese, place it on oil-fried croûton and bake in a hot oven until the cheese warms and its edges begin to slacken and melt slightly. Don't over-bake as this will ruin the natural texture of the cheese. Transfer immediately to a large serving plate and surround with a few sprigs of dwarf frisé (curly endive) or, failing that, rocket. Dot with small cubes of apple and walnut kernel, and dress with a vinaigrette of walnut oil and cider vinegar, adding, if desired, a teaspoon of honey to the dressing.

- Cook some fresh asparagus spears until just tender, allow them to cool, chop into attractively shaped diagonal lengths, add some chopped prosciutto or ham, roasted pine nuts, plumped sultanas (golden raisins) and then loads of fresh pea sprouts. Dress with plain yoghurt and lemon juice, and some shredded mint if you find it refreshing.

- Greek fetta salads traditionally contain chunky pieces of tomato, cucumber and celery. Dotted with black olives, they are finished with olive oil and vinegar, and with teaspoon-sized chunks of fetta.

- Tossed together, boiled artichoke hearts, sliced prosciutto, small black Niçoise or brown Ligurian olives, and chunky pieces of fresh goat cheese are lovely placed on a bed of Cos lettuce or radicchio. The dressing should be Mediterranean in feeling, such as a rich olive oil and red wine vinegar, or try placing olive oil in the blender with basil; the puréed 'basil oil' (page 22) is thick and pungent and looks wonderful poured over almost any salad.

- Mixed blanched vegetables are wonderful in the early summer when many of the tiny dwarf vegetables are available. In boiling, salted water, cook until tender some baby carrots, baby star or pencil zucchini (courgettes), both green and yellow, dwarf eggplants (aubergines) (sometimes these must be sliced to size), baby turnip, baby green beans and snow peas (mangetout) or sugar peas. If still in season, add dwarf golden or red beets, though these must be cooked separately because their colour bleeds. Rinse the vegetables under cold water, drain well and either drizzle with oil and vinegar or, better still, try a light mayonnaise into which you blend canned tuna and some of its brine. This tuna mayonnaise, tossed through the vegetables, gives a really unique flavour, and colour can be added to the top in the form of chopped herbs such as chives, chervil or parsley.

- Smoked chicken or turkey is readily found in butchers and delicatessens. Long, elegant slices of the breast meat look wonderful alongside wedges of roasted, peeled red capsicum (bell pepper) — for a colourful effect, intersperse with yellow capsicum when in season — a wedge cut lengthways from a peeled avocado, and half a mango, cut in strips or simply chunk-cut and turned inside out on its skin. If you are avoiding mayonnaise, these flavours go well with the traditional raita flavours of India — stirred plain yoghurt with a dash of white vinegar and chopped mint.

- A classic favourite chicken salad is the Waldorf, which combines shredded cooked chicken with chopped celery, crisp cubes of apple and walnut kernels. Bind with mayonnaise.

- Try slivers of any cooked poultry — chicken, duck, guinea fowl or pheasant — mixed with shredded celery and carrot, roasted pine nuts, plumped sultanas (golden raisins) and grated lemon or orange zest. Spoon onto a nest of mixed greens or within a border of radicchio, lamb's tongue (*mâche*), rocket or baby spinach leaves.

- And then there's *mesclun*. This is the southern French name given to small-leaved salad greens when they are mixed together. Nowadays many greengrocers do their own mix, so you don't have to buy each lettuce in full quantity, and most mixes are sold by weight.

    The colours, often enhanced by a few flower petals, make an ideal base for all sorts of toppings, both hot and cold. The list is almost endless, but I recommend the following:

    ~Hot chicken breasts, seared on the barbecue, served on a nest of *mesclun* and dressed with a hot vinaigrette and crispy bacon (page 112).

    ~Barbecued or pan-fried (in olive oil) fresh sardines. Deglaze the pan with vinegar or lemon juice, add oil and chopped parsley, then spoon over the sardines on a nest of *mesclun*.

    ~Toss mixed cooked and cooled seafood — mussels, clams, prawns (shrimp), yabbies (crawfish or écrevisses) or bugs (slipper or hammer-head lobsters) — with diced tomato and capers, then spoon over nests of *mesclun* with oil and cider vinegar in the dressing.

See also: Aside from the salads in this section, see also Warm Salad of Tandoori Prawns and Fish (page 73), Rice Noodle Salad with Mixed Seafood (page 77), Chicken Salad with Bacon and Pine Nut Dressing (page 112), Thai Beef Salad (page 138).

CREATIVE SALAD DRESSINGS

Everyone at some time or another gets bored with their own salad dressings. One summer, I took to opening the cupboard and asking my guests to make the dressing. The results were spectacular. Mind you, some of my friends are great cooks! Try these clever ideas:

ITALIAN STYLE

In general, the Italians make the simplest salad dressings. In Italy it is common to simply set cruets of olive oil and vinegar on the table for the diner to drizzle directly over the salad in the ratio that he or she prefers. No salt, no pepper, no other ingredients.

The result depends like no other dressing on the beauty of the basic produce, and Italy makes some of the best. Extra virgin olive oils vary tremendously in flavour, colour, pungency, pepperiness and viscosity. Vinegars are normally made from red wine, occasionally from white, and the area around Modena produces beautiful balsamic vinegars, matured over long periods in varying sizes of oak, juniper and cherrywood casks (a set of seven per series in fact, with a transference from one to the other as the evaporation gives off 'the angel's part' as it matures).

Balsamic vinegar, available from specialist Italian groceries and good supermarkets, is one of the treasures of gastronomy, and can be bought in varying ages of maturity. I have seen them up to 40 years old in Modena, where young women still use it as part of their dowry.

FRENCH STYLE (VINAIGRETTE)

The French combine oils and vinegars of all types, depending on the region they come from. Olive oil is prevalent in the South, peanut in the North, but don't forget the walnut oils of the South-West or the beautiful, but slightly more difficult to find, hazelnut oil. The classic ratio is said to be three parts oil to one part vinegar, or to taste. Chances are if you're not used to olive, walnut or hazelnut oils, you'll cut these heavier oils down to a ratio of two to one. The French love to rub the bowl with garlic rather than add it chopped, but they often add chopped shallots (not spring onions). Then they add a little mustard, salt and pepper. The best vinaigrettes are emulsified to a creamy consistency by whisking the oil into the rest briskly.

Variations then start with the changing of the vinegars. There are many types of vinegar from different sources— red wine, white wine, sherry, Champagne. There are others infused with fruit or vegetable flavours, ranging from shallots, green pepper or chilli oil to the sweeter variations with honey, raspberries or red or black currants. Leave out the vinegar if you wish, but replace it with another acid, such as lemon juice, because dressings need a good balance of acidity to be worthwhile.

Additions then follow, and these are endless. Most obvious are chopped herbs, which give a fresh, crisp pungency. The grassy herbs, known as *fines herbes* — chives, parsley, chervil and tarragon (French tarragon, never Russian) — and basil are the best. Eggs are added both raw (to bind the emulsion and make it creamier) and hard-boiled, with or without other additives such as croûtons, chopped anchovies and bacon. Bacon is often crisped and added with the fat it renders — this particularly suits the firmer greens like Cos (Romaine), radicchio, dwarf frisé (curly endive) and dandelion. Pine nuts, walnuts or hazelnuts (particularly in marriage with the appropriate oils) are common additions, as are the vinegary but not-too-hot pink peppercorns. Summer berry fruits are often tossed in with the appropriate vinegars — fresh redcurrants dropped into salads dressed with redcurrant vinegar are my particular favourite.

MAYONNAISE-BASED DRESSINGS

Apart from dressing a potato salad or maybe a salad of shredded carrot, I find mayonnaise too rich as a dressing. I believe it needs lightening, and the choice is then to lighten with yoghurt, whipped cream (this is aeration only: the taste appears lighter, the ingredients are in fact richer) or a little vinaigrette. For green salads, I actually prefer starting with the vinaigrette base and making it creamier with the addition of a little mayonnaise rather than vice versa. The base flavour of the mayonnaise may be changed by the addition of curry (powder or paste), chopped mint (ideal with the yoghurt-mayonnaise combination), chopped dill (good with fish), tomato paste or even orange juice (combined with a little zest of orange, a whipped cream-diluted orange mayonnaise is excellent to dress fresh asparagus). Mayonnaises can also have chunky things mixed through them to dress larger articles such as fish or meat — hence the invention of sauce tartare with chopped olives, capers and hard-boiled eggs, or the classic sauce Andalouse, which is a tomato paste-tinted mayonnaise rich with chopped tomato and green and red capsicum (bell pepper).

ASIAN CONNECTIONS

Current trends have brought into our repertoire all sorts of marriages between European ingredients and Asian. It is not unusual to make an oil and vinegar-based dressing and add a touch of soy or, better still, a touch of sake or mirin (Japanese rice wine). The Chinese stores offer a rice vinegar too — it's heavier and a little more bitter than normal vinegar. It adds a slight meaty taste a little reminiscent of balsamic vinegar. When adding soy or mirin to a dressing, play with the ratios to get the pungency and flavours you like; it is possible you'll need to add a little sugar or honey to counteract the alcohol and/or the bitterness.

Further exploration of the Asian countries brings us to the flavours of everybody's current favourite cuisine, Thai. A julienne of lemon grass is quite acceptable in a salad, but goes better when the acidity is obtained from lemon or green lime juice rather than vinegar. Sprigs of fresh coriander (cilantro) give a peppery taste, as do nasturtiums, but this is not so much the dressing as an addition to the greens.

FRESH FRUITS

Fresh fruits can be attractive scattered through a salad, but here we are not talking of the use of fruit as an addition but rather as part of the dressing. I've already discussed the various fruit vinegars on the market, but my friend, French cook and author Madeleine Kamman, taught me to make my own infusions. For example, she soaks chopped pineapple in white vinegar, leaving it for a night or a week, then throws it away as she gets bored with it, or when it ferments or goes bitter (usually not before three weeks in a sealed bottle).

Madeleine, whose creativity astounds me, uses puréed fruit as a base for emulsifying interesting salad dressings. She purées the fruit she has chosen and then, tasting as she goes, adds oil and vinegar, lemon or orange juice, mustard, sugar, maybe chutney, and keeps tasting it until she gets it right. Puréed mango is one of her passions for a dressing, because it gives not only a wonderful tropical flavour, but also a creamy texture. She blends it with vinegar and a little oil when aiming for a light, fresh approach; she adds cream or sour cream if she wants a full-bodied, gutsier sauce consistency. She throws in shredded basil if she feels it needs freshness, or curry powder if meats like chicken are included in the salad. I've seen her throw a handful of fresh, unpeeled cumquats in a blender and mix them with a little marmalade and cream, but I cannot to this day tell you how she finished, and nor probably can she. The best thing we can all learn from Madeleine is to open up to the possibilities.

GRAVELAX-STYLE DRESSINGS

More than any other nation, except perhaps the Americans, the Scandinavians love sweetness in their salad dressings. Their classic gravelax dressing was devised to accompany marinated raw salmon, but thinned out (and in my opinion less sweet), it makes an ideal change for dressing a simple green salad. It is made by combining 3 tablespoons French mustard and a dash of powdered mustard with 2 tablespoons sugar, 2 tablespoons white wine, 3 tablespoons chopped dill and whisking well with 8 tablespoons light olive or peanut oil. Thin it to an acceptable consistency with more oil, and you'll find the creamy, dill-laden sauce a delight over iceberg or mignonette lettuce. (This makes a large quantity — make half or store in a bottle.)

CHEESES IN DRESSINGS

Stilton, Roquefort or other blue cheeses make a change, albeit a rather powerful one, to salad dressings. The mayonnaise for potato salad benefits from a large injection of mashed blue cheese, particularly if the smoky taste of crisped bacon is one of the major additives. Oil and vinegar combinations become creamier with a little blue cheese too, but be careful — substitute goat cheese or ricotta or mascarpone for a less palate-boggling combination. If blue cheese is to your liking on a green salad, make sure you use strong-leafed lettuces with a crispy disposition, so they don't wilt under the onslaught. The combination is likely to benefit from crispy croûtons too, and if it has croûtons and chopped anchovy fillets, you are making a variation of Caesar salad, although the traditional Caesar has chopped Gruyère, not blue cheese. Try blending some basil and walnuts to a paste in a mortar and pestle, then thinning to dressing consistency with yoghurt, or ricotta cheese and yoghurt. One trick that will give this dressing a unique taste is to stir in a little liquid smoke (found in some specialist barbecue shops) with the seasonings of salt, pepper and paprika. That reminds me that thinned down pesto would make a good base for a salad dressing, too. Particularly over sliced tomatoes.

Anyone still think salad dressings are boring ...?

SALAD OF SMOKED TROUT
WITH HORSERADISH CREAM DRESSING

Serves 6

2 tablespoons garlic or almond flakes, or both
mesclun (mixed salad greens)
2 smoked trout
1 tablespoon capers
2 Roma (plum) tomatoes, seeded and cubed
12 stalks asparagus, boiled and drained

The sauce
250 ml (8 fl oz) cream
1 heaped teaspoon creamed horseradish
salt and pepper
a little white or cider vinegar
3–4 tablespoons oil

Deep fry the garlic and/or almond flakes in hot oil until golden; remove quickly and place on paper towelling to drain. Divide the *mesclun* and arrange it attractively over the base of each plate. Skin the trout, lift the flesh from the bones, and distribute in medium-size pieces over the *mesclun*. Scatter or arrange the capers, tomatoes and asparagus over the *mesclun* and trout. Drizzle with the horseradish cream sauce.

The sauce: Place the cream in a bowl and stir in (without whipping the cream too much) the horseradish; season to taste with salt and pepper. Thin to a sauce consistency with a few drops of vinegar to taste and about half of the oil. Drizzle over the salads. Drop the remaining oil here and there over the salad leaves.

MIGNONETTE AND WATERCRESS SALAD WITH LIME VINAIGRETTE

Serves 6

1 head mignonette (butter lettuce)
garlic to rub the bowl
75 g (2½ oz) long sprigs watercress (be careful to avoid thick stalks)

The lime vinaigrette
juice and grated peel of 2 green limes
1 tablespoon sherry vinegar
½ teaspoon ground cumin seed
¼ tablespoon ground cardamom
½ tablespoon Szechuan peppercorns, crushed
salt and pepper
125 ml (4 fl oz) light olive oil, or to taste

Separate the leaves of the mignonette; wash and drain well. Place in a garlic-rubbed bowl with the watercress.

The lime vinaigrette: Combine all the dressing ingredients in a bottle. Shake well, then taste for tartness. If the limes were too large, making the vinaigrette too acidic, adjust with extra olive oil. Shake again before pouring over the greens. Do not make too far ahead of time, since this dressing loses its freshness and does not keep well.

Variation

As it is, this is more of a mid-meal salad than an appetiser, so add a few seared scallops or cubes of tuna — either raw or marinated for half an hour in the dressing, or simply pan-fried — for a more substantial dish.

WATERCRESS, LAMB'S TONGUE LETTUCE AND ROCKET WITH SMOKED ALMONDS AND PEARS

Serves 4

1 small pear, peeled, halved and cored
poaching liquor: 250 ml (8 fl oz) white wine, 125 ml (4 fl oz) water and
125 g (4 oz) sugar

The salad

125 g (4 oz) watercress
10 large lamb's tongue lettuce sprigs (mâche or corn salad)—double this if
you can find the new 'land' (dwarf) variety
handful of rocket leaves
about 15 smoked almonds (available in cans)

The dressing

4 tablespoons hazelnut oil (or one of the less pungent extra virgin olive oils)
1 tablespoon blackcurrant or raspberry vinegar
½ teaspoon powdered mustard
salt and pepper

Heat the poaching liquor and add the pear. Cook until tender (about 4–12 minutes, depending on ripeness), then cool in the syrup. This may be done well ahead. When needed, pare into citrus-sized segments.

The salad: Wash the greens, after picking out any stalks of the watercress that are too thick, and picking the little root ends off the lamb's tongue lettuce. Dry, well-rolled in a tea towel, then place in the salad bowl. Add the pear pieces and the smoked almonds. Dress only at the last minute.

The dressing: Combine the ingredients, shake well and change the balance of oil and vinegar to your taste. Leave aside until needed, but shake or whisk again before pouring over the salad.

Variation

Try scattering shredded smoked chicken, left-over turkey or confit of duck breast pieces through this salad.

MIXED GREENS WITH DRIED FIGS AND DUCK SKIN CRACKLINGS

Serves 4–6

3 dried figs
poaching liquor: 300 ml (10 fl oz) water and 3 tablespoons sugar
skin of 2 duck fillets or 6–8 strips of bacon rind
mixed greens, enough for 4 or 6 people (choose mostly pungent, dark greens,
plus radicchio if you want a contrast)
roasted pine nuts (optional)

The dressing
rendered duck fat from the skins
2–3 tablespoons olive oil
1 tablespoon balsamic, sherry or red wine vinegar
salt and pepper

In advance: Poach the figs in the water and sugar until softened and moist, but still chewy. Allow to cool in the syrup, then slice each fig into four or five segments, depending on size. Meanwhile, start crisping the duck skins. Roll the skins, then slice them into slivers. Cut in half any strands that are longer than about 2.5 cm (1 in). In a small frying pan, heat the skin from cold, rendering the fat as you go and continuing to cook until the skin crisps (bacon rind may need a little oil to start with). When cooked, remove the pan from the heat and keep aside for later.

To serve: When ready, reheat the duck skin. Meanwhile, wash the greens, dry well, and place in a bowl with fig segments and pine nuts, if using. When the duck skin is hot and crisp, remove with a slotted spoon and transfer to the greens. Over heat, add the oil to the rendered duck fat, then the chosen vinegar. Working quickly, season to taste with salt and pepper, then pour the hot vinaigrette over the greens. Toss quickly and serve immediately.

HAIL CAESAR!

Food is fashion — and at the rate it is sidling back into favour, the Caesar salad might just be the salad of the decade. It's been creeping up on us, becoming a force on the bistro menus, regaining its classic popularity . . . but without the pretension.

Strange new beginnings for that one-time favourite of large hotel dining rooms in the era where fashion dictated that the maître d' came to the table with the flambé dish and performed culinary 'magic' at the table before delighted diners, flourishing bottles of alcohol, silver spoons and oversized Florentine pepper grinders.

The original Caesar salad had this kind of high drama — salad servers poised in the air, Worcester sauce poured from on high, starched cuffs pulled back to highlight the abrupt snap of the wrist as it broke the perfectly coddled egg over the large wooden bowl, and all to the oohs and aahs of guests who wondered how the perpetrator achieved such marvels that were absolutely, but absolutely, out of reach of the mere mortals entranced by the scene.

These are now things of the past — culinary kitsch of an order quite forgotten in the new regime. But this is definitely how it all began. Not in the US, as many think, but in the Mexican town of Tijuana, where, just over the border from the southern Californian town of San Diego, people from the affluent but prohibitionist North went South to play.

The noisy, brassy bordertown was in its heyday when Caesar Cardini, an itinerant Italian who had settled in Tijuana, opened his restaurant to cater to the droves of hungry Northerners who flooded into the sleazy Mexican town to drink forbidden cocktails, gamble in cheap casinos and stroll in the market places and piazzas. It was 1927 when he created his 'aviator's salad' to honour fliers at nearby Rockwell Field in San Diego. As it increased in popularity, the salad became known by Cardini's name, and was taken back to California to become the darling of the local restaurants. Years later, it has become known as an American classic, for it travelled quickly, and restaurants across the US found it essential to have a 'Caesar's famous salad' of their own.

If the most famous came from Chasen's in Los Angeles, the greats in New York were no slouches, and Jack's (where the Worcester sauce was omitted), the Four Seasons, the Waldorf (which already had a classic in their great Waldorf salad of chicken, celery, mayonnaise and walnut kernels) and 21 all had versions in their heyday.

After World War II, when the 'Yanks' had liberated Europe, and everything American was chic, travellers swapped recipes for the 'great American classic', and the Caesar salad swept the world. The fashion changed when table service began to be considered passé, and more sophisticated diners took the emphasis in grand dining rooms away from steak.

But the wheel has turned full circle, and Cardini's little masterpiece is showing up everywhere, coming to the table — pre-plated — in any number of 'chic' little bistros, its way paved by the return to more strident flavours. As with everything, however, there are huge variations in the standards. Some omit the Worcester sauce, others add bacon (perhaps taking the hint from the Worcester sauce, and confusing the ingredients with oysters Kilpatrick?). Versions omitting the anchovies abound, particularly on Anglo-Saxon tables where few regard the salty little critter with the love and esteem shown to it in the Mediterranean. Nobody omits the garlic croûtons, for on their crunch lies the crux of the salad's fame, but some replace the Parmesan cheese with Gruyère cubes, and in modern versions the grated Parmesan is quite often replaced by shaved Parmesan — to give it this year's look no doubt. Food is fashion, as I've said before.

The most destructive fault, and the one most likely to leave afficionados shaking their heads, is the tendency to get lazy and substitute chopped hard-boiled egg for the perfectly coddled egg that Cardini had considered *de rigeur*.

Versions come and go, but food buffs know that a great Caesar salad is made only with Cos lettuce. Not with iceberg, and *never* — God forbid — with the soft, absorbent lettuces like mignonette (butter lettuce). The long-leafed Cos, also known as Romaine, has long, strong, thin leaves that are resistant to wilting. Only Cos gives the perfect result, for only with Cos does the creamy dressing sit as a velvety Parmesan-textured coating to the crispy leaves beneath.

For the rest, give the real thing the credit it deserves. In the base of the bowl just place a couple of anchovies, halved if you like, and mash them a little with the back of a spoon as you add the oil and a good few drops of lemon juice (never vinegar). Add a touch of salt and pepper and then the one-minute-only coddled egg, broken up with a spoon to catch the creamy centre of the yolk. Add a pinch of mustard, a dribbling of Worcester sauce and the croûtons, which have been rubbed with garlic, then fried in olive oil (not extra virgin this time!). Stir again and add the washed and perfectly drained Cos leaves. Spill over all the quarter cup or so of grated Parmesan. Toss again and add some shaved Parmesan as a bonus if you must, but never in place of the grated. Now to the table fast to do honour to your guests.

Caesar salad can be made as a starter or as a separate salad course after something strong and flavoursome, most often steak or roast beef. Above all, it's just a great salad — go to it!

CAESAR SALAD

Serves 4–5

1 head Cos lettuce, as small and yellow as possible
2 slices bread, rubbed with garlic
light olive oil, for frying

The dressing
2 anchovy fillets
1 clove garlic, crushed
1 whole egg, boiled for 1 minute only (known as a coddled egg)
150 ml (5 fl oz) olive oil (a good, but not extra virgin, olive oil)
juice of a lemon
freshly ground black pepper (no salt!)
1 scant teaspoon Worcester sauce
1 teaspoon grated Parmesan for flavour

The garnish
2–3 teaspoons grated Parmesan cheese (the classic method)
125 g (4 oz) Gruyère cheese, cubed, for decoration (the classic method), or better still, shaved pieces of fresh Parmesan (the modern method)

Separate the Cos leaves; wash and dry well. Remove the crusts from the bread, then cut into cubes and fry in light olive oil. Drain on paper towelling.

The dressing: Place the anchovy fillets in a bowl and mash partially with a fork. Add the garlic and the coddled egg, then whisk in the olive oil, lemon juice, freshly gound black pepper, Worcester sauce and 1 teaspoon grated Parmesan.

To serve: Place the Cos in a salad bowl. Classically, the croûtons and the cubed Gruyère are then tossed through, but the modern tendency is to use grated Parmesan in the dressing and shavings of fresh Parmesan across the top instead of Gruyère cubes.

Re-mix or shake the dressing before pouring over the salad just as it is served.

FASTA PASTA

Pasta is one of the great all-time speedy dishes, and it doesn't take much to broaden your range . . . no wonder it has become such a ubiquitous dish. Long gone is the need to depend on the sloppy stuff in a can—from the age of ten both my daughter and son saw no problem at all in boiling some fettuccine in a pot of salted water, draining it, and adding whatever they uncovered in the fridge or cupboard to make a sauce. Bacon, a sure-bet from the meat cabinet, was always a preferred addition, along with a chopped onion and a can of peeled tomatoes. If they felt like it, they could readily turn their hand to a mean carbonara with the bacon crisped in a pan and the cream added and brought to the boil. They soon mastered the fact that the egg is broken in only at the last minute, and only off the stove, ready for a quick stir and a last minute grinding of black pepper just as they ran to the table.

Pasta is great at its most simple, with butter and Parmesan cheese, or with chopped garlic, olive oil and Parmesan. It's wonderful with any left-over fish, a combination of seafood and fish, or simply squid or octopus rings, garlic, tomato (optional), parsley and olive oil.

Pasta takes to almost any vegetable you care to add, yielding a variety of dishes as obvious as tomato, onion and basil, or as esoteric as radicchio leaves softened in butter with the addition of chopped boiled chestnuts. I've tasted sauces of prawn (shrimp) combined with tomato and macadamia nuts, of poached brains combined with walnuts, and once with lemon, orange and lime julienne in a citron juice and cream sauce. I've thrown in left-over chicken, finishing it off with bacon, onion and tomato, or with red, green and gold capsicum (bell pepper) strips, capers, black olives, shredded chilli, sun-dried tomatoes and the best olive oil. In the home of Giuliano Bugialli, my mentor in all things Italian, I've even tasted a meat sauce cooked with chocolate — and if you think that's some crazy modern twist called *Nuova Cucina,* you're wrong; the recipe is a medieval classic.

Leeks with cream go with pasta, mud crab goes with pasta, squid braised in its ink and highlighted with shredded chilli goes with pasta, cream and champignons with chopped spring onion (scallion) and parsley go with pasta.

. . . And you can do a 'pasta fasta'; try the following recipes as appetisers, which is their correct place in Italian cuisine, or as simple one-course meals with loads of flavour and a minimum of fuss.

TAGLIATELLE WITH ASPARAGUS

Serves 4–6

400–500 g (12 oz–1 lb) tagliatelle (mixed green and white excels here)
100 g (3¹/₂ oz) unsalted butter
250 ml (8 fl oz) cream
small bunch asparagus, cut into 3 cm (1¹/₄ in) lengths
salt and pepper
grated Parmesan cheese

Cook the tagliatelle in boiling, salted water until cooked but firm to bite (*al dente*).

Meanwhile, in a large frying pan, heat the butter, add the cream and asparagus; let the cream thicken a little as the asparagus cooks (2–3 minutes). Season with salt and pepper, then stir in the drained tagliatelle.

Serve immediately with grated Parmesan.

Variations

Choose mixed green baby vegetables — whatever is in season. Try chopped celery, zucchini (courgette), baby peas, asparagus tips and lengths of chopped baby beans, and, if you want more colour, add diced carrot. All bar the zucchini must be blanched first to soften them. In a cream sauce like this, I love to julienne two colours of zucchini — green and yellow — leaving their skins on for colour. Just sauté them in butter until they soften, then add the cream and continue as above. You can also add chopped chives or spring onions (scallions). They bring up the colour and help to 'point' the flavour.

When using mixed vegetables as above, you may choose to omit the cream and use just butter and a couple of tablespoons of olive oil. Try using 25 broad beans, 6 tablespoons cooked peas, 500 g (1 lb) asparagus tips, 3 slices prosciutto (diced) and 4 sliced spring onions (scallions), finishing with shredded leaves of basil. Add 120 g (4 oz) macadamia nuts for a unique crunchy texture.

SPAGHETTI WITH SUN-DRIED TOMATOES AND CHILLI

Serves 6

500 g (1 lb) spaghetti
¹/₂ red capsicum (bell pepper), cored, seeded and cut lengthways into natural sections
¹/₂ green capsicum (bell pepper), cut as above
¹/₂ yellow capsicum (bell pepper), if available, cut as above
150–180 ml (5–6 fl oz) extra virgin olive oil
6 slices sun-dried tomato, shredded

1 small hot red chilli, shredded
2 cloves garlic, finely chopped
3 spring onions (scallions), sliced
2 tablespoons capers
20 Ligurian (small brown Italian) olives
3 slices prosciutto, diced (optional — may be a vegetarian pasta dish if preferred)
freshly ground black pepper
15 shredded basil leaves, or ¹/₂ cup plucked coriander (cilantro) leaves

Bring a large saucepan of salted water to the boil and cook the pasta until *al dente*. Drain well.

Place the capsicum under a hot griller until black and blistered; peel off the skin and cut flesh into strips. When ready to cook, heat 90–120 ml (3–4 fl oz) olive oil in a large frying pan and heat, stirring all the time, the vegetables, capers, olives and prosciutto (if using).

Toss the spaghetti through the sauce until well coated, season with lots of freshly ground black pepper, add the remaining oil to moisten the pasta, and toss through the chosen herb. Basil is more strictly correct, as it is Mediterranean like the rest of the flavours, but coriander gives a peppery, fresh taste in keeping with the flavours of modern cuisine.

SPAGHETTI ALLA PUTTANESCA

Serves 4–6

500 g (1 lb) spaghetti
4 tablespoons olive oil
1 small onion, finely sliced
3 cloves garlic, finely chopped
3–4 anchovy fillets, roughly chopped
5 large tomatoes, peeled and diced, or 600 g (1¹/₄ lb) canned tomatoes
10 pitted black olives (120 g (4 oz) weighed whole), roughly chopped
2 heaped tablespoons capers, well rinsed
shredded peel of half an orange
juice of 1 orange
salt and pepper
pinch of red pepper flakes (optional)
3 heaped tablespoons chopped parsley

In a large pot of boiling salted water, cook the spaghetti until *al dente*; drain well.

Heat the olive oil in a large frying pan and add the onion, garlic and anchovy. Sauté until the onion softens, but has not coloured. Add the chopped tomatoes and bring to the boil. Reduce the heat and simmer for 4–5 minutes, stirring from time to time, and adding the black olives, capers and orange rind. Add the orange juice and blend well. Season to taste with salt and pepper, and a pinch of red pepper flakes (if using). Stir in the chopped parsley. When ready, stir the drained spaghetti into the sauce and serve immediately.

Variation

The above is the typical puttanesca (literally, 'whore's spaghetti'). Variations are often seen with either tuna or pancetta (Italian-style bacon) added. The tuna is added just at the end so it does not mash up; if adding bacon, it should be cut into bite-sized pieces and crisped when frying the onion.

PENNE WITH OLIVE, CAPSICUM AND WALNUT SAUCE

My favourite green olive pasta sauce is with cream (see Variation), but since all the health warnings have us on a Mediterranean diet, try this version given to me in New Orleans by the Tabasco company.

Serves 4

400 g (12 oz) penne or spaghetti
4 tablespoons olive oil, plus a little extra
3 tablespoons butter
1 small red capsicum (bell pepper), finely chopped
1 clove garlic, finely chopped
1 cup pitted green olives, very finely chopped
³/₄ cup walnut kernels, roughly chopped
3–4 tablespoons chopped parsley
¹/₂ teaspoon Tabasco
salt

Bring a large pot of salted water to the boil and cook the penne or spaghetti until *al dente*; drain. Meanwhile, heat the olive oil and butter in a saucepan. Stir in the capsicum and garlic, then the olives and walnut kernels. Add the chopped parsley and Tabasco; season with salt. Toss through the hot, drained penne or spaghetti, adding a touch of olive oil if the pasta needs moistening. Serve immediately.

Variation

Omit the red capsicum and parsley, be a little more generous with the green olives, still include the Tabasco, chop the walnuts a bit finer to match the olives, and finish the dish by heating a good 250 ml (8 fl oz) cream with the sauce just before tossing in the pasta.

SOUPS

SOUPERIOR STARTERS

Soup. The very word creates a picture of winter, of interior warmth, and even feelings of nostalgia, as we imagine ourselves rubbing our hands together, coming in from the cold, and being soothed by the wonderful welcome of a huge bowl of hearty broth.

Its heartiness may make soup special, but things change when you plan a three-course meal. I picture minestrone as a one-course Sunday night meal around a fire, with lots of crusty bread, perhaps a cheese and salad course, and loads of coffee and cake. Soup may seem an ideal entry to a winter meal, but care must be taken to see that it remains light enough to be followed by other dishes, and that it is glamorous enough to make an occasion of a dinner party.

It is easy to distinguish the three main types of soup:

1. Those in which meat and vegetables, vegetables alone, or fish and vegetables float as pieces in the liquid they were cooked in — these are termed broths.
2. The creamed or puréed soups, usually of vegetable. These may appear on the menu as *Crème de* or *Velouté de* and the name of the vegetable. *Velouté* means velvety, and refers to the thicker, richer texture in the soup obtained by using stock instead of water as the basc.
3. The consommé, a meat- or fish-based essence, served clarified — a procedure using egg whites to ensure the soup is clear and limpid. The garnish that is typically served floating in it gives it its classic name.

I have included some of each — hearty winter soups, light soups such as the Fresh and Smoky Oyster Soup (also very quick to prepare), elegant soups such as the Ragoût of Shellfish, and a delicious cold one for summer.

FRENCH ONION SOUP GRATINEE

Serves 6

50 g (1¹/₂ oz) butter
6 large onions, sliced into rings
1 heaped tablespoon plain (all-purpose) flour
1.3 L (2 pt) water
2 beef cubes

salt and pepper
12–16 slices French bread stick, oven dried
90 g (3 oz) Gruyère cheese, grated

Melt the butter in a large saucepan and fry the onions until they are as brown as possible (about 10–12 minutes). Add the flour, toss to the bottom and fry, not leaving any white flecks. Add the water and bring to the boil, then reduce the heat and simmer for 20 minutes, or until the onions are well softened. Crumble in the beef cubes to give flavour, and season with salt and pepper.

While the soup is cooking, dry out the slices of bread in a warm oven until they are quite hard, otherwise they will go soggy in the soup. For this reason, never toast them.

To serve: Pour the soup into bowls. Stir in a tiny bit of grated cheese and then completely cover the top of each bowl with as many pieces of bread as will fit. Scatter plenty of cheese on top and place under a hot griller to gratinée (about 4–8 minutes; the cheese should be melted and browned on top).

FRESH CHUNKY TOMATO SOUP

Serves 8

1 kg (2 lb) very red, fresh tomatoes, preferably Roma (plum)
3 tablespoons oil or 2 tablespoons butter
1 small onion, finely chopped
1 L (1³/₄ pt) water
1 scant tablespoon tomato paste
1–2 teaspoons brown sugar
4 spring onions (scallions), chopped (including the green part)
4–5 tablespoons mixed chives and parsley, chopped
salt
coarsely ground black pepper

Core the tomatoes, drop them momentarily into boiling water to loosen the skin, then peel and chop roughly. In a large saucepan, heat the butter or oil and sauté the onion for a moment. Add the tomatoes and water; bring to the boil. Simmer for 5 minutes and taste before stirring in the tomato paste and seasoning with salt and a little brown sugar to reduce the acidity. Just before serving, add the chopped spring onions and copious amounts of chives and parsley. Finish by coarsely grinding black pepper over the soup. Spoon into bowls and serve hot.

HUNGARIAN-STYLE MEAT AND CABBAGE SOUP

I like to make this soup the day before, allow it to cool and remove the fat that sets on the top. It seems even more flavoursome the next day!

Serves 8

1 ox tail or 600 g (1¼ lb) gravy beef, cubed
a little flour for dredging
60 g (2 oz) lard or margarine
1 onion, cut into 8 pieces
1 L (1¾ pt) beef stock plus 2 L (3½ pt) water
1 beef cube
1 bay leaf and 3 stalks parsley, tied together
2 cloves garlic, sliced
1 carrot, cut into wedges
1 parsnip, cut into wedges
200 g (7 oz) dried cannellini or kidney beans, soaked for 4 hours
or 1 x 300 g (9½ oz) can red kidney beans, drained and rinsed
¼ cabbage, coarsely shredded
salt and pepper

Trim the meat, particularly the skin-like outer layer, and dredge in flour; pat off excess. In a soup pot, heat the lard or margarine and brown the meat well. Add the onion and fry until brown. Cover with the beef stock and water, crumble in the beef cube, and add the bay leaf, parsley and garlic. Bring to the boil, then reduce the heat and simmer slowly for 1½ hours, skimming the froth from the top carefully. (If the liquid is only just simmering, less scum rises.)

Add the carrot, parsnip and beans (if using canned beans, add with the cabbage). Continue to cook for a further 1 hour, or until the meat is tender. Add the cabbage (and kidney beans, if canned) and simmer for a further 20 minutes. Remove the parsley and bay leaf, and season to taste with salt and pepper.

CLEAN-OUT-THE-FRIDGE MINESTRONE

All Italian cookbooks have a recipe for minestrone, but the best technique I learned came from cleaning out the fridge after cooking classes. The idea is to use what you have, although you do need carrots, turnips and onions as the staple vegetables, and celery, zucchini (courgettes) and beans are pretty much essential to keep up the Italian authenticity.

Simply bring the peeled and chopped vegetables to the boil with a good covering of water. If keeping the colour bright is a priority— which it never really was to the Italians— keep the zucchini aside for later addition. Flavour the water with tomato paste (or a can of peeled tomatoes), because vegetable water alone is not rich enough for a 'gutsy' soup. The good old beef cube helps too. If you can possibly soak some cannellini beans for a couple of hours before starting, do so, or cook them for half an hour in the water while you're peeling and chopping the other vegetables.

Italian minestrone rarely features cabbage or parsnip, but if they're in my fridge — in they go. Make sure the broth is well seasoned and tasty. If you like real stand-up body in your soup, add a bit of macaroni or other pasta in the last 10 minutes. The whole procedure takes a lazy 2 hours or so, with no attention necessary after the chopping. By the time you've cleared the fridge, you'll probably have enough for 12 people — so much the better, as it freezes well. Don't forget the Parmesan cheese to pass around at the table.

Variation

The classic southern French Pistou soup is like minestrone with a dash of pesto (pistou) in it. To turn the already great into the sublime, they spoon a swirl of pesto into the soup. (Note, if using pesto, do not serve Parmesan as a garnish.) If you truly are the laziest cook in the business, you can use canned pesto — if not, simply peel 3 cloves garlic, blend to a paste with 40 leaves basil in a food processor, add 2 tablespoons Parmesan cheese, then pour 6 tablespoons olive oil into the machine as it's whirring. Season well. Refrigerate any left over to stir through spaghetti for another night's treat!

OLD MOTHER HOLUIGUE'S FOOLPROOF FORMULA FOR CREAMED VEGETABLE SOUPS

Creamed (or puréed) vegetable soups are the best known soups of the world. If a vote were taken, I suspect tomato soup would come up everyone's top favourite, with pumpkin a close second. But in fact, from asparagus to zucchini (courgette) or our celeriac example (page 58), the steps we go through to make them are exactly the same.

1. **Choose the vegetable**, whatever it may be, and in whatever combination. Traditional methods rarely mix vegetables in creamed soups, preferring the full-bodied flavour of one vegetable. However, there are certain vegetables, notably onions, celery and leeks, that combine well with most vegetables to give them texture and an injection of flavour. As single vegetable soups for six people, the best are:

   - 600 g (1¹/₄ lb) brussels sprouts
   - 1 large bunch celery, including the leaves
   - the root 1 large or 2 small celeriac (root celery)
   - 1 large bunch watercress
   - 1 bunch spinach
   - 5 large tomatoes
   - 1 kg (2 lb) pumpkin
   - 600 g (1¹/₄ lb) asparagus
   - 4 leeks plus 1 potato (thin leek soups) or 4 leeks (white only) plus 3 potatoes (smooth, thick Vichyssoise)
   - 1 celeriac (root celery) and 1 bulb fennel combined
   - 500 g (1 lb) baby turnips
   - 500 g (1 lb) non-fibrous (smaller) parsnips
   - 600 g (1¹/₄ lb) fresh peas plus a small lettuce.

   Prepare them in the simplest way — peeling only if necessary, removing stalks or deveining, cutting away woody or fibrous parts, then cutting into cubes for speedier cooking.

2. **Fry** a diced onion in butter until it is soft but has not changed colour, then add the chopped vegetable. Frying the vegetable brings out its colour, particularly in green, red and yellow vegetables — this is important for broccoli or brussels sprouts, which have a tendency to grey in the cooking and look unappetising.

3. **Add the thickener.** Decide whether you really need a thickener — means you need to know whether you are working with a starchy or a leafy vegetable. If you are guessing, remember root and tuber vegetables (carrot, parsnip, turnip, pumpkin, potato, celeriac (root celery), Jerusalem artichoke, etc.) are starchy and require no thickening; most others, particularly green and leafy vegetables, do need thickening. Green peas are the notable exception.

   If you decide to use a thickener, you must choose whether you want to thicken with potato or flour. Potato is a more natural choice, and is good with watercress, spinach, green zucchini (courgette), yellow squash or leek. Simply peel and cube the potato and cook it with the vegetables. To thicken with flour, sprinkle the vegetable in the pan with 1–2 heaped tablespoons flour, then toss it down to the base where it joins with the butter to form a *roux*. This is good with spinach or any leafy vegetable, such as sorrel, although potato is more commonly used.

   There is a further choice, between potato flour or rice flour, cornflour (cornstarch) or arrowroot (very common with tomatoes, but the main reason critics spurn canned tomato soup). These products are excellent for catching up on thickening when caught short, for they are always blended in a cup with a little water and, unlike flour, can be added at the end of the cooking time.

4. **Add the liquid**. For vegetable soup, the liquid can be water, chicken stock, vegetable stock, milk, or a combination. Water makes a less sophisticated, family-style soup; vegetable stock is appropriate but not much different, and hardly worth the trouble.

   Chicken stock is an important alternative as it gives body, viscosity and richness to the soup that comes from its gelatinous, somewhat fatty texture. Don't fool yourself — a chicken cube is high on chicken flavour, but low on viscosity, and therefore never a substitute for real stock in making soups. Never underestimate how much better soups taste with real chicken stock, but don't think it's an imperative. With pumpkin, for example, I find it gives an almost sickening richness, and I prefer to make my pumpkin soup with half milk, half water. The milk enriches a little, but also blankets the sharpness of pumpkin, bringing, for example, a green pumpkin flavour down to one more similar to a butternut. Milk also enhances the colour, as it does with celeriac (root celery) or Jerusalem artichoke.

5. **Add the flavourings.** Unlike casserole-making, few flavourings are needed, but salt, pepper and herbs, and perhaps beef/chicken cubes or tomato paste, are added at this stage.

6. **The cooking time**. Bring the soup to the boil, then reduce the heat so it doesn't aerate or, in the case of a milk base, curdle, and simmer gently until the pieces are mashable against the side of the saucepan.

7. **Purée the soup**. If the vegetable has many fibres or strings, chances are the fibres will jam and damage a blender or wand (Bamix-style) blade. In this case, the mouli is the classic utensil used to purée a soup. If the vegetable is not fibrous, the wand is extremely good because you work directly in the pot; the blender is fine but often you need to do two batches; the food processor works for anything without a large potato content, where it has a tendency to work up gluten. When you have puréed the soup, return it to the pot and correct for thickness and seasoning.

8. **Add the garnish.** Some garnishes cook in the puréed soup — asparagus tips after the rest of the stalk has made up the soup; a few sliced mushrooms after the rest are puréed; slivers of red capsicum (bell pepper); 2 tablespoons tapioca in tomato soup, and so on. But most often the garnish is added to the soup in the tureen or soup bowls — drizzled cream, grated nutmeg, chopped chives or other greens, sliced lemon in spinach soup, or a large dob of yoghurt. A garnish is to enhance the soup; it may complement, contrast, or add an element of surprise. For example, garnish white cauliflower soup with blanched florets of both cauliflower and broccoli, or lift a pumpkin soup by adding a couple of whole tiger prawns (shrimps) in the garnish (the juice you cooked them in can go in the broth). Pesto gives an injection of summer, the capsicum (bell pepper) garnish on the Roasted Corn Soup (page 61) gives both a dash of colour and a spiked flavour of chilli.

CELERIAC OR JERUSALEM ARTICHOKE SOUP

Serves 6

50 g (1¹/₂ oz) butter
1 onion, chopped
1 large or 2 small celeriac (root celery)
or 600 g (1¹/₄ lb) Jerusalem artichokes, peeled and chopped
350 ml (11 fl oz) water
1 L (1³/₄ pt) milk
salt and white pepper

The garnish

200 ml (7 fl oz) cream and some chopped chives, pea sprouts or chervil

or

250 g (8 oz) yoghurt spiced with ¹/₂ teaspoon each of cumin powder, turmeric, ground coriander and paprika

Heat the butter in a soup pot and sauté first the onions, then the celeriac or Jerusalem artichokes. Add the water and milk, then season with salt and pepper. Bring to the boil, then reduce the heat and simmer gently for about 20 minutes, or until tender enough to mash against the side of the saucepan.

   Purée the soup in a blender or with a mouli, then return to the saucepan and thin with a little more water if necessary. Check the seasoning, pour into a soup tureen or individual bowls and garnish either with drizzled cream and chopped greens, or spiced yoghurt. If using the two-soups method (page 60), the yoghurt garnish is not applicable; use the cream, but stir it in.

FRESH PEA AND LETTUCE SOUP

Serves 6

1.5 L (2¹/₂ pt) water or light chicken stock
50 g (1¹/₂ oz) butter
1 small leek or 1 onion, chopped
500 g (1 lb) fresh peeled peas
1 small mignonette (butter lettuce)
1 cup parsley leaves, stalks removed
salt and white pepper
2 teaspoons sugar

The garnish
200 ml (7 fl oz) cream
8 snow peas (mangetout), each cut diagonally into six pieces

Bring the water or chicken stock to the boil. Meanwhile, heat most of the butter in a large saucepan and sauté first the chopped leek or onion, then the peas (until they turn a vivid green). Pour the boiling chicken stock into the saucepan, then break up the mignonette roughly and toss it in along with the parsley. Cook until peas are tender, usually 15 minutes, depending on the quality of the peas. Season with the salt, pepper and sugar.

   Purée the soup, then return it to the saucepan and add half the cream. If serving on its own (as distinct from the two-soups-in-a-bowl method on page 60), ladle into bowls and garnish with drizzled cream and a julienne of snow peas that have been tossed in the remaining butter (which you have melted) until shiny. If serving with a second soup, stir the cream into the soup and pour into the bowl using the jug method described on page 60.

BOWLED OVER!— TWO SOUPS IN A BOWL

Few things can so simply give greater impact to a dinner party than the colourful idea of serving two different soups in one bowl. The only thing to remember is to choose two soups of similar viscosity, which means the technique is at its most infallible with puréed vegetable soups like those on pages 56–59. Find a combination of soups where both the colours and the flavours go well together. You may choose to combine green tomato and red tomato, pumpkin and leek, cauliflower and broccoli, fresh pea and spinach, leek and spinach, or corn and spinach. For all these soups, you must omit the garnish and rely only on the decorative effect of 'feathering' one colour into the other. For soups where cream is the garnish, stir the amount of cream into the original recipe.

Both soups are made separately, and the way to combine them is to pour them from two jugs into either side of the soup bowl at once. If one soup seems to be 'overtaking' the other, pour this one more slowly until the other catches up. The mechanics are very simple — you need not even practice in advance. Just remember that the two soups need to be of the same thickness; if not, boil one down or thin one out to even them up. To get a decorative, 'feathered' effect at the point where the soups join, simply use the end of a teaspoon to 'draw' one soup through the other.

ROASTED VEGETABLE SOUP WITH SAFFRON-TINTED CREME FRAICHE

A thick vegetable soup that follows the formula for puréed vegetable soups, but differs in sophistication and flavour as the vegetables are oven-roasted to acquire a rich, caramelised flavour that adds an interesting innuendo to the result.

Serves 8

$^1/_2$ *small butternut pumpkin (optional)*
2 small eggplants (aubergines)
2 onions
2 small or 1 large red capsicum (bell pepper), cored and trimmed
2 large tomatoes

4 tablespoons olive oil
water, to cover
2 small cloves garlic, finely chopped
2 sprigs thyme and 1 bay leaf, tied together
2 sprigs parsley
salt and freshly ground black pepper
¹/₂ teaspoon dried chilli flakes

The garnish
200 ml (7 fl oz) saffron-tinted crème fraîche or
saffron-tinted olive-oil mayonnaise
thin croûtons of sliced French breadstick, fried in olive oil

Halve all the vegetables, leaving their skin on — even the onions. Brush the vegetables with oil and place first the pumpkin (if using) in the oven at 200°C (400°F) for 10 minutes, then the eggplants for a further 10 minutes, then the other vegetables for 20 minutes (i.e. 40 minutes in all if using pumpkin, 30 minutes if starting with the eggplants).

When ready, remove the vegetables, cool a little, then peel the pumpkin, onions and capsicums. Chop very roughly. Transfer all the vegetables to a soup pot, along with any caramel left on the baking tray. Pour in the water, making sure it covers the vegetables by 6 cm (2¹/₂ in). Add the garlic, the thyme and the bay leaf, and throw in the parsley. Bring to the boil; season with salt, pepper and chilli flakes. Reduce the heat and simmer slowly for about 30 minutes, then remove thyme and bay leaf.

Purée the soup, then return it to the saucepan and reheat. Check the seasoning. Thin with more water if necessary, but return any addition to the boil for 1 minute. Ladle into bowls and drizzle with the saffron-tinted *crème fraîche* or mayonnaise. Serve with the croûtons on the side.

ROASTED CORN SOUP
WITH CAPSICUM CHILLI PUREE
Inspired by a recipe of Californian chef and author, Joanne Weir.

Serves 8

The soup
12 medium ears of corn, husks on, or 440 g (14 oz) can corn kernels, drained
300 g (9¹/₂ oz) butter
5 cloves garlic, unpeeled
600 ml (1 pt) chicken stock
300 ml (10 fl oz) cream
salt and pepper
40 g (1¹/₂ oz) polenta (cornmeal)

The capsicum chilli purée

2 red capsicums (bell peppers), roasted and skin removed
3 small bird's eye hot red chillies, or 2 larger chillies, roasted,
then skin and seeds removed
1 scant tablespoon tomato paste
3 tablespoons olive oil

The soup: (can be prepared in advance). Soak the corn (don't remove the husks) in water for 20 minutes, then drain. Pull aside some of the husk and insert 25 g (1 oz) butter into each ear of corn, then pull back husk to cover the corn again. Roast the corn and the unpeeled garlic in the oven at 190°C (375°F) for 30 minutes, or until tender. Remove husks and scrape all the kernels from the cobs. Peel the garlic.

In a food processor or blender, purée together the corn, garlic and (cold) chicken stock, in batches. Strain through a mouli or sieve to remove the corn kernel skins. Alternatively, use canned corn kernels and uncooked, peeled garlic, finely chopped. In this case, add these to the stock and cook for 5 minutes before passing through a mouli.

In a saucepan, combine the soup and cream, and stir to heat through. Season to taste with salt and pepper. Add the polenta and cook for a further 2 minutes, in which time the polenta will cook and thicken the soup. Thickness will also depend on the starch content of the corn. Regulate the thickness either with a little extra stock, or a little extra polenta.

To serve: Ladle soup into individual bowls and garnish each serving with a trail of capsicum chilli purée through the soup.

The capsicum chilli purée: (can be prepared in advance). In a food processor, purée the capsicums, chilli, tomato paste and oil. Set aside until needed.

RAGOUT OF SHELLFISH

An elegant ragoût in which the shellfish sit whole as a garnish; more a broth than a soup.

Serves 6

6 scampi (langoustines)
6 yabbies (crawfish or écrevisses)
1.5 L (2¹/₂ pt) fish stock or light chicken stock
¹/₂ small carrot, cut into small batons (sticks)
18 mussels, scrubbed and beards removed
18 small prawns (shrimp), peeled but with heads still on at least 6
about 24 scallops, cut in half horizontally (if they are small, leave them whole)
a few broccoli florets
18 small snow peas (mangetout), topped and tailed
salt and pepper
sprig fresh dill, chopped

With scissors, cut out the softer membrane of the underside of the tail of the scampi and yabbies. Pull this away, thus freeing the tail flesh for easy eating with a fork, and close back the tail, leaving the rest of the carcass intact.

Heat the stock and cook the carrot in it until tender (about 2 minutes). Add the scampi for 3 minutes, then the yabbies for 2 minutes along with the mussels, which open into the soup. Add the prawns, scallops and broccoli for 1½ minutes, then the snow peas for about 30 seconds. Season the broth to taste with salt and pepper. Ladle the fish and vegetables into large soup bowls, then cover with the liquid. Sprinkle with chopped dill. Serve with a spoon and fork.

Note: Mix and match the seafood according to availability; tiger prawns and cubes of fish may also be used.

FRESH AND SMOKY OYSTER SOUP

Serves 4

700 ml (24 fl oz) fish stock
julienne of mixed vegetables: ½ small carrot, ½ stalk celery, 4 green beans,
3 snow peas (mangetout)
24 fresh oysters (These may be 'broken' oysters from an oyster supplier. Keep the water that comes with them; better still, if buying from an oyster supplier, ask for extra natural juices.)
salt and pepper
1 can smoked oysters, drained well on paper towelling
200 ml (7 fl oz) cream (optional)
2 tablespoons chopped parsley

Bring the stock to the boil and cook the vegetables in it for about 3 minutes, or until tender. Add the juice from the oysters, then season to taste with salt and pepper. Add the smoked oysters, cream (if using) and chopped parsley. Simmer for about 2 minutes to heat through. Place the fresh oysters in four soup bowls, then ladle the hot soup over them. Serve immediately.

Variation

For a fresh-tasting soup, you may omit the smoked oysters. If you have trouble getting fresh oyster juice, it is possible to make this soup with canned oysters. Place the brine in the soup early, but drop in the drained oysters for only a few seconds, to heat. If cooked even slightly, oysters become rubbery.

AMERICAN-STYLE SALMON CHOWDER

Serves 6

60 g (2 oz) butter
1 large onion, chopped
1 clove garlic, finely chopped
3 large tomatoes, peeled and chopped, or
1 can Roma (plum) tomatoes, chopped
1 L (1³/₄ pt) fish stock
2 large potatoes, peeled and cut into 1 cm (¹/₃ in) cubes
400 g (12 oz) salmon fillet, skinned and cut into 1 cm (¹/₃ in) cubes
2 tablespoons chopped dill
3 tablespoons chopped parsley
4 spring onions (scallions), finely sliced
salt and pepper
crusty bread

Heat the butter in a large saucepan and sauté the onion and garlic until softened. Add the chopped tomato, stir well, then cover and simmer for 3 minutes. Add the fish stock and half the potatoes. Cook for 20 minutes, then mash the mixture a little with a potato masher before adding the rest of the potatoes. Cook for 10 minutes, then add the fish, herbs and spring onions and cook for a further 5 minutes. Season to taste with salt and pepper. Ladle into large soup bowls and serve with crusty bread.

LAKSA

Serves 6–8

5 shallots
4 cloves garlic
3 small bird's eye hot red chillies or 2 larger hot red chillies
2 stalks lemon grass
2 x 4 cm (1¹/₂ in) pieces fresh ginger, peeled, plus
small piece galangal (Thai ginger), if possible
coriander (cilantro) roots
400 ml (12 fl oz) can of coconut milk
1 heaped teaspoon Tom Yum paste (sweet and sour soup base)
1.5 L (2¹/₂ pt) fish stock
3 makrut (Kaffir) lime leaves
4 large dried Chinese mushrooms, soaked, or 6 small fresh champignons, sliced
50 ml (1¹/₂ fl oz) Thai fish sauce, or to taste
juice of 1 large or 2 small green limes
50 g (1¹/₂ oz) bean thread noodles, soaked in water

The seafood
about 15 tiny prawns (shrimp)
8–10 larger prawns (shrimp) (they may be cutlets,
or peeled with their heads left on)
150 g (5 oz) ling, blue eye, orange roughy (sea perch) or other large-lobed,
white-fleshed fish, sliced finely (chill well first to help)
8 large scampi, or Dublin bay prawns, yabbies (crawfish or écrevisses),
or bugs (slipper or hammer-head lobsters). Large seafood pieces may be
halved lengthways if too expensive for 1 per person, but are very
decorative in the bowl whole
6–8 large scallops (optional)

The greens
choose some Vietnamese greens, or break 2 small bok choy into leaves.
*(I have been known to use rocket, lamb's tongue lettuce (*mâche*) or mizuna*
if I have them in the fridge.)
¹/₂ bunch fresh coriander (cilantro)

Slice the shallots, garlic and chillies. Slice the tender part of the lemon grass, then cut a couple of long thin pieces of the root lengthways. Place about three-quarters of the sliced ingredients in a grinder (or mortar and pestle) along with all the ginger and about 6 coriander roots; grind almost to a paste.

Open the tin of coconut milk without shaking, and spoon about 3–4 tablespoons of the thick part from the top into a soup pot. Add the ground ingredients, then the Tom Yum paste, and fry until aromatic. Add the rest of the coconut milk as well as the fish stock, makrut lime leaves and mushrooms, and bring to the boil. Reduce the heat and simmer for 6–8 minutes. Flavour with the fish sauce and lime juice, then add the soaked noodles.

Add the seafood in turn, depending on the time you think it will take to cook (i.e. thicker seafood like prawns first, scallops and tiny prawns last), and the greens in turn (i.e. thicker ones first, followed by thinner-leaved greens). Place the freshly plucked leaves of coriander directly into the bowls. Ladle the soup into the bowls, making sure the larger seafood pops out for a prettier presentation.

NASTURTIUM CREAM SOUP

A very different cold soup, inspired by Ricki Holt.

<u>Serves 6</u>

1 small carrot
¹/₂ stalk celery
¹/₂ small leek (white only)
2 cups nasturtium leaves
200 ml (7 fl oz) cream
a few nasturtium flowers, for garnish
salt and pepper

Peel the vegetables and dice into tiny pieces (called *brunoise*). Place half the nasturtium leaves in the base of a blender. Scald half the cream and pour onto the leaves; blend to a purée, seasoning with salt and pepper. Repeat the process with the other half of the ingredients. Pour into the bowls. Add the *brunoise* and garnish with the nasturtium petals. The soup can be served hot or cold, frothy or settled, but it loses its green colour if reheated.

SEAFOOD

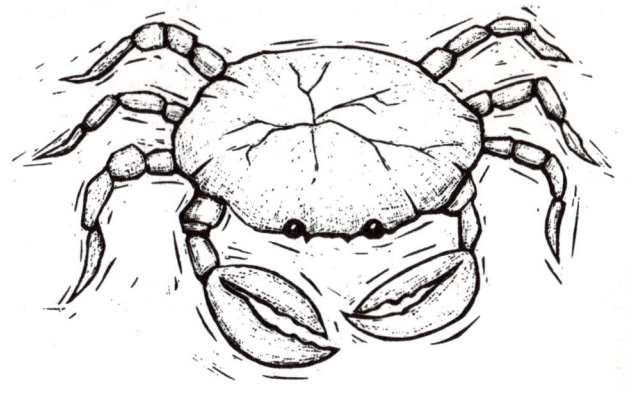

SEAFOOD SAVVY

Scallops, oysters, prawns (shrimp), school prawns, pippis (clams) and periwinkles, mussels, lobsters, scampi (langoustines), Moreton Bay bugs (slipper or hammer-head lobsters), yabbies (crawfish or écrevisses), marrons (large freshwater crayfish), sea urchins, abalone, crabs, squid. The world's coastlines are rich in seafood, many varieties of which we have not even explored as possible delicacies for the table.

Pippis are great for tomato pasta sauces; periwinkles more problematic to use, but good presented like buttery snails or garlic prawns, in their shells. Here, however, we only have the space to deal with the more commonly used seafood.

If you get a chance to open oysters yourself, so much the better. Most cooked seafood dishes benefit from the addition of oyster juice in the sauce. Cooked oysters are traditionally not as prized as those eaten raw, but a few recipes in this chapter may change your mind.

Prawns are highly rated and ubiquitous, but their expense of late sees them scarcer in the home kitchen. Green prawns are readily available, so you should never have to recook those already cooked (thus automatically toughening them). Remember, most prawns are frozen as soon as they are caught, and some shops may even re-freeze them. Brightness of colouring, buying only as many as you need now, and making sure you know when they came into the shop are your best guarantees of quality. Always cook the heads and carcass peelings in water with a little wine, then strain and freeze. This can then be used to enhance sauce or soufflé flavours. Do not forget to devein them (i.e. remove the gritty black intestine).

Scallops are, unfortunately, becoming similarly expensive. It is more common now to find them in their shells; if removed from their shells, they are of better quality when they are not soaked in water to plump up their weight (the good ones are called 'dry-shucked'). Try to buy the largest ones you can. If buying them in their shells, remember to discard the outer band of gristle, keeping only the 'eye' and the 'coral'.

Mussels are popular, and easy for the home cook to cope with. Most nowadays come from hatcheries and need little scrubbing for barnacles. Remember to remove the beard (holding the back of a knife to it and pulling is the easiest way), and never soak them or you lose the sea-water inside. Move them briskly around the sink to keep them shut while cleaning; discard any that remain open — they are dead.

Yabbies, scampi, Moreton Bay bugs and the unique West Australian marrons have almost interchangeable uses in cookery. Remember to devein them — because of its muddy environment, the yabby bears a particularly gritty vein. If the scampi, marrons or bugs are large enough, they lend themselves to halving lengthways and grilling.

Lobsters are expensive, and are now mostly confined to restaurants, or the home grill for special occasions. Beware the frozen tails — they seem a good buy, but their membranes refuse to detach for grilling and successful carving. They are better under sauces.

COMMON TECHNIQUES FOR COOKING SEAFOOD

As with fish (and meat, for that matter), seafood can be steamed, boiled, poached, grilled, barbecued, pan-fried, deep-fried (floured, crumbed or battered), casseroled and braised. If your aim is to invent dishes with these different methods, use the guidelines mentioned with fish and meats, but remember the following: *the suitability of a given cooking method is highly related to timing.* Most seafood can only stand a minimum of cooking, or it becomes rubbery.

This may mean just cooking it less than the equivalent style of fish or meat dish, but often it requires thinking through a compromise method. Take the classic dish, Lobster à l'Americaine. The flavour of the braised-style sauce is determined by the long simmering of the sauce ingredients. This does not mean certain seafood cannot be braised, it means understanding the compromises needed to create the effect. For example, in Lobster à l'Americaine, the carcass and claws are simmered along with the tomatoes and onion to give a lobster flavour to the sauce; the lobster meat is only bathed in the mixture for enough of time to cook through.

Suitability may well include other factors — the shape of the food, the texture, and some vitally important detail that seems trivial, such as will it fall apart? can it be turned? will it toughen? will it dry out? This is possibly why the common methods of seafood cookery are searing on a barbecue or frying in a cast-iron pan (ensure the barbecue or pan is extremely hot, otherwise weeping takes place and the plan to brown the outside and keep the centre undercooked is quickly lost), deep-frying in crumbs (I shudder at the thought, but the method has sense — it keeps the moisture in and crisps only the covering), and steaming (a moist environment, thus no drying out of the food).

Seafood requires some knowledge — particularly as regards preparing it for cooking. Never underestimate the help of a good, knowledgeable supplier. Ask. He or she will be delighted to help.

OYSTERS WITH PISTACHIO NUT BUTTER

Ingredients are per person

12 oysters
100 g (3¹/₂ oz) unsalted butter
2 tablespoons pistachio nuts, shelled, skinned and chopped
2 tablespoons finely grated lemon rind
1 clove garlic, crushed
4 slices prosciutto, cut into thin slices
freshly ground black pepper

Remove the oysters from their shells; wipe the shells dry. Cream the butter and add the pistachios, lemon rind and garlic. Wrap some prosciutto around each oyster. Replace each oyster in its shell, cover with pistachio butter and grind pepper on top. Grill gently or place in a hot oven until the butter melts.

Variations

Replace the prosciutto with chopped, crisped bacon, add a bed of cooked spinach and substitute Worcester sauce for the pistachio butter, and you have the classic recipe for Oysters Kilpatrick. Closer to the method above, change the pistachio butter to hazelnut butter and you have a great flavour. You can also omit the prosciutto and the bacon, change the pistachio butter to hazelnut butter — this is a great flavour marriage with a bed of spinach. There is much to play with in this simple recipe.

OYSTER SPRING ROLLS

Serves 6

24 oysters
6 water chestnuts, finely chopped
1 slice fresh ginger, finely chopped
6 spring onions (scallions), finely chopped
¹/₂ teaspoon sesame oil
¹/₂ teaspoon light soy sauce
3 large spring roll wrappers, cut into four
oil, for deep frying

The garnish
12 spring onions (scallions), green stems attached

Remove the oysters from their shells. In a bowl, combine the finely chopped water chestnuts, ginger and spring onions with the sesame oil and soy sauce. Add the oysters. Divide the mixture evenly among the spring roll wrappers, allowing 2 oysters per portion, and roll up, carefully folding in the sides to enclose. Brush the edges with water to seal. Deep fry for 2–3 minutes in hot oil; drain and serve immediately.

Variations

The fact that spring rolls fry and crisp means they can adapt to stronger flavours than the original Chinese tradition suggests. Try a modern version with spinach and finely chopped sun-dried tomatoes. You may then prefer to add firmer-textured seafood such as prawns (shrimp) and scallops, rather than just oysters.

SAUTEED SCALLOPS
WITH APPLE AND MANGO SAUCE

Serves 4

12 scallops
½ Granny Smith apple, unpeeled
½ mango
40 g (1½ oz) butter
200 ml (7 fl oz) dry alcoholic cider
200 ml (7 fl oz) cream, preferably with 45 per cent milk fat
salt and pepper

Separate each scallop from its coral. Chop the corals, apple and mango into tiny, tiny squares (*brunoise*). Melt the butter in a medium-sized saucepan and sauté the corals, apple and mango for about 45 seconds, keeping crunch in the apple. Remove from the pan and keep warm. Reheat the saucepan to very hot, then sauté the scallops for 2 minutes. Remove from the pan and mix with the fruit.

Deglaze the pan with the cider, stirring up the sediment at the base of the pan. Add the cream and stir until it is reduced to sauce consistency. Season the sauce with salt and pepper. Divide the scallops amongst 4 shells or small plates and spoon the sauce over them.

Note: If you leave out the cream, you can keep the unctuous quality of the sauce by whisking in 25 g (1 oz) unsalted butter in its place. Remove from the stove to do this; increased heat melts the butter and serves to decrease its ability to 'bind'.

TEA-SMOKED SCALLOPS

If you cannot find scallops already smoked, try this easy home-style method. They are great as part of a cold seafood platter.

36–48 scallops

The marinade
250 ml (8 fl oz) dry alcoholic cider
1 heaped teaspoon sugar
salt

The smoking process
4 tablespoons heavily perfumed tea (such as Lapsang Souchong)
1 teaspoon sugar

Place the scallops in a bowl and cover with the marinade ingredients; leave for a minimum of 1 hour, or overnight.

Line the base of a wok with foil, then place the tea and sugar in a pile on the foil. Drain the scallops and pat dry with paper towelling. Place them on a round cake rack, then set the rack in position over the tea. Put the lid on the wok, place over heat and allow some smoke to build up. Reduce the heat and smoke slowly until the scallops dry and colour. Depending on their size, with this hot smoking method the scallops are ready in 8–10 minutes. Turn them once to even the cooking, and press one between the fingers to judge whether they are ready. Never overcook — they can go very rubbery.

To serve: Drizzle with a tiny bit of oil to soften the skin formed by the smoking. When they are served simply like this, I often add a little finely chopped apple and walnut and bind together with a minimum of mayonnaise. If you prefer, simply serve with lemon juice, or toss in a full vinaigrette with chopped parsley and chives through it.

GRILLED SQUID WITH AN ASIAN TOUCH

Serves 4

8 small squid tubes
a little oil
1 red capsicum (bell pepper), cut into julienne
250 ml (8 fl oz) white wine vinegar
125 g (4 oz) sugar

The garnish
4 small bird's eye hot red chillies or 2 larger chillies, shredded
16 mint leaves
16 sprigs coriander (cilantro)
75 g (2¹/₂ oz) roasted peanuts

Clean the squid, if necessary, and slit tubes down one side so they will lie flat. If very large, cut into 2 or 3 large slices lengthways. Brush lightly with oil and barbecue (tentacles too — they curl and look great), or cook on an oiled cast-iron grill for 1–2 minutes per side. Remove and slice into strips, then transfer to a bowl with the red capsicum. Combine the white vinegar and sugar and toss through the salad.

To serve: Pile the salad attractively on individual plates. Garnish liberally with the hot chillies, mint leaves, coriander and roasted peanuts.

WARM SALAD OF TANDOORI PRAWNS AND FISH

A wok-cooked stir-fry, but pan-frying will also make a success of this simple warm salad with Indian flavours.

Serves 4

1 fillet orange roughy (sea perch), blue eye or other large-lobed, white-fleshed fish
12 green prawns (shrimp), peeled and deveined, but with tails on
3 tablespoons tandoori spices (a commercial brand mix will suffice)
75 ml (2¹/₂ fl oz) peanut oil
2 handfuls baby spinach leaves, washed
1 handful pea sprouts (or use other mesclun salads to plump out the mixture)
4 tablespoons sultanas (golden raisins), soaked in water and drained
16 snow peas (mangetout), the largest ones cut in half diagonally

The garnish
4 tablespoons garlic (cloves sliced diagonally), deep fried
2 tablespoons flaked almonds, deep-fried
fresh coriander (cilantro) leaves
a few fresh mint leaves

The sauce
200 ml (7 fl oz) plain yoghurt thinned with 3 tablespoons water and 1 tablespoon lemon juice
6 mint leaves, chopped
salt

Slice the fish into long fingers to about the size of the prawns. Coat the prawns and fish with tandoori spice mix. Leave for 1 hour. When ready to cook, heat the oil in a wok or frying pan and fry the prawns and fish for 2 minutes, then quickly add the spinach, pea sprouts, sultanas and snow peas. Cook for just a moment. Pile into small pyramids on a nest of pea sprouts on individual serving plates. Top with the garlic and almonds, and garnish with the fresh herb leaves.

The sauce: Combine the thinned yoghurt and mint; add salt to taste. Serve in a sauceboat.

TIGER PRAWNS IN COCONUT BATTER

Serves 6

30 large green prawns (shrimp), peeled and deveined, but with tails on
500 ml (16 fl oz) beer
500 ml (16 fl oz) ginger ale
salt and pepper
about 1 teaspoon grated fresh ginger, or to taste
plain (all purpose) flour
6–8 tablespoons desiccated coconut
6–8 tablespoons shredded coconut
peanut oil, for deep frying

Butterfly the prawns, being careful not to cut too deep. Combine the beer and ginger ale in a large mixing bowl. Whisk in the grated ginger, and season with salt and pepper. Using a whisk, gradually incorporate enough flour to obtain the consistency of thick cream.

In another large bowl, mix equal amounts of desiccated and shredded coconut together. Lightly flour the prawns, making sure they are completely covered, then shake off excess. Dip the prawns in the batter, shaking off excess, then roll in the coconut mixture. Heat the peanut oil in a frying pan and gently deep-fry the prawns for 4–5 minutes, or until golden.

Drain on paper towelling for 30 seconds, then serve with a mayonnaise which has been lightly flavoured with curry powder.

STEAMED PRAWNS, TAHITIAN STYLE

Serves 5–6

1 kg (2 lb) green prawns (shrimp), peeled and deveined, but with tails on
250 ml (8 fl oz) cream
2 teaspoons brandy
1 small onion, chopped very finely
2–3 tablespoons light soy sauce
1 tablespoon cornflour (cornstarch)
4 spring onions (scallions), chopped

Place the prawns on the rack of a steamer, or on a plate which you can put in a covered vessel to act as a steamer. Set aside until needed.

In a small saucepan, heat the cream, brandy and onion. Cook until the onion softens, then add the soy sauce. Bring back to the boil, stirring. Mix the cornflour with a little water in a cup, to make a paste. Stir the paste gradually into the sauce; keep stirring until the sauce boils and thickens.

When ready to serve, steam the prawns over fast-boiling water for about 1–1½ minutes. Toss through the sauce, adding the spring onions. Serve on small plates, or pour into a large clam shell and serve at the table.

PRAWNS AND EGGPLANT
IN TAMARIND CHILLI SAUCE

*A recipe with a Malaysian touch from Beh Kim Un of
Monsoon Restaurant, Melbourne, Australia.*

<u>Serves 6</u>

The shrimp floss
2 tablespoons dried shrimp (available in packets from Asian supermarkets)

The tamarind chilli sauce
· 125 ml (4 fl oz) tamarind juice or lime juice
180 g (6 oz) palm sugar or 125 g (4 oz) raw sugar
2 small red chillies, finely chopped
1 teaspoon salt

The prawns and eggplants
3 tablespoons vegetable oil
2 medium eggplants (aubergines), unpeeled and cut into large cubes
salt
18 very large green tiger prawns (shrimp) or 12 scampi (langoustines)

The garnish
banana, padana or aspidistra leaves (optional)
90 ml (3 fl oz) coconut milk

The shrimp floss: Place the dried shrimp in a food processor and blend until the shrimp is finely chopped and triples in volume. At this point, it can be placed in a jar and kept for weeks. You may choose to use the whole packet, rather than 2 tablespoons, because the blades of some food processors find it hard to pick up small amounts.

The tamarind chilli sauce: In a saucepan, heat the tamarind or lime juice, add the palm or raw sugar and stir until dissolved. Add the chillies, shrimp floss and salt, and reduce over heat until the mixture is two-thirds its original volume. Set aside until needed.

This mixture will keep for 2 weeks in the refrigerator sealed in a jar or may be frozen. The clever cook will find many uses for this spicy sweet sauce.

The prawns and eggplants: Heat the oil in a frying pan and fry the eggplant cubes. When their flesh is well-seared, reduce the heat and cook until just softened. Salt lightly; keep warm.

Boil or grill the prawns, having spiked each one on a satay stick along its length to keep the tails straight. Peel each prawn, leaving head and tail on.

To serve: Garnish the base of the serving plates with the leaves. Transfer 3 prawns (or 2 scampi) to each plate and spoon the fried eggplant cubes over or alongside. Coat with tamarind sauce. Drizzle a little coconut milk over each for a refreshing contrast of flavours.

YABBIES WITH MEDITERRANEAN FLAVOURS

Serves 6

90 ml (3 fl oz) extra virgin olive oil
5–6 tablespoons julienne of mixed vegetables: choose from carrot, turnip,
green beans, snow peas (mangetout), celery or leek
30 yabbies (crawfish or écrevisses) — I am presuming cooked, because this is
typical in many markets, but if raw, cover the pan for a moment after frying to
allow them to cook through. You may prefer to use green tiger prawns (shrimp)
or scampi (langoustines)
salt and cracked black pepper
about 12 black olives (depending on size), pitted and diced
2 tablespoons chopped Italian parsley

Heat 3 tablespoons of the oil and sauté the vegetables until they soften, but retain a slight crispness. Add the yabbies and reheat (or cover and cook through). Season with salt and pepper (stronger on the pepper) then add the olives and parsley just as you are about to lift them from the pan. Arrange attractively on individual plates, then drizzle with the remaining unheated olive oil. Serve immediately. Rice or couscous may be served as an accompaniment.

GRILLED SCAMPI WITH MANGO AND PASSIONFRUIT CHUTNEY

Serves 6

12 large scampi (langoustines) or 18 large green tiger prawns (shrimp), peeled
and deveined, but with heads and tails on
a little olive oil
salt and pepper
1 tablespoon dried herbes de Provence

The mango and passionfruit chutney
¹/₂ mango, peeled and finely diced
¹/₂ Granny Smith apple, peeled and finely diced
1 shallot, pink-fleshed if possible, finely chopped
1 tablespoon chopped coriander (cilantro)
¹/₂ bird's eye hot red chilli, very finely chopped
2 tablespoons olive oil
¹/₂ tablespoon vinegar
salt and pepper
2 passionfruit

Slice the scampi lengthways and keep the flesh in the shells, or devein the prawns. Slide a satay skewer along each prawn or scampi to help keep them straight while cooking. Drizzle a film of oil over the seafood, salt and pepper lightly, then scatter with the *herbes de Provence*. Set aside for 1 hour.

Cook the scampi or prawns on a hot barbecue or cast-iron grill for about 2 minutes in all, or until tender. (The scampi are cooked on the flesh side only; the prawns turned).

Place 2 scampi, or 3 prawns, on each plate, with a heaped spoonful of chutney alongside. Serve immediately — the scampi or prawns should be sizzling hot.

The mango and passionfruit chutney: Combine the mango and apple in a bowl; stir in the shallot, coriander and chilli. Add the oil and vinegar, then season with salt and pepper. Stir in the pulp and juice of the two passionfruit.

RICE NOODLE SALAD WITH MIXED SEAFOOD, VIETNAMESE STYLE

Serves 6

*250 g (8 oz) vermicelli rice or bean thread noodles
(sometimes known as glass noodles)*
*500 g (1 lb) mixed cooked seafood: yabbies (crawfish or écrevisses) and/or
scampi (langoustines) and school prawns (baby shrimp)*
4 asparagus stalks, peeled and cut diagonally into 2.5 cm (1 in) lengths
$^1/_2$ stalk celery, finely sliced
10 large or 15 small snow peas (mangetout), topped and tailed
*2 tablespoons dried shrimp, rehydrated for 30 minutes in hot water
(if large, cut in half diagonally)*
$^1/_2$ red capsicum (bell pepper), diced
2 heaped tablespoons (about $^1/_2$ small can) diced water chestnuts
6 spring onions (scallions), sliced
2 hot red chillies, shredded
leaves of $^1/_2$ bunch fresh coriander (cilantro)

The dressing
2 teaspoons grated or finely chopped fresh ginger
90 ml (3 fl oz) mirin or sake
2–3 tablespoons light soy sauce (less if heavy soy)
2 tablespoons fish sauce
juice of 2 green limes or 1 lemon

The garnish
extra coriander (cilantro) leaves
1 tablespoon dried onion flakes
4 tablespoons roasted or deep-fried cashew nuts

Well before dinner, place the rice noodles in a bowl, in as flat a layer as possible, and cover with boiling water. Allow to cool, then drain the noodles and place on paper towelling to dry well.

Peel the (cooked and cooled) seafood, deveining as necessary. Blanch the asparagus and celery in boiling, salted water until just tender, adding the snow peas just before draining. Refresh under cold water; drain well.

The dressing: Place the grated ginger in a bowl, add the mirin, soy sauce, fish sauce and lemon or lime juice; mix well.

To assemble the salad: Add the noodles, vegetables and seafood to the dressing. Leave for 1 hour to blend the flavours, then add the coriander leaves and chilli. Toss well and pile on plates. Top with fresh coriander leaves, onion flakes and cashews.

Variation

The salad works very well with shredded chicken, crisped Chinese sausage or smoked ham instead of seafood. Topping variants include crisped (i.e. deep fried) shrimp floss (page 75), roasted peanuts, freshly deep-fried onion chips and/or garlic flakes, or toasted sesame seeds. Mint is refreshing added to the coriander leaves.

SEAFOOD COUSCOUS

This couscous is served almost identically to the classic meat-based Moroccan dish (page 144), except it is topped with an assortment of colourful vegetables, cut in small strips so that they are eye-appealing, cooked along with an assortment of light seafood.

Serves 6

The seafood
about 30 mussels
18 green tiger prawns (shrimp) or
36 smaller (school) prawns (shrimp)
500 g (1 lb) squid tubes
300 g (9¹/₂ oz) blue eye, ling or other large white fillet of fish
24 scallops

The vegetables
2 firm, very red tomatoes
¹/₄ cucumber
1 small or ¹/₂ large carrot
¹/₂ green capsicum (bell pepper)
¹/₂ red capsicum (bell pepper)
2 onions

The couscous

500 g (1 lb) couscous
250 ml (8 fl oz) boiling water
90 ml (3 fl oz) olive oil
pinch of salt
1 L (1³/₄ pt) fish stock
(ask your fishmonger for some bones, or maybe they sell stock)
3 sprigs dill

The garnish

A small bowl of harissa (available in good delicatessans, or use the recipe on page 147) or chilli paste or 1 medium hot red chilli, shredded
2–3 tablespoons chopped parsley

The seafood: Clean the mussels and remove beards; place in an empty saucepan, cover with the lid and place the pan over heat until they open (about 3 minutes). Set aside. Peel and devein the prawns, leaving the heads and tails on 1 or 2 per person for decoration. Slice the squid tubes and cut the fish into cubes. Set aside with the scallops.

The vegetables: Peel, seed and dice the tomatoes. Cut the cucumber, carrot and capsicum into small strips. Peel and slice the onions. Set aside, covered in plastic wrap, until dinner.

The couscous: Before dinner, tip the couscous into a bowl and pour 250 ml (8 fl oz) boiling water and the olive oil over it. Add the pinch of salt. When swollen and cooled a little, run your fingers through the couscous to remove any lumps. Transfer to the top of a couscousier or place in a piece of muslin in a colander which can fit over a saucepan as a steamer.

Place the fish stock in the base of the couscousier or steamer, then add the carrot and onion. Bring to the boil and simmer for 5 minutes, then add the capsicum, cucumber, tomato and dill.

For all this time, use the steamer over the top to steam and heat the couscous. Place the seafood in with the stock for the time it needs to cook, in this order: the fish cubes and scallops, then the prawns, if they need cooking (if not, then reheat with the mussels), then the squid. The fish and scallops take 2–3 minutes, the prawns take 1–2 minutes and the squid only 30 seconds. Add the drained mussels last, only to reheat.

To serve: Spoon some couscous onto the base of each plate (a wide old-English style soup bowl is ideal) and ladle the seafood over. Season the stock with salt and pepper, and perhaps a little mussel juice, but remember that this is salty. Garnish with parsley, and scatter the shredded chilli over the top (if using). Serve the chilli paste or harissa on the side. Fork the harissa through the broth as you eat, a little at a time, to your taste. (It's hot!)

PAELLA

This great Spanish classic contains meat, chicken and mixed seafood.

Serves 8

1 small chicken, cut into small pieces
1 carrot, peeled and halved
1 onion, peeled and halved
8 king prawns (shrimp)
8 scampi (langoustines)
10 mussels
16 scallops
200 ml (7 fl oz) olive oil
1 onion, chopped
1 clove garlic, sliced
250 g (8 oz) calamari rings
200 g (7 oz) green beans
200 g (7 oz) peas
1 red capsicum (bell pepper), sliced into strips
1 tomato, peeled and chopped
100 g (3¹/₂ oz) ham, chopped into bite-sized pieces
150 g (5 oz) chorizo sausage, chopped into bite-sized pieces
100 g (3¹/₂ oz) lean pork, chopped into bite-sized pieces
400 g (12 oz) rice, preferably Calrose or Arborio
¹/₂ teaspoon saffron stamens, plus a pinch of powdered saffron
a few drops lemon juice
salt and pepper
3 tablespoons chopped parsley

Boil the chicken, carrot and onion. When cooked, remove the chicken and save the broth. Cook the prawns, scampi and mussels in their shells in a small amount of water: 3–4 minutes for the prawns and scampi; 1 minute for the mussels.

Heat a small amount of oil in a large frying pan and sauté the onion and garlic until golden. Add the calamari and cook for 1 minute, then add the beans, peas, capsicum, tomato, ham, sausage and pork.

At the same time, cook the rice in the remaining olive oil in a paellera (a flat paella pan) until transparent. Add the food from the frying pan, arranging the ingredients evenly through the paellera. Measure 1 L (1³/₄ pt) of liquid from the chicken and seafood broths and bring to the boil in a saucepan before adding to the paellera. Add the saffron stamens and lemon juice. Season with salt and pepper. Arrange the chicken, prawns, scampi, mussels, raw scallops, parsley and strips of capsicum on top. Bring to the boil then reduce heat and simmer for 15 minutes.

Check the seasoning, and add saffron powder if you want a deeper colour. Remove from heat and stand covered with a cloth for 5 minutes before serving.

MUSSEL POWER

Mussels are the Belgians' favourite seafood, and perhaps only the people of northern France love them as much. Strange, as they are some of the cheapest seafood available, and perhaps the easiest to cook. Perhaps what has put many of us in Anglo-Saxon countries off them is the English tradition of sousing them in a vinegary solution that made them impossible to use in cooking.

Nowadays, most good fish shops and supermarkets sell mussels. Many are still fished from the deep, and can be old and bear quite a few barnacles, which need to be scraped off with the back of a knife under a tap. But a new interest in farming mussels, in very much the same manner as oysters are farmed, now gives us controlled breeding, controlled size, and, since they are raised well above sand level and away from rocks, a much cleaner shell.

Now all the cook has to do is give them a quick dip under some water, only a cursory scrubbing, and remove the beard, that hairy protrusion from the side of the shell. The easiest way to do this is to hold it securely between the back of a small knife and your thumb, and pull firmly. If they are to be used shelled in a dish, they can be opened in an empty (ungreased) covered saucepan placed directly over the heat; if they are to be served in their shells, just follow the recipe.

Avoid the large mussels on the market known as green-lipped mussels; they are generally fairly tough. I don't recommend them for the type of recipes below; they work better cold in salads, or served as stuffed mussels with a diced ragoût of cooked capsicums (bell peppers), onion and garlic tucked into the shell and a drizzling of olive oil.

The first recipe most of us learn for cooking mussels is Moules Marinière, in which a little chopped shallot and white wine is placed in the base of a saucepan and boiled for a moment before the mussels are placed in the saucepan to open. When they are opened, they are cooked. They are then seasoned with some freshly ground pepper — never salt — and a scattering of chopped parsley. That is all that's needed for the mussel-lovers of the world to tuck in with joy. Moules Marinière is served in a wide soup plate with a spoon to eat a little of the juice as you go. Those that don't relish the salty sauce often mellow it by stirring 150 ml (5 fl oz) cream into the juice before serving.

For a further change, try cider instead of wine (in this case, the cream is almost obligatory). Try also making a little ragoût in the base of the saucepan by frying a little peeled tomato and some red capsicum (bell pepper) along with onion. This can be made with or without wine, and thus has less juice.

I have also made mussels on a base of three colours of capsicum (bell pepper) — green, red and yellow — dicing the capsicum (bell pepper) and some onion, ignoring the wine, and relying only on chopped parsley and a good grind of the pepper mill before spooning the vegetable over the mussels, with a minimum of liquid only. The following three mussel dishes have a more esoteric approach to flavouring mussels.

STUFFED MUSSELS FROM ISTANBUL

The traditional Turkish way to cook this speciality is to prise the mussels open, catching any juice that falls, then stuff them with cooked rice pilaf. Tie them with string so they cannot open, and steam them until cooked (3–4 minutes). Cut the string, stack them into a pile in a large casserole dish, sprinkle with chopped parsley, and reheat them before serving. This is delicious, and certainly more moist, but somewhat tedious and difficult. The following recipe is a more conventional method, relying on an unusual flavour combination to be of enough interest to speak for itself.

Serves 6

36 mussels, scrubbed and with beards removed

The stuffing
75–90 ml (2¹/₂ –3 fl oz) olive oil
1 large onion, grated
3 tablespoons pine nuts
3 tablespoons currants or sultanas (golden raisins)
1 teaspoon sugar
180 g (6 oz) short-grain rice
2 large tomatoes, peeled and roughly chopped
pinch of allspice
salt and freshly ground black pepper
chopped parsley and dill
375 ml (12 fl oz) water with a little mussel juice (watch the salt content) or fish stock

Place the mussels in an empty saucepan and heat for 3–4 minutes until they open. Remove and discard half of each mussel shell, leaving the mussels tucked into their saved shells. Strain the mussel juice.

The stuffing. Heat the oil in a saucepan and sauté the onion until softened, but not browned. Add the pine nuts, currants or sultanas and sugar, and stir for a moment. Stir in the rice until it is well greased. Add the tomatoes, allspice, salt and pepper to taste, then the parsley and dill and the liquid. Bring to the boil, then reduce the heat. Cover the saucepan with a lid and cook the rice for about 12 minutes, or until tender.

To serve: Spoon a little of the rice stuffing up and around the mussels in their shells. If the dish is made in advance, reheat covered with foil and try not to dry out. To keep the moisture, mix a little extra parsley and dill in olive oil and drizzle it over the mussels before covering and reheating.

THAI-FLAVOURED STEAMED MUSSELS

Serves 6

40 mussels, scrubbed and with beards removed
about 15 leaves baby spinach, cut in wide strips
150 g (5 oz) tiny white champignons, sliced

The sauce
1 tablespoon raw sugar
$1/2$ teaspoon palm sugar
3 tablespoons hot water
2 teaspoons fish sauce
2 stalks lemon grass, tender part only, chopped
2 cloves garlic, finely chopped
$1/2$ teaspoon chopped ginger
1 small red chilli, finely chopped

The garnish
1 bunch Thai or sweet basil leaves, shredded
$1/4$ bunch coriander (cilantro) leaves, shredded
2 small bird's eye hot red chillies, sliced

Place the mussels in an empty saucepan and cover with the saucepan lid. Steam the mussels open by placing the pan directly over heat (2–3 minutes, depending on size). Remove when just cooked, and place aside a few whole mussels for decoration. With the remaining mussels, break off half of each shell, retaining only those in which the mussels nestle. Blanch the spinach leaves and mushrooms; drain well.

The sauce: Dissolve both sugars in the hot water; stir in the fish sauce and chopped ingredients.

To serve: Place a little spinach and mushroom around each mussel in its shell, then warm in the oven for a couple of minutes. Pour the dressing over, and garnish with sliced chilli, basil and coriander. Serve immediately.

MUSSELS WITH CURRY

Serves 4

2 tablespoons olive oil
1 onion, very finely chopped
4 teaspoons mild curry powder or paste
4 cloves garlic, crushed
2 tablespoons each carrot, celery and red capsicum (bell pepper),
very finely diced, then mixed
48 mussels, scrubbed and with beards removed
250 ml (8 fl oz) dry white wine
500 ml (16 fl oz) cream
1 tablespoon shredded threads of coconut,
soaked in water for 2 hours to soften

Heat the olive oil in a large saucepan. Stir-fry the onion, curry powder or paste, garlic and vegetables until the vegetables are well-greased, then add the mussels, keeping the heat high. Stir for a few seconds.

Add the white wine and simmer for a few seconds. Add the cream and cook over medium heat until the mussels open (about 5 minutes). Using a slotted spoon, transfer mussels to a serving plate. Pour the sauce over the mussels, sprinkle with coconut threads and serve.

FISH

FOR THE LOVE OF FISH

Over the years, I have found people to be less daring with fish than with any other major ingredient. Pan-frying is the norm, yet with the wonderful array of fish now available, and medical advice that fish is an important part of a healthy diet, the clever cook must be able to handle it much better than this. More knowledge of the subject will give the less self-assured greater confidence.

WHEN IS A FISH FRESH?

1. **Whole fish:** The skin should be shiny; flesh around the gills should not only shine, but send off reflected lights in a number of colours (blue, pink, gold) other than the main colour. Eyes should be shiny, never cloudy. A coating of slime — that is, a slippery feeling like that which makes a cake of wet soap slip from your hand — is natural. Tackiness, however, is a sign of old fish. Most fish (other than those kept on ice for long-distance travel) should be flexible when held. Fish should never smell unpleasant, and certainly must not have a smell of ammonia.

2. **Fillets:** Fillets must never be dehydrated or look dry around the edges. Nor should they be sitting in water or watery trays. A frozen fillet is very spongy to the touch (and its texture will be similarly spongy when eaten), and will not spring back when pressed. A slight squeeze will make it emit water. In a good fillet, the flesh must be true to colour, mostly white or pinky-white, but you do need to get to know the fish — bream is slightly yellow/grey, tuna is pink or pink/grey. The smell should be 'clean' even though fishy, with no odour of ammonia.

TECHNIQUES FOR COOKING FISH

1. **Deep frying:** When fish is deep-fried, it is usually coated with a batter: egg and breadcrumbs, or at least flour. There are many types of batters, the lightest being Japanese tempura batter, in which corn-flour (cornstarch) is mixed with flour, and ice cubes added just before use. Of the European batters, the best are made with beer or soda water — these are always crisper than the egg or egg and yeast-based ones.

    The fish is deep-fried in oil — usually peanut or a bland oil. The oil should always be at least 8–10 cm (3–4 in) deep. Ensure the oil is hot — a deep-fry thermometer should read 190°C (375°F). If you don't have a thermometer, test the oil with a piece of fish. It should sizzle well and rise immediately to the surface. Timing depends on the thickness of the fish; it should be kept to a thickness whereby it is cooked in the time the batter takes to become a golden brown. Never overcrowd. Drain well on brown paper; sprinkle with salt.

2. **Pan-frying**: Pan-fried fish is shallow-fried. The fish is usually floured lightly, the excess patted off, then fried in a frying pan in butter or margarine. The Mediterraneans fry in oil, but oil is not as readily absorbed by the fish and tends to remain as a pungent film on the food. There is much to be said for browning fish in margarine, as it does not burn as readily as butter, but if the butter is to be used as a sauce (e.g. in trout with almonds, meunière recipes, etc.), replace the margarine with fresh butter after frying. Fish in egg and breadcrumbs sometimes uses a pan-fry method, but unlike deep-frying, it is then cooked in butter, not oil.

3. **Grilling:**
   Under the griller: Only fish that sit on their tummies (whiting, gurnet, garfish) are suited to this method, because if the fish has to be turned during cooking, the underside will have softened and the skin will be broken. If the fish is thicker in the centre than the tail, score a few slashes into the flesh on each side to help the heat penetrate, then brush with oil to prevent drying. Adjust the height of the grilling rack to the thickness of the fish so they don't burn while cooking.
   On a char grill or barbecue: Grilling small fish is tricky if the skin is thin (whiting, red mullet), although if well oiled, it is possible. Oil the grill and the fish, and flour the thinner-skinned fish, or those you think might break up — and never turn too early.

4. **Baking**: Both small and large fish can be baked in the oven, with or without a small amount of liquid (usually white wine, water, fish stock, or even milk) in the base of the pan. If baking without liquid, butter the pan very well. Most fish baking can be done at 200°C (400°F), but the longer the fish is in the oven (depending on size), the more likely it is to dry out. Only thicker-skinned or smaller fish bake well without the top drying out. Many cooks put a piece of buttered foil over the baking tray to seal in some steam, but if this covering is in place for the whole time the method is strictly steaming, not baking.

5. **Steaming**: Of all the steamers on the market, the Chinese bamboo is the cheapest. It is highly effective, provided it is wide enough. It also has an advantage in that you can superimpose layers (a maximum of three unless you change their places during cooking). Aluminium steamers tend to turn the fish grey and give it a metallic taste. Avoid this by laying the fish on a bed of seaweed, herbs or celery leaves. Steaming is ideal for large-lobed slices cut across the

fillet (a 130 g (4 1/2 oz) slice is perfect per person), such as salmon, ling, blue eye, cod, or a fillet of barramundi, dhufish or orange roughy (sea perch). It is suited to fine-fleshed fish only if cooked to a minimum.

Steaming tends to keep fish succulent, but sauces need to be made separately. Simple sauces, from drizzling with extra virgin olive oil to vinaigrettes with herbs or the more sophisticated Hollandaise, are the most suitable. Interest may be added by serving on a bed of vegetables — sautéed leeks, warmed chopped tomatoes, julienne of vegetables — before saucing.

Encasing in foil or a paper parcel, and then either cooking in the oven or over a barbecue, is another method of steaming. In this case the liquid is trapped in the parcel — usually the natural fish juices combined with citrus juice and/or butter or oil is enough to suffice as a sauce. For more detail, see 'Wrap it Up!' on page 101.

6. Poaching:

Whole fish: Fish should never be boiled. Poaching cooks the fish from 60°C (140°F) upwards, but optimum cooking is at around 90°C (200°F). The classical poaching liquor, *court-bouillon,* is a vegetable-flavoured water, with a touch of acidity (usually vinegar, sometimes wine) to hold the flesh of the fish together. Use chopped celery, carrot and onion, 3 stalks parsley and 3 peppercorns, but no bay leaf, as dry ones are musty (for more detail see page 98).

Fillets: A *court-bouillon* is not typically used with fillets, which often have no skin, and which, unlike larger fish, take so little time to cook that they are unlikely to fray on the outside while cooking through. Fillets are more usually poached in a mixture of half white wine and half water. Milk is sometimes used as an alternative to reinforce the whiteness of the fish, but it tends to form scum. It is also possible to poach fillets in fish stock, reducing the cooking liquid when the fillets are removed, and 'mounting' the sauce with butter, to which you may add herbs or crushed tomato.

WHEN IS THE FISH COOKED?

Overcooked fish means dry fish, which can become very sinewy and stick to the roof of your mouth. The culprit is invariably the beginner who cooks it for one or two minutes more 'just to be sure'. To test whether a fillet is cooked, simply check the fish has turned opaque; a milky white colour must replace the translucence. A whole fish must be tested at its thickest part, the shoulder or hump. The edge of a knife should penetrate to the spinal column readily, and, if slightly turned, could lift the flesh from the bone.

JAPANESE-STYLE TEMPURA OF WHOLE BABY SNAPPER

Serves 2 (or 4 as part of a many-course Japanese banquet)

1 x 750 g (1 lb 8 oz) snapper or bream, cleaned and scaled. Use 2 fish of the same size if doubling; a larger fish is hard to cook through in this manner.

The dipping sauce
125 ml (4 fl oz) light soy sauce
125 ml (4 fl oz) water
1 tablespoon mirin or sherry
a few pieces shredded, peeled fresh ginger
a few rings sliced spring onion (scallion)
hot chilli sauce of your preference (sambal oelek, commercially bottled chopped chilli, or chilli sauce)

The tempura batter
1 egg
enough cold water to make a little more than a cup of liquid (including the egg)
1 tablespoon cornflour (cornstarch)
250 g (8 oz) sifted plain (all-purpose) flour
vegetable oil, to deep fry the fish
6 ice cubes

Prepare the fish by patting it dry with paper towelling and snipping off the fins. Combine the ingredients of the dipping sauce and place ready in a serving bowl, alongside a bowl of chilli.

The batter: Break the egg into a large bowl, and whisk with the cold water. Add the cornflour and plain flour, and blend well. Use a large whisk to do this, but stir rather than use a whisking action — this avoids whisking air into the batter. The Japanese blend only lightly; a slight lumpiness is typical of their style. Allow the batter to rest until needed — a minimum of 30 minutes, but no more than 1 hour.

When ready to use and the oil is heating, throw in the ice cubes, stir once to cool the mixture, then pass the fish through the batter (expect a thin coating only for tempura — this is not a fish and chip shop style batter).

Lower the fish carefully into the hot oil. Cook until the batter is golden brown (4–5 minutes), and the fish will be cooked. Insert an egg-lift or long spatula under the fish, and transfer carefully onto brown paper to drain excess fat, then to the serving plate. Use the egg-lift to gather up any left-over fried batter pieces in the oil, and scatter over the fish. Serve with the dipping sauce and the bowl of chilli sauce.

LING WITH MACADAMIA NUTS AND BASIL

A pan-fry method.

<u>Serves 4</u>

4 x 130 g (4¹/₂ oz) pieces ling or John Dory, turbot, jewfish, cod, barramundi,
blue eye, or orange roughy (sea perch)
200 g (7 oz) fresh green beans, as small as possible
100 g (3¹/₂ oz) butter
salt and pepper
30 g (1 oz) macadamia nuts, coarsley chopped
about 15 basil leaves, shredded
few drops basil oil (optional) (page 21)

Dry the fish well with paper towelling so it will fry better. Cook the beans in boiling, salted water until just tender; drain. Heat 2 tablespoons butter in a pan large enough to hold the fish snugly; sauté the fish for about 2 minutes on the first side, and a further minute on the second side, or until cooked. Season with salt and pepper, then transfer to serving plates and keep warm.

   Discard any burnt butter from the pan, then add the remaining butter. Add the nuts and stir until golden, then stir in the beans to reheat. Add the shredded basil, season with salt and pepper, and spoon the butter sauce over the fish.

Note: The fish may be rubbed with basil oil before cooking, or a little oil can be poured into the sauce for a more intense flavour.

BLUE EYE PROVENCAL

A steamed dish served on a bed of vegetables.

<u>Serves 6</u>

6 x 130 g (4¹/₂ oz) rectangular pieces of blue eye,
orange roughy (sea perch) or ling
4 tablespoons olive oil
1 small or ¹/₂ large eggplant (aubergine), prepared as above
1 small zucchini (courgette), unpeeled and diced into 1.5 cm (¹/₂ in) cubes
4 large, very red tomatoes, peeled, seeded and diced
salt and pepper
4 tablespoons extra virgin olive oil, for dressing
3 tablespoons roughly chopped chives

Heat some water in the base of a steamer and place the fish on the rack in the steamer. Cook until opaque, usually about 6 minutes, depending on the thickness of the fish.

   Meanwhile, heat the olive oil in a frying pan and quickly sauté the eggplant, adding the zucchini as the eggplant cooks, then finally the tomatoes (the latter just to heat so they don't change too much or lose their shape). Season with salt and pepper.

To serve, spoon about 3 heaps of the vegetable mixture onto each warm plate, taking care to leave any liquid behind. Place a piece of fish on top of each vegetable bed. Drizzle a little extra-virgin olive oil over each fish, and garnish with chives.

Variation

If the fish fit snugly in the pan, place them on top of the vegetables in the frying pan, cover, and steam them directly in the pan. However, if the fit is a squeeze, it is better to cook the fish pieces separately.

The recipe above takes great care to undercook the tomatoes, thus keeping them as small cubed units. If you prefer to create the effect of a bed of ratatouille under the fish, double the tomatoes, chop them roughly, cut the eggplant and zucchini into larger pieces, and cook all the vegetables together for a longer period to allow them to render in the traditional style of a ratatouille. You may also choose to add a little onion and diced red capsicum.

WHITING GRENOBLOISE

A pan-fry with a light self-saucing garnish.

Serves 6

12 whiting fillets, skinned, or sole, John Dory or trout fillets, skinned
90 ml (3 oz) peanut oil
200 ml (7 fl oz) dry white wine
juice of 1 lemon
100 g (3¹/₂ oz) unsalted butter, softened
1 tablespoon tiny capers, rinsed
peeled flesh of 1 lemon, diced
salt and pepper
1 tablespoon chopped dill

Fold the fillets upon themselves, (former) skin side inwards. Pan-fry in hot oil, nicest side up, until golden. Place the lid on the pan and cook through (a further 2 minutes). Transfer to hot plates and keep warm. Discard the oil and add the wine and lemon juice to the pan. Bring to the boil and reduce by half, then remove from heat. Add the butter in pieces, whisking quickly to bind the sauce. Add the capers and diced lemon, then season lightly with salt and pepper. Spoon this sauce over the fillets, and garnish with the dill.

GRILLED SWORDFISH OR FRESH TUNA WITH TOMATO

A grill, barbecue or pan-fry method.

<u>Serves 2</u>

2 swordfish or tuna steaks
1 tablespoon olive oil
2 small, red, fleshy tomatoes, peeled, seeded and cut into small dice
4 spring onions (scallions), including the green part, sliced
juice of 1 lemon plus the peel, grated in fine threads
salt and freshly ground black pepper
a little extra virgin olive oil

About 1 hour before dinner, rub the fish steaks with olive oil, then set aside. Place the tomato in a saucepan with the tablespoon of olive oil, the spring onions and the lemon peel. Cover and set aside.

When ready to cook, sear the fish on both sides on a well-heated barbecue, cast-iron grill or frying pan. Depending on size, the fish will need about 3 minutes on the first side and 1 1/2 minutes on the second. After turning, add salt, pepper and a few drops of lemon juice. Gently heat the tomato mixture, making sure it retains its shape and fresh taste.

To serve, scatter the tomato and spring onion mixture over the plates. Nestle the fish in the centre, drizzle with extra virgin olive oil and season with freshly ground black pepper. Serve with boiled, parsleyed potatoes.

SALMON A L'UNILATERALE

A pan-fry method. The French word, unilatérale, *meaning cooked on one side only, denotes the technique. This dish is traditionally made with salmon, as people enjoy the crisp skin, but the clever cook might generalise to other thick-fleshed fish with good skin texture, such as barramundi.*

<u>Serves 4</u>

4 x 130 g (4 1/2 oz) slices Atlantic salmon or ocean trout fillet,
skin on, at room temperature
a little oil
a little sea salt

Lightly oil the flesh of the fish. Heat the pan and cook the fish skin side down for about 18 minutes. Use a moderate heat only and ensure the skin crisps but does not scorch. Halfway through cooking, sprinkle a little sea salt over the flesh side. When the fish is cooked, it should feel warm to the touch and have begun to go from translucent to opaque. Do not overcook.

Transfer the fish to plates and serve alongside Caramelised Witlof (page 160), creamed leeks, or any other vegetable you feel complements the fish. The fish may be served simply, or dressed with olive oil, Hollandaise or beurre blanc (page 106). It's great, too, served on a bed of couscous with sliced preserved lemon (page 146) and olive oil.

STEAMED ATLANTIC SALMON ON A BED OF LEEKS WITH HOLLANDAISE SAUCE

The classic steamed fish, this time on a bed of vegetables.
The interested cook might compare steaming it traditionally with poaching it. See the difference.

Serves 6–8

4 tablespoons butter
4 leeks, washed, trimmed and sliced (use a little of the lighter green part)
6 (or 8) x 130 g (4¹/₂ oz) pieces Atlantic salmon fillet
salt and white pepper

Hollandaise sauce
150 g (5 oz) unsalted butter
3 egg yolks
4 tablespoons cold water
salt and white pepper
2 teaspoons lemon juice, or to taste

In a large frying pan with a lid, heat the butter and sauté the leeks until softened but not coloured. Place the salmon pieces on top, salt and pepper lightly, then place the lid on the pan to steam the fish. Reduce the heat and steam for about 6–8 minutes, depending on the thickness of the fish. Transfer the salmon pieces and their bed of leeks to 6 (8) plates and spoon the Hollandaise sauce over the fish. Serve with two or three pieces of steamed or boiled potatoes and the remaining Hollandaise in a sauceboat.

Hollandaise sauce: (can be prepared an hour or so in advance and reheated). Melt the butter gently in a small saucepan; remove from heat.

In a second saucepan, break the egg yolks and add the water. Using a wire whisk, stir well over low heat with a brisk figure of eight movement until the mixture fluffs up to twice its volume and begins to thicken. Beware coagulation of the egg — lift the saucepan above the heat, whisking briskly, to avoid any scrambling, then continue to cook until the mixture thickens to the consistency of light mayonnaise. When ready, lift from the stove and continue whisking until the saucepan cools a little.

When the saucepan with the egg is about the same temperature as the saucepan with the butter (that is, you can rest you hand comfortably on the sides of each), dribble the butter bit by bit into the egg, stirring all the time to incorporate. The slow addition of the butter and the thickness of the egg mixture are the two factors that control the thickness of the sauce. When all the butter is added, season with salt, pepper and lemon juice. Set the sauce aside, but never refrigerate — a Hollandaise will reset.

To reheat the sauce: Stir-heat the sauce in the same way it was made, until it returns to temperature, taking care not to heat much above lukewarm , as the butter can melt and spring out of suspension (i.e. separate).

Variations

Change the leek to chopped tomato, or spinach (add nutmeg), or rings of fennel. Fennel appreciates a little chopped preserved lemon through it (page 146), a little sliced over the top, and a drizzle of extra virgin olive oil as an alternative to the Hollandaise.

SALMON OR OCEAN TROUT WITH RED WINE ONION SAUCE

A steamed method, served on a bed of vegetables.

<u>Serves 4</u>

4 x 130 g (4¹/₄ oz) pieces Atlantic salmon or ocean trout fillet

The red wine sauce
35 g (1¹/₂ oz) butter
2 large onions, sliced finely into rings
1 rounded tablespoon plain (all-purpose) flour
600 ml (1 pt) red wine
250 ml (8 fl oz) water
salt and pepper

Lay the pieces of salmon or ocean trout on the rack of a steamer. Bring the water in the steamer to the boil, and, about 6–7 minutes before serving, lower the salmon over the water and steam for 3 minutes. Remove the salmon from the steamer and lay on a board for 2 minutes, so it can finish cooking in its own heat while you serve.

Place a ring of the red wine sauce and onion in the centre of each plate and, with the help of an egg-lift, carefully lay the salmon on top. Serve with boiled potatoes, or sliced potatoes in cream, and one green vegetable.

The red wine sauce: Heat the butter in a frying pan or wide-based shallow saucepan and fry the onions. Continue to fry without browning until they soften, then sprinkle with flour. Stir the flour to the bottom, continuing to stir until it sticks to the base of the pan, then add the wine and water.

Bring to the boil, then reduce the heat to a very low simmer and cook the sauce for 25–30 minutes. During this time, the wine will reduce, but keep the simmer low enough not to reduce the wine so much that the sauce gets too thick. At the end of cooking time, if the sauce is too thick, add a little water. Season with salt and pepper only when the final consistency is reached.

PINWHEEL OF SALMON
WITH WATERCRESS SAUCE

A sophisticated steamed dish for the more ambitious cook.

<u>Serves 6</u>

fillet of salmon, cut from one side only of a medium-large
(about 2.3 kg/4¹/₂ lb) fish, scaled, but with skin on
6 tablespoons mixed julienne of green beans, carrot and turnip
6 slices smoked salmon
salt and pepper

The watercress sauce
1 tablespoon chopped shallots
2 tablespoons white wine
3 tablespoons water
100 g (3¹/₂ oz) unsalted butter
salt and pepper
1 cup watercress leaves

The salmon: (prepare a couple of hours before dinner so it firms its shape). With tweezers, remove any remaining bones from the salmon. Slice the fillet lengthways into strips about 2.25 cm x 15 cm (1 in x 6 in). One fillet should easily yield 6 of these strips. Blanch the julienne of vegetables in salted water until flexible; drain well. Cut the smoked salmon to fit along the fresh salmon strips. Pat gently into place, then place a layer of vegetables on top of the smoked salmon. Roll into pinwheels and fix with a satay skewer. Set aside, covered with greaseproof paper.

When ready to serve, place the salmon in a steamer, cover again with the greaseproof paper, and steam over hot water until just cooked (2–3 minutes, depending on thickness). Do not overcook; latent heat will finish the job.

The watercress sauce: Cook the shallots in the white wine and water. When cooked down to two tablespoons of liquid, whisk in the butter very quickly so that it incorporates, but remains unctuous. Season with salt and pepper, then stir in the cress leaves until they wilt. Never heat this beurre blanc style of sauce too much as it will turn to melted butter.

To serve: Spoon a little sauce onto the base of six plates, and place the pinwheel of salmon on top. Serve with steamed potatoes or a vegetable of your choice.

Variation
Although less modern than the watercress sauce, a classic Sauce Hollandaise (page 93) also suits this dish and is even strong enough in flavour to allow for the tarragon in a Sauce Béarnaise.

SALTIMBOCCA OF FISH WITH PROSCIUTTO

A pan-fry based on the classic Italian veal recipe.

<u>Serves 4</u>

4 x 120 g (4 oz) pieces snapper fillet
20 sage leaves
4 slices prosciutto, sized to wrap fish
flour, for dredging
100 ml (3¹/₂ fl oz) olive oil

Mixed herb pesto
about 40 mint leaves, chopped
about 40 small basil leaves, chopped
2 cloves garlic, finely chopped
40 ml (1¹/₃ fl oz) extra virgin olive oil
salt
coarsely ground black pepper

Trim any skin or bone from the fish. Evenly distribute the sage over the four pieces and wrap each piece with a slice of prosciutto. Dredge in flour, patting off any excess. Heat the olive oil and sauté the fish for 30 seconds, turning once. Place the pan with the fish in the oven and cook at 170°C (335°F) for 4 minutes, or until medium rare. Remove the fish from the pan and place directly onto the plates. Drizzle the herb pesto over or around the fish and decorate with coarsely ground pepper and some potatoes or a green vegetable of your choice.

The mixed herb pesto: Place the herb leaves and garlic in a small food processor. Process until very finely chopped, then feed the olive oil down the funnel. Salt lightly.

BLACKENED FISH WITH MANGO AND LYCHEE COMPOTE

A barbecue hotplate or pan-fry method based on Cajun traditions from New Orleans, with the exotic addition of tropical fruits.

<u>Serves 6</u>

6–8 teaspoons commercial 'blackened fish' spices, or combine 1 teaspoon each sweet paprika, onion powder, cayenne pepper, garlic powder and ground black pepper with 2¹/₂ teaspoons salt and ¹/₂ teaspoon each powdered thyme and oregano
6 fillets of firm white-fleshed fish (flounder, trevally, garfish, whiting, bream)
150 g (5 oz) unsalted butter, softened
film of oil for the pan

The mango and lychee compôte
2 mangoes, ripe but not too soft
10 lychees, peeled and coarsely diced
flesh of half a large avocado, cubed (optional)
juice of 1 lemon or 2 limes
salt and cracked black pepper
50 g (1¹/₂ oz) macadamia nuts, roughly chopped
2 level teaspoons shredded coconut
3–4 tablespoons natural yoghurt
2 small bird's eye hot red chillies, shredded
3 spring onions (scallions), sliced
3 tablespoons mixed shredded coriander and mint leaves

Place the well-combined spices or commercial mix in a bag and shake a light coating over the fish. Heat a barbecue hotplate or heavy black cast-iron pan to extreme heat. When smoking, smear the fillets with butter. Lightly oil the pan, then cook the fish for 3–5 minutes, turning once, until slightly dry-scorched and charred.

Serve immediately, smeared with more butter, and with the compôte alongside.

The compôte: Halve the mangoes, remove the stone, then peel and cube the flesh. In a bowl, combine the mango cubes with the lychee flesh and avocado (if using). Souse with the lemon or lime juice; season with salt and pepper. Add the chopped nuts and coconut and bind with the yoghurt. Fold in the chilli, spring onions and herbs just before serving.

Variation
When mangoes are not in season, try pineapple, lychee and avocado, or simply pineapple alone.

LAWFUL POACHING

The traditional way to poach fish is to immerse it in flavoured water — the theory is that if it goes into water alone, the flavour of the fish will be washed away. The classic poaching liquor — *court-bouillon* — contains onion, carrot, celery, a few peppercorns and three or four sprigs of parsley. Some cooks add a bay leaf. I find them too pervasive and somewhat musty.

A true *court-bouillon* has a touch of vinegar in it. Like vinegar in poached eggs, the acidity of the vinegar keeps the flesh together, for fish flesh is delicate and may be plucked apart — the very reason we choose to poach in the first place rather than boil. If the *court-bouillon* is to be used in the sauce, the vinegar should be replaced by white wine, but give thought to the amount of wine you may also be adding to the sauce — too much acidity is the number one fault in fish sauces.

A clever cook knows that if a poaching liquor is to add flavour to a fish, there is little use in adding vegetables at the same time as the fish. It is better to cut them small, cook them in the water until their flavour is well infused, strain them out so they don't stick all over the fish, and have the poaching liquor ready-made before you start.

If you prefer not to bother with a *court-bouillon,* remember the idea is to poach in something flavoursome, rather than in water. This may be as simple as water or fish stock enriched with a little wine, or water in which you've boiled a few herbs. Dill and fennel are the most usual; Kombu and Dashi seaweeds are common Japanese flavourings.

Most individual-sized fish lend themselves to poaching. River trout, mullet or Australian salmon (also known as bay trout), whiting, Murray perch, pike, jewfish and Atlantic salmon are among the best. Small snapper poaches well — but beware the larger snapper, for in the time the larger ones take to cook, the delicate flesh on the head can pull away completely from the bone structure. Large Murray perch, kingfish, nannygai, trevally and trumpeter poach quite well; large snapper, coral trout and sweetlip are better baked.

Cooking time depends on the thickness of the fish, not its weight (compare a snapper to a long, slim pike). Test the flesh at the thickest part — usually the hump behind the gill — by piercing with a knife blade, which should be able to reach the bone structure without effort. Remember, optimal cooking is at 90°C (200°F), and does not take place under 60°C (140°F), so check that the water is just simmering. Timing takes practice, but, fortunately, overcooking shows up less in poaching than in any other method, because the fish remains moist.

With all that theory behind you, try poaching a salmon steak and serving it with Hollandaise sauce (page 93), and compare the steamed and poached results. You can poach a mullet or a trout and then make a sauce or a white *roux,* adding a little white wine, a ladleful or two of the (vinegar-free) *court-bouillon,* and finishing with cream and mixed shellfish. You can poach a small snapper and sauce it with Champagne and cream, with a garnish of champignons and watercress. Or you may want to make a beurre blanc (page 106) and pour it over a perfectly poached pike.

TRUITES EN MEURETTE

An unorthodox poaching method from the wine-loving Burgundians, who stop water washing away the flavour of fish in their own way — in red wine. The clever cook will notice that the poaching liquid is simmered well before the fish is added, to rid it of its acidity.

Serves 6

The poaching liquor
4 tablespoons butter
1 onion, chopped
$^1/_2$ small carrot, sliced finely
1 tablespoon plain (all-purpose) flour
750 ml (25 fl oz) red wine
1 clove garlic, finely chopped
bouquet garni
salt and pepper

The garnish
100 g (3$^1/_2$ oz) continental bacon, cut into bite-sized pieces
100 g (3$^1/_2$ oz) champignons, sliced

The fish
6 brown (or other river) trout, each 150–200 g (5–7 oz)

The poaching liquor: (can be made in advance). Heat the butter and fry the onion and carrot until golden brown. Add the flour and stir to a *roux.* Add the wine, garlic and bouquet garni, and season with salt and pepper. Bring to the boil, then reduce heat and simmer, covered, for 30 minutes, to blend the flavours. Strain out the solids and retain the liquid, adding a little water if there has been too much evaporation and the liquid is too thick to poach the fish in.

The fish: When ready to cook the fish, fry the bacon and champignons in a pan large enough to hold the fish. Pour in the strained poaching liquid and return to the boil. Poach the trout in this liquid, keeping the temperature just below boiling point to prevent the delicate flesh coming apart. Baste occasionally if the fish is not fully covered. Test fish at their thickest point to see if they are cooked. Depending on thickness, they take about 8–10 minutes.

Transfer trout and garnish to serving plates. Reduce the poaching liquid to sauce consistency. Coat the fish with the sauce, and serve remaining sauce in a sauceboat.

WRAP IT UP!

Wrapping fish in parcels, whether it be fillets, small whole fish, or larger fish which can later be portioned out, is an ideal method for cooking fish. It keeps the aromas circulating in the steam, keeps the moisture in the fish, and means cooking without pots. It also means little preparation, and preparation which can be done well ahead. The method, of course, is steaming. It is the same as when the fisherman wraps fish in wet newspaper to cook in the campfire beside of the stream, but its modern versions are with foil and greased parchment paper, or steaming in paperbark — an age-old Aboriginal method akin to the Pacific Islander or African method of baking in banana, pandana or other leaves.

The simplest foil method is to place a large fish (snapper, nannygai, red emperor, sweetlip, bay trout or trevally) in a suitably sized buttered piece of foil and garnish with the ingredients you like most. A lemony version would use slices of lime or lemon under and over the fish, a herb that marries well over the top (try branches of dill or fennel), lemon juice, salt and coarsely ground black pepper, and a few knobs of butter. Fold in the edges of the foil and cook in the oven at 200°C (400°F) for about 45 minutes for a 1.5 kg (3 lb) fish.

A Mediterranean version of this is to garnish with slices of firm red tomatoes, seasoned with shredded basil leaves and scattered with tiny black olives. The foil should be oiled and the fish drizzled with a couple of tablespoons of extra virgin olive oil. You could also add a few mussels (steamed first in an empty saucepan and plucked from their shells) and/or prawns (shrimp) to give a different effect.

A Provençal recipe I use frequently places blue eye fillets in foil, along with olive oil, halved stoned black olives, sprigs of chervil, black pepper, a drizzle of olive oil, and some artichoke hearts. If doing individual pieces of about 125–140 g (4–5 oz), or whole fillets of around 30–40 cm (12–16 in) in length, the timing is the same, providing the thickness is the same. Simply seal them well and cook in the oven at 200°C (400°F) for 10–12 minutes. To serve, add a little freshly chopped chives and chervil for freshness, and garnish the dish with a spoonful of Italian black olive paste on the side.

Small, individually packaged fish are known as 'papillotes'. Papillotes can be made using foil, but look best in well-buttered or oiled greaseproof paper. Choose the strong baking-parchment type, tear off a piece the length of the fish (or fillet or piece of fish) and fold it in half lengthways. Then, with scissors, trim off the square edges to make an oval package. Unfold the paper and put the fish on the right-hand side. Garnish with your chosen ingredients, then neatly pleat together the two sides of the paper. Start from the left-hand top of the fold and proceed towards the right, and then down and around the paper. Small folds every 4–5 cm (1½–2 in) give a neat finish and hold the fish well. If it's airtight, the paper swells and browns attractively in the oven as the fish cooks. Small fish need about 20 minutes at 200°C (400°F), but this method is more usually used for fillets (10–12 minutes), or rectangular fleshy pieces of fish (12–15 minutes, depending on the thickness of the piece).

Try the flavours suggested with the large fish above, but also try simple combinations such as a little butter into which you have mashed chopped herbs, some ground black pepper and a drizzle of lemon or lime juice. Add a leaf or two of fresh spinach, or a julienne of mixed vegetables, fried first until softened, and then scattered over the fish with butter and lemon juice or some lemon slices. Try a daub of pesto, an extra teaspoon of olive oil and some cooked baby vegetables. Try left-over ratatouille stuffed in the boned-out centre of a small whole fish. Try Thai flavourings such as 2 tablespoons green lime juice mixed with ½ teaspoon fish sauce, 3 drops sesame oil, some finely chopped lemon grass and whole coriander (cilantro) leaves, with or without a little coconut milk to mellow it.

For a Japanese effect, smear the fish fillet with (very little) wasabe, some very finely grated onion and ginger, and a dash of half light soy, half mirin or cooking sake. Or try chunks of tomato, shredded basil, coarsely ground pepper and extra virgin olive oil. Above all, vary the plot — wrap and seal in advance and bake when required. For maximum impact, serve each diner a package to open at table.

Remember, the minute you trade the oven for the barbecue, or decide to use a large whole fish for 6–8 people (i.e. a 1.2 kg /2½ lb fish or larger), it is imperative to change back to foil for its toughness and security. All the recipes above can be done in foil if preferred.

POULTRY

POULTRY PANACHE

As consumers, we are now offered more choice from the poultry industry than ever before. Free-range is a viable alternative to battery-bred, and specialists even supply maize-fed birds, after the style of the famed chickens of Bresse, France.

Duck suppliers are following suit, although Peking ducks still dominate the market. Unfortunately, their fat content makes them more suitable for Peking Duck and other Chinese recipes than for the largely French-based methods of European recipes. Their breasts are quite unsuitable for treating like rare steak, and whole birds are not much more suitable for roasting fast and rare in the French manner. However, cooks keen to follow the French style continue to use them, and we can now buy duck breasts in most good poultry stores.

Compare the results you obtain when roasting a duck French style at 225°C (435°F) for 50 minutes, with the East European style at 225°C (435°F) for 15 minutes, then 180°C (350°F) for 1 hour 15 minutes, and finishing with another 5 minute burst at 220°C (425°F) to crisp the skin. The textures are completely different and, although I'm French-trained, I know the latter suits Peking ducks much better, though it's less in fashion.

Baby chicks (*poussins*) are more readily available in larger cities; pigeons and guinea fowl are still largely confined to restaurants. However, farmed quails and pigeons have a burgeoning market, and are now inexpensive. However, remember these birds are hatchery and not 'game'; they don't have muscular, sinewy flesh, and thus cook in a fraction of the time that most international recipes propose.

Is it any wonder that chicken is such a kitchen favourite? Popping a chicken in the oven and deglazing the sediment at the base of the pan to make a gravy is the simplest recipe! Variations include putting garlic, butter and sage in the cavity (fabulous, too, in quails); finishing the gravy with fried dual colours of capsicum (bell pepper) and tomato, stirred in with the juices to make a simple chunky sauce; or rubbing the chicken with powdered ginger and salt, placing some chopped fresh ginger in the cavity, and then mixing the juices with cream for a soft, unctuous sauce that goes with rice rather than roast potatoes.

For casseroles, pre-cut portions mean the home cook doesn't even have to joint a chicken. However, a word of warning — most apportioned chickens are cut straight down the backbone. This spinal column makes the curved pieces of chicken hard to brown. Using good kitchen scissors, the clever cook will slice this line of bone away before commencing. Using the method on page 148 you can easily put together a casserole with red wine, onions and bacon in typical *coq au vin* style, or with white wine and cream, or cream and champignons. Try cooking the pieces with beer or orange juice instead of wine (page 108). With both these liquids, I prefer to finish with cream, reinforcing the beer with a couple of crushed juniper berries, or the orange juice with a few sultanas and a final garnish of julienne of peel and a dash of Grand Marnier.

Pre-cut portions come into their own with the smaller cuts — breasts, wings and the thigh and drumstick combination known as the Maryland. These not only enable you to serve only the pieces that please, but to cook them in the speedy manner that only small cuts will allow. For fabulous fast family food, the clever cook can't do better than to look to the recipes in this chapter featuring breasts and Marylands.

The breast is sold both on the bone and off. On the bone, it has the drawback referred to above, and it is harder to eat. For recipes other than casseroles, the best choice is the boneless breast fillet. In the interests of lowering cholesterol, the breast is now sold with skin or without. Again, a warning — the skin, with its natural fat content, keeps the chicken flesh moist as it is cooked so rub skinless fillets with oil before placing them on the barbecue or in the pan, or use a marinade.

Most marinades include one or more ingredients that will caramelise and glaze the meat over heat, adding an eye-appealing crustiness to the finished result. Breast fillets are the best buys for quick preparation; they barbecue well and are sensational on a corrugated cast-iron grill. Most chefs simply rub the fillet with oil or herbs, grill it, then serve with an accompanying vegetable. Eggplant (aubergine) and capsicum (bell pepper) are a common choice because with an olive oil topping they reflect the popular Mediterranean flavours. And then there's the pan-fry, with its many varieties of sauces made from deglazing the base of the pan.

The Maryland is another easy cut to handle; it can be cooked whole, or separated into drumstick and thigh. To do this, turn the leg over to the underside, and find the tiny band of white gristle that indicates you are at the true centre of the joint. Cut here, and the knife will slice through the meat easily, without having to cut through bone.

There are many ways to use the Maryland. Along with wings, it is often rubbed with honey and soy and baked in the oven. Try also placing Marylands (as well as a couple of breasts on the bone) in a large ovenproof dish, daub them with a generous portion of unsalted butter, pour the juice of a lemon over the top, sprinkle with paprika, push in six or eight sprigs of thyme or rosemary here and there, and bake at 190°C (375°F) for 35 minutes. Serve the cooked portions at the table directly from the dish, spooning the buttery sauce over the top. There is no simpler dish in summer when the heat has your cooking energies at an all time low. Serve with crusty bread — it's impossible not to want to blot up the sauce.

Marylands, wings and the now popular spare ribs — which for the most part can be bought from the supermarkets already marinated and ready to go — are suitable for the barbecue, but with smaller chickens (1 kg (2 lb) spatchcocks), baby chicks and quails, buying them whole and preparing them using the traditional *crapaudine* method is not to be overlooked. The idea is to tuck the two legs into the parson's nose, then cut the backbone free with two scissor lines on either side of the backbone from the neck up to the parson's nose. Remove the backbone, leaving the parson's nose intact to pin the legs in place. (For quails, the legs are not tucked, and the backbone should be removed in its entirety). Open the bird out flat and give it a whack with a mallet to break the breastbone. The flattened bird is then ready for the barbecue; cook it first on the skin side to give it a good brown colouring and the marks of the grill, then turn it over to finish its cooking. Make sure the flesh doesn't scorch or toughen while cooking through. Herbs (rosemary, fennel) and oil are great additions.

Leathery poultry is the product of the naive cook, and is to be avoided at all costs. All too often the cook who fears a pink, undercooked interior adds a couple of extra minutes to cooking time 'just to be sure' — this is all the time it takes to turn it into a dry, stringy-textured piece of meat. Be it a large roast bird or a pan-fried fillet, the trick is to test with a skewer and catch those juices just when they turn from pink to yellow — but on no account to dry the juices away — and the poultry will be at its very succulent best.

TRI-COLOURED CHICKEN FILLET WITH TARRAGON BEURRE BLANC

A poached method, although it can also be pan-fried.

<u>Serves 4</u>

4 chicken breasts, skinless
750 ml (25 fl oz) chicken stock
300 g (9¹/₂ oz) broad beans (shelled weight)
2 medium tomatoes, peeled, seeded, and cut into small dice

The tarragon beurre blanc
3 shallots, finely chopped
150 ml (5 fl oz) white wine
2 tablespoons vinegar
100 g (3 1/2 oz) butter, cut into pieces
4 sprigs fresh tarragon, chopped
salt and white pepper

Gently poach the chicken fillets in the chicken stock for 15 minutes. Cook the broad beans for 3–4 minutes in boiling, salted water; drain. Pop off their grey–green skins, and set aside in a small saucepan with a knob of butter, to reheat later. Repeat this process with the tomatoes in another saucepan.

The tarragon beurre blanc: In a saucepan, heat the shallots, wine and vinegar until the liquid is reduced to 3 tablespoons. Whisk in the butter vigorously, bit by bit, over a low heat. (As with all beurre blancs, the reduction may be done in advance, then brought quickly to the boil for the addition of the butter when ready to serve.) Stir vigorously to melt the butter, but never heat enough to allow it to turn to grease; the sauce must be unctuous and yellow. Quickly stir in the tarragon, season with salt and pepper, and serve.

To serve: Slice the chicken breast and fan it over one side of the plate. Reheat the broad beans and place on another side. Place warmed diced tomato on the third portion. This is the tri-coloured effect that gives the dish its name. Pour the tarragon butter sauce around the edge of the plate.

Note: The atmosphere in the above recipe is very definitely French. Watch how three different vegetables and a change of saucing ingredients bring the three colours of the next recipe to a result that is very definitely Asian.

ASIAN MARINATED CHICKEN BREAST WITH BOK CHOY

A pan-fry or barbecue method. This is my favourite way to serve baby bok choy as a vegetable — use it for other dishes.

Serves 4

4 chicken breasts, skinless

The marinade
125 ml (4 fl oz) light soy sauce
125 ml (4 fl oz) water
1 tablespoon dry sherry
2 tablespoons olive oil

The vegetables
2 bunches baby bok choy
(allow 2 small whole bok choy per person — a bunch is normally three)

2 red capsicums (bell peppers), roasted and peeled
about 75 ml (2½ fl oz) olive oil
2 cloves garlic, sliced horizontally
3–4 drops sesame oil
coriander (cilantro) leaves (optional)

Remove and discard the smaller fillets that are attached to the chicken breasts. Lay the breasts on a plate and pour over the marinade ingredients. Leave for about 1 hour, then remove and pat dry; keep the marinade.

Meanwhile, blanch the bok choy for 30 seconds in boiling, salted water; drain well and set aside. Slice the roasted capsicum into large strips.

When ready to serve, heat a cast-iron pan or other heavy pan well, then add 3 tablespoons oil. Add the capsicum and heat, stirring; remove and keep warm. Pan-fry the chicken breasts, adding a little oil if necessary, for about 4 minutes on the first side, 2 minutes on the second. See that they sear well on the outside and remain undercooked, but not pink, on the inside. Transfer to a board, cover with a bowl for 1 minute, then carve into slices.

Drizzle a little more olive oil into the pan and reheat the bok choy, turning so that the oil glazes the leaves. Add the garlic and lightly brown, then pour in the marinade. Bring to the boil, stirring up any sediment that has formed in the base of the pan, and add the sesame oil.

To serve: Place a bed of capsicum on the base of each plate, fan the chicken fillet over this and serve the bok choy and sauce alongside. Garnish with coriander leaves, if using.

Note: You may use a corrugated cast-iron grill or barbecue to cook the capsicum and chicken, but a pan is necessary for the bok choy.

CHICKEN MARYLANDS WITH ORANGE SAUCE

A quickly cooked casserole with a light sauce, suitable for serving at any time of the year. The Maryland pieces are convenient but the dish can also be made with a whole, apportioned chicken.

Serves 6

40 g (1½ oz) butter
4 chicken Marylands, divided at the drumstick (i.e. into 8 pieces)
3 oranges
125 ml (4 fl oz) water
salt and pepper
150 ml (5 fl oz) cream or 2 tablespoons butter

In a frying pan, heat the butter and fry the chicken pieces until golden. Meanwhile, take some rind from the oranges and cut into thin matchsticks (about 2 tablespoons in all). Squeeze the juice. Add the orange juice, water and the rind matchsticks to the chicken. Cover, reduce the heat and simmer for 20 minutes, then transfer the chicken to a serving plate and keep warm. Season the liquid with salt and pepper, then boil down to sauce consistency, whisking in either the cream or butter to thicken.

Spoon the sauce over the chicken and serve with saffron-flavoured Rice Pilaf (page 170) or angel hair pasta.

SPICY LIME CHICKEN

A barbecue or pan-fry dish.

Serves 4

4 chicken Marylands

The marinade
125 ml (4 fl oz) light olive oil
90 ml (3 fl oz) green lime or lemon juice
$^1/_2$ small onion, finely sliced
2 cloves garlic, crushed
1 teaspoon Tabasco sauce
salt

Place the chicken Marylands in an ovenproof dish or oven bag. Mix together the ingredients of the marinade and pour over the chicken. Refrigerate overnight, covered with plastic wrap if in a dish.

When ready, place the chicken on a wire rack and grill it on a barbecue. Grill the skin side first, then, when well-browned, turn and finish the cooking at a lower heat on the second side. This should take about 20 minutes in all. If you prefer, panfry the chicken in 50 g (1$^1/_2$ oz) butter with 2 tablespoons light oil.

Serve with the more traditional barbecue salads — green, coleslaw or potato.

Variation:

Try this dish with small birds (spatchcocks, baby chicks) *en crapaudine* (page 106). If barbecuing any chicken piece without a marinade, remember to oil the flesh first.

CHICKEN FILLETS WITH VEGETABLE JULIENNE AND TARRAGON

A quick and easy pan-fry.

<u>Serves 6</u>

8 tablespoons julienne of mixed vegetables of 3 or 4 colours: carrot, turnip,
celery, leek, beans or snow peas (mangetout)
6 chicken breast fillets, skinless
55 g (2 oz) butter
salt and pepper

The sauce
250 ml (8 fl oz) chicken stock, or vegetable stock made from 1 stalk celery, end
of 1 leek, 1 chopped carrot, salt and pepper, boiled together, then strained
3 shallots, finely chopped
1 tablespoon white wine or tarragon vinegar
4 sprigs fresh tarragon, chopped
2 tablespoons soft butter

Soften the julienne and make it flexible either by blanching for 2 minutes in boiling, salted water, or by pan-frying in a little extra butter. Make a small slit horizontally along the chicken breasts and stuff the julienne into the pocket, allowing a little to protrude and show. Fold the remaining flesh over without pressing it fully closed.

Heat the butter in a frying pan and gently place each fillet in the pan, former skin side down first. Pan-fry until a pale golden colour, then, using a spatula or egg lift and your hand to help keep them together, turn the fillets carefully and cook on slightly reduced heat. This should take about 9–10 minutes in all. Season with salt and pepper only after turning. Transfer the chicken to plates and keep warm.

The sauce: Add the shallots to the pan and stir for a moment to soften, then deglaze the pan with the vinegar. Stirring up the sediment, add the stock and tarragon, and boil down to make a light sauce. Quickly whisk in the softened butter, either on or off the stove.

The sauce must no longer reach the boil because the butter will lose its thickening properties if it melts totally. Season with salt and pepper.

To serve: Spoon the sauce over the chicken, and serve with rice or the vegetable of your choice.

Variation

Like many other dishes in this style, the sauce may be finished with cream rather than butter. This changes the effect from a lighter sauce to a richer one. This recipe is also excellent with large white-fleshed fillet of fish, or salmon, using the butter sauce rather than the cream. See the next recipe, which also works with fish fillets (preferably long, thin, white-fleshed fish such as John Dory, sole or whiting).

STEAMED CHICKEN WITH MARINATED DUCK LIVERS AND SULTANAS

<u>Serves 4</u>

12 large duck livers
3 tablespoons sultanas (golden raisins)
225 ml (7¹/₂ fl oz) sweet white wine (Noble Riesling, Sauternes,
Spatlaese Riesling)
4 plump chicken breasts, skin removed
salt and pepper
85 g (3 oz) unsalted butter

The duck livers: Remove any sinew from the duck livers and break each into two lobes. Place in a small bowl with the sultanas, cover with the wine and allow to stand for about 45 minutes.

The chicken: For a neater presentation, remove the smaller fillet of each chicken breast; otherwise, tuck it well under the breast. Plump the breasts into nice rounded shapes, and place on the rack of a steamer.

When ready to cook, place the rack over hot water in the steamer and steam for 8–10 minutes, depending on size. Remove the rack from the steamer and rest for 2 minutes before serving, to equalise the cooking.

To assemble the dish: As the chicken steams, remove the duck livers from the bowl and shake off any liquid; set aside the sultanas and the wine. Heat about 40 g (1¹/₂ oz) butter in a pan just large enough to hold the livers snugly, and fry them to a crusty brown on the outside. Make sure that they remain a light pink on the inside or they toughen. Add the sultanas as you fry, stirring so they do not burn.

When the pan has a good sediment on the base (the wine sugars should caramelise slightly), add the wine. Bring to the boil, stirring up the sediment. Season with salt and pepper, then add the remaining butter, stirring it in to give the liquid a sauce consistency. (The term for this is 'bind' or 'mount' the sauce with butter.)

To serve, place a chicken breast on each plate, spoon the livers and sauce over one end and serve with a green vegetable and potato of your choice.

Variation

You may choose to serve the livers and sultanas cooked in this way over pan-fried (not steamed — the grey colour is unattractive) duck breasts. It also makes a successful sauce for a roast chicken instead of the more mundane gravies.

WARM CHICKEN SALAD WITH BACON AND PINE NUT DRESSING

A typical modern favourite — a warm salad in which the chicken is cooked on a barbecue, or in a pan or cast-iron grill.

Serves 6

3 slices bacon, chopped
1 tablespoon pine nuts
6 tablespoons olive oil
2 tablespoons vinegar
salt and pepper
mixed salad greens (mesclun) — enough to make a colourful nest on the base of each dinner plate
oil, for frying
6 chicken breast fillets, skinless

Sauté the bacon lightly in a pan until crisp and rendered; empty into a bowl. Add the pine nuts to the pan and toss until golden, then put in the bowl with the bacon and add the oil and vinegar. Season with salt and pepper, and set aside.

Lay out the plates and pile the middle of each with a handful of mixed greens. To cook the chicken, smear a film of oil on a pan, corrugated cast-iron grill or barbecue and fry the chicken fillets for 3 minutes on each side. Place the hot chicken on top of the salads — either whole or, for a more formal look, sliced lengthways and fanned out. Quickly stir the dressing and pour over the chicken. Serve immediately so the *mesclun* retains its crispness.

STIR-FRIED CHICKEN WITH SWEET WALNUTS

One of the few true Chinese-style stir-fry methods in this book.

Serves 6

1 tablespoon cornflour
1 tablespoon soy sauce
1 tablespoon water
1 tablespoon dry sherry
1 teaspoon grated ginger
2 cloves garlic, finely chopped
3 chicken fillets, cut in strips
3 tablespoons vegetable or peanut oil
100 g (3¹/₂ oz) abalone (oyster) mushrooms
20 beans, sliced in two
4 spring onions (scallions), sliced at 5 cm (2 in) on the diagonal
12 large spinach leaves, stalks removed

18 snow peas (mangetout)
1 chicken stock cube, crumbled into 100 ml (3 1/2 fl oz) water
about 20 sweet walnuts (available from Asian delicatessans)
3–4 drops sesame oil

The noodles
50 g (1 1/2 oz) bean thread or rice noodles

Mix the cornflour to a smooth paste with the soy sauce, water, sherry, ginger and garlic. Place the chicken strips in a bowl, add the marinade and set aside for 30 minutes.

When ready, drain the chicken and keep the marinade aside. Heat a wok, then quickly add the oil and first fry the mushrooms and beans, then the spring onions. Remove the vegetables, add more oil to the wok, and quickly fry the chicken strips. When the flesh turns white, return the vegetables, then add the spinach and snow peas. Toss until the spinach wilts, then add the marinade and chicken stock. Bring to the boil, simmer for a moment, stirring, then add the walnuts and sesame oil.

To serve, place in the centre of a plate piled with deep-fried bean thread or rice noodles.

The noodles: Heat a large quantity of oil in a deep-fryer. Just before starting the stir-fry, lower the noodles into the hot oil. It will immediately swell, turn white and double in volume. Toss once with a wire ladle or slotted spoon, then remove and place on serving platter.

THAI CHICKEN CURRY
An easy version of an Asian favourite.

Serves 6

1 chicken breast fillet, cut into large, chunky pieces
3 chicken thigh fillets, cut into large, chunky pieces
280 ml (9 fl oz) can of coconut milk
2 tablespoons peanut oil
1/2 onion, very finely chopped
12 peeled shallots, left whole
1 stalk (fleshy part only) lemon grass, finely sliced
1 clove garlic, finely chopped
2 teaspoons green curry paste
1 piece (about 2 cm or 3/4 in) fresh green ginger, or Siamese ginger (kha)
2 makrut (Kaffir) lime leaves
1 can straw mushrooms, drained, with half the brine kept aside
50 ml (1 1/2 fl oz) Thai fish sauce (nam pla), or to taste
3 small branches fresh green peppercorns, or 1 teaspoon canned peppercorns
2 small green or red chillies, shredded

The garnish

¹/₂ bunch each fresh coriander (cilantro) or Thai basil leaves, and mint
6 tablespoons peanuts
¹/₂ small cucumber, unpeeled and sliced

Do not shake the coconut milk; carefully spoon 2 tablespoons of the thicker part into the bottom of a saucepan and heat, along with 2 tablespoons oil. Sauté the onion, shallots, lemon grass and garlic for a moment, then stir in the curry paste. Stir-fry the chicken pieces until well-coated. Add the ginger, lime leaves and straw mushrooms, then cover with the remaining coconut milk and the mushroom brine. Simmer for 3–4 minutes, then season with the fish sauce. Stir in the green peppercorns and the chillies and simmer at just below boiling point until the chicken is cooked (about 8 more minutes).

Serve on a bed of boiled rice in wide soup bowls, and top with plenty of fresh coriander and mint leaves, a few peanuts and some cucumber slices on the side.

Note: For a more correctly Asian preparation, use a mortar and pestle to grind the onion, lemon grass, ginger, 2 teaspoons coriander roots and half the chilli together first, then proceed as above. Use chicken on the bone rather than fillets, slicing across the bone into large chunks — the Asians are right in believing that the bones add sweetness to the flavour and gelatine that binds the sauce. The choice is yours . . .

CHICKEN A LA NICOISE

After reading Old Mother Holuigue's Foolproof Formula for Casseroles on page 148, the clever cook should be able to devise his or her own classic red wine coq au vin *recipe, or create a version with riesling, paprika, or anything else that's fancied. The method is the same — it's all in the choice of ingredients. Adding the traditional vegetables of the South of France changes its name, and serves to remind us that ingredient changes are all that is necessary to give the dish a totally different flavour.*

<u>Serves 6</u>

90 ml (3 fl oz) olive oil
2 x 1.6 kg (3¹/₄ lb) chickens, jointed, or 10–12 chicken pieces
1 onion, diced
1 heaped tablespoon plain (all-purpose) flour
350 ml (11 fl oz) dry white wine
350 ml (11 fl oz) chicken stock or water
1 tablespoon tomato paste
2 cloves garlic, finely chopped
bouquet garni with extra thyme or a sprig of oregano

6 medium, very red tomatoes — 4 peeled and chopped, 2 unpeeled and quartered
salt and freshly ground black pepper
18 small black olives
6 anchovy fillets, halved lengthways or chopped

In a large frying pan, heat the olive oil and brown the chicken pieces. Add the onion and cook until softened, then, if dry, add a little more oil. Sprinkle on the flour, stirring until it sticks to the base of the pan, where it will lightly brown, too. Add the white wine and chicken stock or water, then the tomato paste, garlic, bouquet garni and the 4 chopped tomatoes. Stir once, season lightly with salt and pepper, then cover and simmer for 50 minutes.

When ready, transfer the chicken to a serving plate and keep warm. Add the olives and anchovies to the pan, then reduce to the desired sauce consistency. Correct seasoning only when reduced. Finally, add the 2 quartered tomatoes to heat through — they should not cook or wilt, as they are the garnish.

Spoon the sauce over and around the chicken. Serve with rice, or flat noodles (tagliatelle) that have been tossed in finely chopped garlic, butter and chopped parsley, or potatoes baked in their skins.

PICK A CHICK

'When in doubt — throw on a chicken,' my mother used to say. 'A good roast chicken is easy, tasty and satisfying. Everybody likes it, and it doesn't take all day.'

Boring? At a meeting with some food-buff friends recently, I asked those present to give me their recipe for a 'simple roast chicken'. It was amazing to see just how different each cook's approach was.

Mike Murphy, publican cook, was first: 'Throw boiling water over it if you want a crisp skin,' he advised. And then, 'Pat it dry, place 4 chopped spring onions (scallions) and a piece of chopped ginger into its cavity, brush it with soy just before it goes into the oven, and cook it for about 45 minutes to an hour at 200°C (400°F).'

Alex Tseng, Chinese restaurateur, chipped in to propose finishing this Chinese-style chicken in the classical manner: 'Serve with wedges of lemon and a small bowl of spicy salt.' Spicy salt, for those not in the know, is salt sprinkled with Chinese five-spice and toasted in a very hot, dry wok until the aroma comes out.

Claire Kearney, cookbook authority par excellence, added another way to get the skin crisp: 'Wash and dry the chicken, squeeze green lime or lemon juice all over it, then stuff the lime or lemon skins into the cavity.' Claire then leaves her chicken to stand uncovered for about 3 hours to dry the skin before roasting it on a rack — sometimes with sprigs of thyme pushed into the cavity, too.

Violet Oon, whose authority on the Nonya food of Singapore is second to none, rubs her chicken in a similar way — with dark soy sauce, lime juice and ground black pepper. She leaves it to stand for an hour before brushing it with melted butter and roasting it. With this sort of colouring macerating the skin, she assures me you can even microwave the chicken and be proud of the way it looks.

My Italian butcher, Jonathon Gianfreda, disagrees with 'stuffing something up the backside', suggesting that even a fairly strong aroma doesn't permeate the bone structure and membranes of the chest wall through to the breast. The debate brings up the classic French masterpiece, *Poulet Demi-Deuil*, which requires large slices of truffle to be placed between the breast skin and breast flesh; with this, Jonathon agrees. There are a couple of reasons why the flavouring should be placed under the skin. First, it perfumes much more strongly than even the largest bunch of strong herbs in the cavity; and second, when locked in by the skin, the chosen ingredient doesn't dry out or get burned by the heat.

Desirable ingredients for using this way range from healthy sprigs of fresh tarragon through to truffle slices, orange zest, wads of grated zucchini (courgette) seasoned and mixed with Parmesan cheese, and the chopped skins of Moroccan salt-preserved lemons (page 146).

Here is Jonathon's method for the 'simple' roast, then. First, the chicken must be a corn-fed, yellow chicken — fatty and well fed. Like Mike, he likes the idea of drying the skin to assure crispness. Jonathon dries his by leaving it in the coolroom before cooking. At home, this means removing any plastic and standing it on a rack in the fridge, with a plate on the shelf below, for the whole day before roasting (at worst, use a hairdrier for a few minutes). Place the chicken, salted and peppered but without grease, on a rack, breast-up, and pop into a 180–190°C (350–375°F) oven for 30 minutes. Then turn the chicken over so it is spine-up with the backside pointing towards the fan, and roast for a further 20 minutes. For the last 10 minutes, turn breast-up again, brush with olive oil and sprinkle with thyme leaves.

Preoccupation with the crisp breast skin leads me to the method of one of my students, Janice Lowe, who is also a Chinese restaurant proprietor. Jan has a 'twice-cooked' method that is somewhat more time consuming, but just as easy, and has the added benefit of giving you a bowl of chicken stock en route.

Her method starts with making stock — place the chicken in a large pot and cover it with cold water and a sliced carrot, onion, a few stalks of parsley, and a couple of peppercorns. Bring slowly to the boil and simmer for about 1 hour, or until the chicken is cooked. Strain and keep the stock for other purposes. Jan then suggests cooling the chicken by propping it so that it drains (i.e. neck down). When cool, it should be well dried in room-temperature air.

The chicken will be at its best if used the same night, or, at least, without refrigeration. Jan's Chinese way is then either to deep-fry it or roast it. To deep-fry, carefully lower the chicken into a hot deep-fry basket of peanut oil. The crisping effect is gained quickly — it will be well browned in the time it takes to reheat. If you prefer to roast the bird, rub the skin with about 2 tablespoons maltose (available from Chinese delicatessens and some health food shops), then place in a baking dish on a rack and roast in the oven at 190°C (375°F) for about 15 minutes, or until the chicken is hot and its skin crisp. This must be done from room temperature — the twice-cooked bird must never be refrigerated if it is to be served warmed through without overcooking.

Chef Phillip Searle uses a different Chinese technique to get crispy skin. He paints the bird with a rich, pasty marinade made up of a piece of bean curd (in its marinade, as found in Chinese supermarkets),

¹/₂ teaspoon each of chopped ginger and chopped gapul (available from Chinese or Asian delicatessens), 2 teaspoons palm sugar, ¹/₄ cup dry sherry or rice wine, ¹/₂ teaspoon orange flower water, ¹/₂ teaspoon rice flour, 1 teaspoon soy sauce and 1 teaspoon grated lemon peel. Combine all the marinade ingredients in a blender and process until smooth, bring the mixture to the boil, then cool it and rub it into the chicken (or duck). Then string the chicken up over a plate to catch the juices, dry it for 2–3 hours in front of a fan, then roast it in the oven at 180°C (350°F) for 40–45 minutes (1 hour 15 minutes for a duck).

This may be stretching the point regarding the 'simple' roast chicken, but all these people are food lovers who find these techniques not at all out of the ordinary — and they guarantee great results.

When pressed for my simplest chicken roast, I have to say that I rub the skin of the breast and leg with powdered Jamaican ginger, then cut about 3 cm (1¹/₄ in) fresh peeled ginger, press it into a large walnut-sized knob of butter and place this into the cavity. I roast, salt and pepper in the same way as the others, then as I remove the chicken, I empty the ginger from the cavity into the baking dish, place the dish on the heat and stir up the sediment with a bit of cream.

If you don't favour a creamy sauce, try this instead. Rub the chicken with olive oil, salt and pepper, and roast in the usual way, but in the last 30 minutes add some halved heads of garlic drizzled with olive oil and wrapped in foil. Each diner unwraps the garlic 'parcels' at the table, and, with the help of a knife, spreads the garlic purée on the chicken to add a pungent flavour. With a recipe such as this, my chosen vegetable has to be a Mediterranean one — a few pieces of roasted eggplant (aubergine) or red capsicum (bell pepper) will do the trick. If I have some fresh sage leaves, I like to throw them quickly into hot butter to wilt for a moment just before I carve the bird — they look great scattered over the chicken, and entice the diner with a healthy aroma. The following recipe is a slighly different version.

CHICKEN WITH FRESH HERBS AND OVEN-ROASTED GARLIC

An oven-roast method that can be adapted to pan-fried or barbecued chicken fillets

<u>Serves 6</u>

3 heads garlic, unpeeled
1.8–2 kg (3¹/₂–4 lb) chicken
3 sprigs fresh rosemary
a good handful fresh sage leaves
250 ml (8 fl oz) olive oil
salt and cracked black pepper
50 g (1¹/₂ oz) butter

Pull 3 cloves from the garlic; peel them, rub them over the outside of the chicken, then place them in the central cavity, along with a small sprig of rosemary and 3 sage leaves. Drizzle the chicken with some olive oil, season with salt and pepper, then press a few rosemary leaves onto the flesh. Place in an oiled baking tray and bake at 175°C (350°F) for 15 minutes.

Peel off the outer layer of skin from the remaining garlic heads to better show the curves of the (unpeeled) cloves within. Hold each head firmly between your hands and twist slightly — while they should still hold together, this will loosen them and help expose them to the heat. Rub the garlic heads well with olive oil, then place in the baking tray around the chicken, pour the rest of the oil over them and place the dish back in the oven for 1 hour. Turn them occasionally, so they brown evenly but don't scorch, and baste them from time to time with a little olive oil from the base of the tray.

When the garlic is ready, transfer it to a plate and keep warm. Raise the heat of the oven to 220°C (425°F) and cook the chicken for a further 5–10 minutes to brown and crisp the skin. Transfer the chicken to a serving platter and surround with the cooked cloves of garlic.

Heat the butter in a small frying pan or saucepan, and stir in the remaining rosemary leaves and sage; spoon the fresh herbs over the chicken breast. Sprinkle the chicken with cracked black pepper and carve at the table.

Serve with potatoes of your choice and some roasted red capsicum (bell pepper), heated on a grill or in a frying pan. To eat the garlic, simply hold the wider end of each clove with a fork and use your knife to press the softened garlic flesh from its skin, or use your fingers to draw each clove through the teeth.

Variation

For less crisp, but slightly easier to handle garlic, see foil-roasted garlic on page 158. For this method, use 1 half-head (horizontally sliced) per person. Readily retrievable with a knife, the flesh can be spread over the chicken as a pungent flavourer. Chicken breasts or Marylands can be barbecued or pan-fried as pieces instead of cooking a whole roast.

CHICKEN STUFFED WITH COUSCOUS

A roast with a Moroccan influence.

Serves 6

The stuffing
400 g (12 oz) couscous
4 tablespoons olive oil
1 teaspoon salt
olive oil, for deep-frying
200 g (7 oz) unblanched almonds
200 g (7 oz) sultanas
12 baby onions or shallots, blanched for 5 minutes in boiling water and drained
1 large clove garlic, finely chopped
2 preserved lemons or limes (available from Asian delicatessens, or see page 146)
2 level tablespoons cinnamon
1 teaspoon coriander seed, crushed
1 scant teaspoon cumin seed

The chicken
1.8 kg (3³/4 lb) chicken
salt and pepper
a little olive oil for roasting

The stuffing: Place the couscous in a bowl and drizzle with the olive oil. Sprinkle the salt over. Pour over enough boiling water to cover it by 1 cm (¹/₃ in). Let it stand for 10 minutes, then fork through it to ensure there are no lumps.

Meanwhile, heat 3 cm (1¹/4 in) depth of olive oil in a saucepan and deep-fry the almonds to a dark roasted brown. (When they crackle and pop, it indicates the inside is well-roasted and crispy.) Stir the almonds through the couscous, along with all the remaining stuffing ingredients.

The chicken: Spoon as much of the stuffing into the cavity of the chicken as possible. Secure with trussing pins or skewers. Place the chicken in a roasting pan, season with salt and pepper, and drizzle with a little olive oil. Roast in the oven for 1 hour 20 minutes, or until juices tested at the thigh run yellow, not pink.

Meanwhile, place the remaining couscous stuffing in a piece of muslin or a tea towel and steam for 1 hour while roasting the bird.

To serve: Place the roast chicken on a serving platter and spoon the steamed stuffing around it. Carve in the usual manner and serve with the stuffing. Pass harissa (page 147) around the table as a spicy condiment. You can also serve this dish with some slices of different coloured capsicums (bell peppers) that have been pan-fried in olive oil, then steamed with the lid on for 10 minutes, or until tender.

SMOKED CHICKEN WITH SAUCE ROMAINE

A sophisticated roast, but a meal without effort for the clever cook, who buys the chicken from a good delicatessen pre-prepared, and has demi-glace and slivered almonds in the freezer, sultanas in the pantry.

Serves 4–6

1.3–1.5 kg (2¹/₂–3 lb) smoked chicken, commercially available both with and without stuffing (your choice)

Sauce Romaine
3 shallots, finely chopped
2 tablespoons white wine
1 tablespoon sugar
1 tablespoon water
350 ml (11 fl oz) demi-glace (page 225) or well-reduced beef stock
30 g (1 oz) sultanas (golden raisins)
30 g (1 oz) slivered almonds
salt and pepper

There are a couple of ways to reheat the smoked chicken without toughening it. The best is in an oven bag at 175°C (350°F), particularly if the chicken is stuffed and therefore has to be heated through more slowly. A stuffed chicken should take around 30–40 minutes, providing it did not come straight from the fridge. For quicker heating, the chicken can be cut into four or six portions, wrapped in foil and reheated. At 200°C (400°F), the portions take around 20–25 minutes (less without stuffing); a whole unstuffed bird takes about 25–30 minutes.

The whole chicken may be carved at the table, with the Sauce Romaine in a sauceboat. If the chicken is in pieces, brush the pieces with sauce first to give them a sheen, and put the remaining sauce in a sauceboat.

The Sauce Romaine: Place the shallots, wine, sugar and water in a small saucepan and reduce the liquid until the sugar starts to caramelise (only about 2 tablespoons left). Add just enough demi-glace to build a sauce — the finished sauce should not drown out a slight aftertaste of the sweet and sour ingredients. Add the sultanas and almonds, and season with salt and pepper.

Variation
Sauce Romaine is also marvellous with boiled ox tongue or pan-fried or roasted venison.

TO BASTE OR NOT TO BASTE?

I believe you should absolutely *not* baste meat while it is roasting, but time and again I read recipes that insist you do. Basting — that is, spooning liquid or fat from the base of the roasting dish, or a marinade, back over the breast from time to time during the cooking period — seems particularly popular with poultry, especially turkeys.

When I question believers as to what they think basting might be doing, most suggest a correlation between basting and succulence. There's an assumption that because the fat or marinade liquid is constantly replenished at the top of the bird, the flesh cannot dry out, and thus it will be more moist and tender. To be true, this would imply that the basting ingredient somehow penetrates the skin.

I truly doubt it. As I see it, the effect would be quite the opposite. My reasoning goes something like this.

You may have noticed that the old advertisements urging you to put your meat in the oven when you go to work and allow the timer to trigger the cooking for your arrival home, have gone by the board. Why? Because when meat goes into a cold oven, the internal juices of the meat flow towards the source of heat. By the time the oven is up to temperature, half the juice in the meat is out on the base of the baking dish — giving you a beautiful basis for a good gravy, but a hopelessly dry, juiceless piece of meat. Meat needs to enter a hot oven to seal — and that means to seal the pores shut, and keep the juices in.

Let's see what this means in relation to basting. We place the bird in a hot oven, and the internal juices immediately start to flow towards the source of heat. When they start to flow from the pores, the first droplets of blood are caught and seared on the skin just as they start to escape. Perfect. The juices are trapped inside for a tender, succulent breast. But now we come along and baste, washing off those little 'plugs' of dried blood that are sealing the pores. A few more drops escape and seal with the onslaught of heat — but then we baste again. Once again we wash away the 'plugs' and lose precious juices from the inside. It's a vicious circle — loss of juice, loss of succulence and the end result, a dry and fibrous breast. The exact opposite of the effect that we were trying to achieve.

In truth, the best way to keep succulence in a bird is to time the cooking properly. A 'just-cooked' bird is a lot better than the bird given 'a few more minutes to be sure'. It is a concept I teach for almost everything I cook, but for anything that may become fibrous (such as bird breasts), it is also a major element in cooking to perfection.

In the case of birds, the breast needs less cooking than the legs, which are more fibrous (they have more muscles and thus need more cooking time to break them down), and are also thicker. Thus, the place to test whether a bird is cooked is the base of the leg — the thicker thigh part, not the drumstick. I prick this part with a roasting fork then lightly press, and, just as the juices can be seen to be running yellow rather than pink, I whip the bird out of the oven before it has any further time to overcook the breast. In the case of turkey, where the disparity between the length of time required to cook the breast and that required to cook the legs is greater, it helps to place foil over the breast and on top of the drumsticks (never the whole bird) to deflect the heat from these areas while allowing the thicker parts to cook through. The foil is removed for the last 20 minutes or so in time to even the colouration.

The best way of all, of course, is to use the (in)famous Buffé cut, which is a turkey sold with breasts and wings on the carcass, but with no legs at all — but a legless turkey is not everyone's choice for the Christmas table!

Back to basting. There is truth in the fact that the rôtisserie chicken is succulent because it is 'self-basted'. This type of basting bears no resemblance to basting of the external skin. Its name comes from the effect gained when the bird is placed on a spit that rotates the bird as it cooks. The movement of the spit sets up a flow of juices inside the bird so that the juices of the more succulent part (thighs) move through to the drier parts (breast area) as the bird rotates. In the Paris Cordon Bleu 25 years ago, when domestic ovens were not fitted with rôtisseries, we were taught to simulate this method by cooking our birds half on the left side, then half on the right, only placing them breast side up for the last 10 minutes to help crisp the skin evenly. This is one way you might try; another is to cook it on a rack, breast side down, again turning it right side up to correct breast colouring for the last few minutes. This latter method works only with a rack, because breast side down in a dry baking pan will burn the breast, and in a layer of grease, will yield a wet, soggy breast skin. The problem with using a rack or a rôtisserie is that there is no gravy of any value. For a good gravy there needs to be a layer of grease in a good, thick baking dish, so that caramelisation of juices can begin on the base of the baking dish. This can later be built upon to make a sauce.

One last word. Basting also has the undesirable effect of softening the breast skin — rarely an asset in a roast chicken. The exception to the rule is when the liquid used contains sugar. Although basting with fat, butter or oil is never, in my opinion, warranted, there is something to be said for basting with liquids such as soy sauce, soy/honey combinations, or orange juice, because the sugars they leave behind will caramelise on the skin and leave it crisp. However, be careful — you don't want to interfere too much, and wash away too frequently those 'plugs' I mentioned earlier.

My rough guideline in this case is to start brushing or spooning the liquid over the bird about one-third of the way into cooking, and two or three times during cooking, then stop basting in the last 15 minutes or so in order to re-establish the final crisping of the skin. If you can turn the chicken from side to side during this operation, so much the better, but don't try this on the rôtisserie, lest all the juices fall constantly to the oven floor and burn.

ROASTED QUAIL

Serves 6

12 small or 6 large quails, or 6 poussins *(baby chicks)*

The marinade
1 tablespoon coriander seed
1 teaspoon cardamom seed
¹/₄ bottle white wine
4 tablespoons light olive oil
1 teaspoon lemon pepper, or coarse ground pepper mixed with grated lemon peel

The marinade: Roast the seeds in a dry frying pan until fragrant, then roughly crush with a mortar and pestle. Place in the bottom of an oblong airtight plastic container and add the wine, olive oil and lemon pepper. Add the quails or poussins, place lid on and leave overnight, shaking the marinade from time to time to mix well and to infuse the quails with flavour.

The quail: The next day, remove the birds from the marinade, place in a greased baking dish and roast them whole in the oven at 220°C (425°F). Allow 15-18 minutes for smaller quail, 25 minutes for larger ones or *poussins*. Serve with the vegetables or salad of your choice.

Variation

This dish is also well suited to barbecuing. After the birds have marinated overnight, cut them open along the backbone and flatten before placing on the oiled grill. To prevent drying, cook with the boney side down for three-quarters of the cooking time (total cooking time being about 12–15 minutes, depending on heat), only turning them flesh side down to brown them. Because of the heat on a barbecue, you may need to baste them twice during cooking with the marinade. Season with salt just before they are turned over.

ROAST DUCKLING WITH HONEY, CARAWAY SEED AND DATE PUREE

A roast with a real difference; not modern, but medieval. Take out all the extras — from cinnamon to demi-glace *— and you have my method for roasting duck; change those extras (glean some possibilities from the recipes in this chapter), and you have your own recipe for roasting duck.*

<u>Serves 4</u>

1.7 kg (3¹/₂ lb) duckling
1 teaspoon caraway seed
¹/₂ teaspoon cumin seed
1 tablespoon honey
¹/₂ teaspoon cinnamon
salt and pepper
60 g (2 oz) butter

The sauce
500 ml (16 fl oz) demi-glace *made with duck neck and giblets instead of beef*
(see recipe on page 225)
¹/₂ star anise
1 small bay leaf
100 ml (3¹/₂ fl oz) red wine
100 ml (3¹/₂ fl oz) orange juice
small piece cinnamon stick
¹/₄ teaspoon caraway seed
the 'essence' of the duck sediment
salt and pepper

The date purée
300 g (9¹/₂ oz) fresh dates, seeds removed
pinch of bicarbonate of soda
small knob butter
salt and pepper
pinch of cumin
scant amount of cream (optional)

To prepare the duckling: Cut off the wings at the second joint (the joint nearer the duckling) and remove the neck. Keep these aside for the *demi-glace*, along with the heart and gizzard. Truss the duckling. Mix the caraway and cumin in the honey and spread over the breast; sprinkle with the cinnamon, salt and pepper. Place in a baking dish greased with the butter and roast at 225°C (430°F) for 15 minutes, then reduce heat to 180°C (350°F) for 1³/₄ hours.

The sauce: Make up the *demi-glace* in the usual way (page 225), but add the piece of star anise and the bay leaf during cooking. Place the strained *demi-*

glace in a saucepan with the red wine, orange juice, cinnamon stick and caraway seed. Bring to the boil and simmer for 30 minutes, reducing by at least a third, then strain. (Sauce may be made in advance to this point.)

When the duckling is cooked, pour off the grease and add just a little water to the baking dish to boil up and scrape the sediment from the base of the dish. Transfer this 'essence' to the sauce; season with salt and pepper. If the sauce is too sweet, add a touch of brandy or sherry.

The date purée: Place the dates in a saucepan with the bicarbonate of soda and butter. Cover with water and bring to the boil, then simmer until tender. Purée through a mouli. Season with salt, pepper, a little cumin and, if necessary, thin with a little cream.

To serve: Cut the duckling into four by first cutting out the spinal column and then dividing each half into a wing section and a leg section. Place a quarter of the duckling on each plate, with the date purée alongside and the sauce in a pool. Serve with creamed sliced potatoes or Caramelised Witlof (page 160).

SAUTEED DUCK FILLETS
WITH BRANDIED CUMQUATS

Serves 4

4 duck breasts (Muscovy ducks are better than Peking;
as they are bigger, you will feed 8)
60 g (2 oz) margarine
2 shallots, finely chopped
16 pickled or brandied cumquats plus 75 ml (2¹/₂ fl oz) of their liquor
300 ml (10 fl oz) chicken stock or, better still, demi-glace *(page 225)*
salt and pepper
60 g (2 oz) butter, softened

Remove the duck skin and wing, if attached. Peking ducks have a tendency to be fatty and the fat will not cook through while maintaining a rare duck flesh. If you prefer to leave the skin on, cook the ducks for 90 per cent of the time on the first (skin) side, then quickly turn them over at the last minute to seal the meat. Done on a high heat, this should crisp the skin.

Heat the margarine and pan-fry the breasts. If the skin is on, use 45 g (1¹/₂ oz) only, and pour off excess fat as it renders. Peking duck breasts cook in about 3 minutes on the first side, 2 on the second (skin off), but Muscovy ducks take longer. The latter may be cooked totally in the pan, or fried to sear then transferred to a 220°C (425°F) oven for 8 minutes. After the cooking time, transfer the ducks to a board and cover them with a bowl to keep warm.

Pour any grease out of the pan then and add the shallots to the pan. Cook until softened, then deglaze with the cumquat liquor. Add the chicken stock or demi-glace. Bring to the boil; reduce to sauce consistency, stirring up sediment from the base of the pan. Add the cumquats to reheat; season with salt and pepper. Give the sauce a sheen by whisking in the softened butter.

To serve, slice the duck breasts, fan over the plates and spoon the sauce around the edge, garnishing one corner of the plate with the cumquats.

Variations

Change the fruit and the wine. Try fresh (or pickled) figs and deglaze with green ginger wine; sautéed peach halves and deglaze with port; fresh redcurrants or bottled blackcurrants and deglaze with port or red wine . . . or any other combinations you can think of.

A similar effect can be obtained with roast duck. Just roast in the usual way, transfer the duck to a board, degrease the dish, then deglaze and continue as above, scraping up the sediment on the base of the roasting pan as you form the sauce. The cumquats (or other fruits) may be heated separately in a small saucepan with a little *demi-glace.*

GREAT STUFF!

So you've chosen to have a traditional Christmas, and you've brought the turkey home. Now, just what are you going to do with it? Chances are from time to time you get sick of your own cooking, so I've asked a few friends to come up with their suggestions for stuffing turkey.

To start with, a word about the cooking and, most importantly, the timing. I'm inclined to prefer smaller turkeys, but then, unlike many of you with larger families, we are never more than eight at the table. I use a 4.6 kg (9 lb) bird (size 46) — the stuffings below will fill the centre and the crop of a bird from this size up to 5.5 kg (11 lb). Any larger, and you should add a further third to the recipes.

Unfortunately, one of the problems with cooking a turkey is that by the time the legs are cooked through, the breast is overcooked. So the best we can do is to protect the breast by deflecting as much heat from this area as we can with foil, and also to try and make the timing so perfect that it comes out of the oven when it is *just* cooked.

Smear both the baking dish and the turkey with butter, season the bird with salt and pepper, place foil over the breast and top of the drumsticks, then roast the stuffed and trussed 4.6 kg (9 lb) turkey in the oven at 220°C (425°F) for 15 minutes. Reduce the heat to 190°C (375°F) and cook for a further 2 hours 45 minutes. For the last 20 minutes, remove the foil. If the breast skin has not browned enough, you can finish the cooking on 220°C (425°F). To test, pinprick the thickest part of the thigh, press, and just as the juices start to run yellow and not pink, remove immediately.

If you choose to cook a Christmas duck instead, start at 225°C (430°F) for 15 minutes, then 185°C (365°F) for 40 minutes per kilo; for goose, start at 220°C (425°F) for 20 minutes, then 180°C (350°F) for 55 minutes per kilo.

GREEK STUFFING

Sauté 2 chopped onions in a little butter, then add 200 g (7 oz) lamb minced with the heart and liver of the bird. Mix with 750 g (1½ lb) cooked rice, 3 tablespoons pine nuts and 2 diced apples. Season with salt, pepper and fresh marjoram or oregano.

GREEN PEPPERCORN AND PRUNE STUFFING

Mix together 300 g (9½ oz) white breadcrumbs made from day-old bread with 1 teaspoon green peppercorns, 200 g (7 oz) pitted prunes (roughly chopped), 3 rashers bacon (diced and crisped), salt, pepper, and the leaves (chopped) from a sprig of fresh rosemary. To bind, stir in 2 eggs, beaten with a fork, and 100 g (3½ oz) melted butter. This is a rich recipe, which Dutch chef Hans Buddungh uses to stuff the crop only. You may like to make more and stuff the whole bird, but in larger quantities it is more suitable to use with a rich goose than a turkey.

OYSTER STUFFING (from an 18th century recipe)

Take 24 oysters, preferably with their juice, and chop into pieces. Add to 150 g (5 oz) white breadcrumbs made from day-old bread (without crusts). Add 90 g (3 oz) butter cut into little pieces, then the grated rind of a small lemon, lots of grated nutmeg, salt and two tablespoons chopped parsley. Bind with the yolk of an egg mixed with either milk or oyster juice. Stuff the crop with the mixture and sew in place. Should there be any left over, it can be rolled into little balls and fried in butter as an accompaniment. Note that this stuffing should not be too highly seasoned lest it drown the flavour of the oysters. Some stalks of finely chopped celery may be added for a crunchy texture.

GEORGES BLANC'S CHESTNUT STUFFING

Soak 500 g (1 lb) dried chestnuts overnight, then drain and cook in 600 ml (1 pt) chicken stock until softened (about 1 hour), or simmer a large can of drained, canned chestnuts for about 15 minutes only (they are quite fragile). Meanwhile, melt 75 g (2½ oz) butter and sauté 2 shallots or 1 small onion (chopped) and add 300 g (9½ oz) mixed pork and veal mince. Sauté until the meat is par-cooked and well broken up. When cooked, purée the chestnuts and 250 ml (8 fl oz) of the liquid and add to the meat. Season with lots of salt and freshly ground black pepper; Georges likes to add chopped truffles, too.

ANN CREBER'S DRIED FRUIT STUFFING

Crumb 180 g (6 oz) day-old wholemeal bread in the food processor. Chop 150 g (5 oz) unsoaked dried apricots and add to the bread along with the chopped leaves of a sprig of rosemary (or ½ teaspoon dried) and a pinch of dried herbs. Season with salt and pepper and stir in 125 g (4 oz) melted butter. This stuffing can either go inside the turkey cavity or the crop, or may even be placed under the skin to keep the breast moist. A few stoned prunes and/or slivered unblanched almonds are a nice addition.

EAST MEETS WEST, TWICE-STUFFED TURKEY

For the cavity: Mix 435 g (13½ oz) canned water chestnuts (drained) with breadcrumbs made from half a loaf of day-old bread (crumbed, without crusts, in a food processor), then add 4 chopped spring onions (scallions), salt, freshly ground black pepper, 1 tablespoon shredded pickled red ginger (available from Asian food markets) and 3 tablespoons melted butter to bind it together.

For the crop: Mix 750 g (1½ lb) raw pork and veal mince with 50 g (1½ oz) raisins soaked in Marsala and seeded. Season with salt, pepper and 1 teaspoon mixed herbs, then bind with an egg. Stuff the crop with this mixture and truss or pin in place. Because the mixture has been put in raw, this front stuffing will set like a pâté and can be carved into slices.

APPLE AND SAGE STUFFING

Sauté 2 chopped onions in a little butter, then add 500 g (1 lb) mixed pork and veal mince. Sauté until the mince is par-cooked and broken up. Transfer to a bowl and add the chopped unpeeled flesh of 2 Granny Smith apples and 2 Golden Delicious apples (the first are tart and resistant to mashing; the second go gooey and delicious). Add 2 tablespoons pine nuts and 3 tablespoons Calvados or dry alcoholic cider. Season with salt, pepper and 4 crumbled sage leaves (or 1 level teaspoon dried).

Optional: Sometimes I add 12–15 prunes; if cooking a goose, this is imperative — but it's rich!

MEAT

HOW TO FRY WITHOUT GETTING PANNED

On holiday in a small town, thinking it was an international classic, and not too technically beyond any chef standing near a Worcester sauce bottle and a bit of garlic, I ordered Steak Diane. I didn't have the foresight to predict that it was easier for him to open a packet of cornflour-based, pretend sauce with powdered garlic, add water, and pour the horrid concoction over the steak. I saw red!

With just the tiniest bit of knowledge about how to make a successful pan-fry, that chef could have had a menu of wonderful freshly made dishes as long as his arm. So can you.

Pan-frying is the most important technique for the hurried cook. From Steak Diane to Pork Chops in Cider, Chicken Fillets with Grapes, or even Beef Stroganoff, the technique is the same — only the ingredients differ. Fast, delicious dishes, with an enormous range of sauces, built simply and quickly with different liquids right in the base of the pan. The pan-fry is only as limited as your imagination.

The success of all good pan-fry sauces depends on the quality of sediment in the base of the pan, so first a few words on successful browning:

- Always use a black pan for a brown sauce, but never for a sauce deglazed with cream. Avoid aluminium, which greys the sauce; for preference use cast-iron or enamelled cast-iron, as good heat dispersal guarantees a better browning.

- Choose a pan the size of what you are cooking. One steak in the middle of an electric frypan is an invitation to burnt butter; one overlapping another is steaming, not frying, and behold — no sediment to make the sauce with.

- Never flood the pan with butter or oil — this prevents the sediment adhering to the base of the pan. And make sure the medium is hot before trying to seal the meat, particularly if the meat is thin or needs to be rare in the centre (prawns, scallops, steaks); less hot for meat that needs to cook through without going leathery on the outside (pork chops, thick-cut fish, chicken Marylands).

- Steak should never be turned more than once; a little more than half the cooking should be done on the first side (the side that faces up on the plate). Salt only once the meat is turned. Salt makes juices run and prevents the meat sealing well. Only the served side is salted and peppered.

Having browned the meat, remove it from the pan, discard any grease (particularly if burnt or speckled), then add the chosen liquid and stir up all the colour you can from the sediment on the base of the pan (this is known as deglazing the pan). Sometimes, particularly for the stronger (brown) sauces, some chopped shallot or onion is fried in a little butter before the liquid is added, as are some garnish vegetables, such as sliced mushrooms.

Years ago, cooks often thickened the sauce by blending a little cornflour or arrowroot with the liquid, but in modern cooking this trend has disappeared in favour of lighter sauces, boiled down enough to condense the liquid and make it syrupy.

Another good technique is to enrich the sauce with a large knob of butter, which serves to bind and lightly thicken the sauce. The trick to 'binding' or 'mounting' with butter rests on letting it melt only to an unctuous yellow, off the heat if the sauce is still hot — any further cooking turns it to grease, which remains as an ugly layer on top of the food.

SOME PAN-FRY CLASSICS

Pepper steak
Impregnate steaks with cracked pepper; fry, flambé in 2 tablespoons brandy, deglaze the pan with cream and reduce to sauce consistency. Season with salt and spoon over the steaks.

Some cooks prefer to deglaze with *demi-glace* (page 225) and mount with a knob of butter, but no cream.

Veal chops or escalopes with cream
Pan-fry the veal, flambé in brandy, then remove. Add fresh butter and pan-fry sliced champignons, deglaze the pan with cream and reduce to sauce consistency. Season with salt and pepper and spoon over the veal. Try this, too, with brains.

Lamb fillets with sweet vermouth
Fry 3 whole lamb fillets (for 6 people). Remove after 3 minutes on each side, then sauté a couple of tablespoons of chopped shallots. Deglaze with vermouth and reduce to sauce consistency, whisking in a 50 g (1½ oz) knob of butter to thicken the sauce. Slice the fillets diagonally, and spoon sauce over.

Medallions of beef fillet (or kangaroo) with port
Fry the meat in butter, flambé in brandy, add sliced champignons or a julienne of tongue and ham. Transfer to plates. Deglaze the pan with port and beef stock. Reduce to sauce consistency, season, mount with butter and spoon over the meat.

Beef Stroganoff

A pan-fried dish of slivered beef fillet fried with rings of onion and champignons and finished with cream — try also slivered beef or veal finished with French mustard and cream.

Fillet of beef (or fish) with green peppercorns

Pan-fry steaks or lightly floured, thick white fish fillets in butter. Transfer to plates. Add a tablespoon of crushed green peppercorns with their brine, then some cream; stir together. Season the sauce with salt and spoon over the steak or fish.

Minute steaks with fruit

(You can also use beef, venison or, for that matter, duck fillets with the skin removed.) Oil the minute steaks; if using venison, leave for 3 hours to tenderise. Pan-fry the steaks. Remove. Deglaze the pan with red wine or fruit vinegar. Add brown stock or *demi-glace* and the chosen fruit (poached cherries, blueberries, fresh figs). Reduce to sauce consistency, season, and spoon over the plate with the fruit. Lay the steak across the top. Venison is great with blueberries, Krakus or a similar brand of bottled blackcurrants, or Stone's green ginger wine with figs; sometimes I use port or marsala to deglaze and then add prunes with the meat.

And that Steak Diane? Fry the minute steak on both sides, season and transfer to serving plates. Add fresh butter, a clove of garlic (chopped) and 2 shallots (chopped). Fry until softened. Deglaze the pan with tomato sauce (ketchup), a dash of Worcester sauce and water. Stir to pick up the meat sediment, and boil to reduce the water by half. Remove from the heat, stir in a knob of butter, and add some chopped parsely. Spoon the sauce over the steaks.

DOUBLE-THICK PORTERHOUSE STEAK WITH BLACK AND GREEN OLIVE BUTTER

A barbecue or cast-iron grill method; can also be a pan-fry.

Serves 6–8

The black and green olive butter
120 g (4 oz) butter, preferably unsalted
2 tablespoons chopped shallots
8 pitted black olives, chopped
8 pitted green olives, chopped
salt and pepper

lemon juice, to taste
1 heaped teaspoon French mustard

The steaks

oil for the grill or barbecue; 60 g (2 oz) margarine if pan-frying
3 double-thickness, aged and well-hung porterhouse steaks, fat removed
salt and pepper

The olive butter: (can be prepared in advance). In a bowl, soften the butter with a whisk and stir in first the shallots, then the olives. Season with salt, pepper, lemon juice and mustard. The butter can be kept refrigerated, though if it will be kept for more than 2 days, omit the shallots.

The steaks: Steaks of this thickness are at their best on a good corrugated cast-iron grill or a barbecue. Pan-frying is the least successful option, although it is possible. If pan-frying, you will need margarine to fry in, as butter at this heat will burn over the time required to cook the meat.

Heat the grill until it radiates a good heat, then oil lightly only as you start the cooking. Never oil as you heat because the oil will burn, and never add too much oil if using a cast-iron grill, as it will negate the corrugations.

Place the steaks on the well-heated grill and cook for a little more than half the time on the first side (about 5 minutes, depending on thickness). When halfway through cooking on this first side, rotate the steaks at a 45° degree angle to create the traditional criss-cross imprint. Turn over and cook for 3–4 minutes on the second side, depending on how well done you like your steaks (the times given here are for a rare, 2.5 cm (1 in) porterhouse steak). Season with salt and pepper only when turned over. Transfer to a wooden board, and rest for 2–3 minutes before carving.

To serve: Carve the steaks into slices, cut slightly on the diagonal, then fan out half a steak per person. Daub with a generous helping of olive butter. It's delicious served with Jansen's potatoes (page 167) and a green salad.

Variations

The olive butter is a classic compound butter — that is, butter with chopped ingredients added to it to give it flavour and texture. Snail butter — with chopped garlic and parsley, and seasoned with lemon juice — is another well-known one; anchovy butter another. Use your imagination to invent others.

MUSTARD-COATED ROAST FILLET OF BEEF

An oven-roast, with a barbecue variation.

Serves 8

1.5 kg (3 lb) fillet, scotch fillet or porterhouse, cut from well-hung beef
2 cloves garlic, slivered
2 heaped teaspoons each of cardamom and
coriander seeds (optional)

about 4 tablespoons cracked black pepper
1 teaspoon salt
3 tablespoons French mustard
4 tablespoons grainy French mustard
3 tablespoons oil

Trim any sinew or fat from the beef, make a few knife slits and insert the slivered garlic. In a mortar and pestle (or a paper bag you can roll over with a rolling pin) combine the coriander and cardamom seed (if using). Grind roughly, leaving a little more texture than powdered spice, then mix with the pepper and salt. Mix the two mustards and spread all over the fillet, using a knife. Spread the spices on a wooden board and roll the mustard beef in them.

Drizzle about 1 tablespoon of oil in the centre of a baking dish. Place the beef in the dish and pour the remaining oil over the top. Roast at 250°C (500°F) for 25–30 minutes, depending on how cooked you like your beef. Rest the beef on a board, covered with a bowl, for at least 5 minutes before slicing. This makes for more tender meat and easier carving, and also helps to keep the meat juices inside the meat. When ready to serve, cut the meat into thick slices. Degrease the pan, leaving any meat juices. Heat the pan, add a little water, and stir up the sediment. Pass through a sieve, and serve 1 tablespoon of this concentrated juice over the meat. Serve with vegetables.

Variation

If you can rig up a spit, turned beef roasts more evenly, but I regularly roast this beef on the usual barbecue rack, turning once or twice, but finishing the cooking with the nicest side facing up. Count on about 20–25 minutes for rare beef of about 12–14 cm (5–5$\frac{1}{2}$ in) in diameter; more if you use a large roast of porterhouse, or if you like your meat well done. Remember the length of the meat doesn't change cooking time; greater or less width does.

CORNED BEEF AND VEGETABLES WITH ONION SAUCE

A classic English stew designed to keep the winter wolves from the door;
a magnificent old-world dish that should not be forgotten. The best cut
to use is the silverside, the long thin muscle from the leg of the beef,
which is first pickled, then rolled or netted. The onion sauce is totally
classic; my difference — or rather a trick I learned from my mother — is
the delicious sweet marmalade that gives not only a lift to the flavour,
but a brilliant sheen to the presentation.

Serves 8

3 kg (6 lb) corned silverside or sirloin
2 bay leaves
3 cloves
4–5 black peppercorns

1 stalk celery (optional), cut into 5 cm (2 in) lengths
1 tablespoon vinegar
3 large carrots, cut into wedges, or 1 bunch baby carrots, left whole
3–4 parsnips, cut into wedges
8 baby turnips, left whole, or 3 large turnips, halved
4 leeks, white part only, halved across, not lengthways
8 baby onions
½ cabbage, cut into large wedges

The onion sauce
5 small or 3 large onions, finely sliced
600 ml (1 pt) milk
65 g (2½ oz) butter
50 g (1½ oz) plain (all-purpose) flour
salt and pepper
pinch of nutmeg

The garnish
2–3 tablespoons thick-cut Seville marmalade

Trim any excess skin from the meat, but not every skerrick of fat. Bring a large stockpot of water to the boil with the bay leaves, cloves, peppercorns, celery and vinegar. Add the corned beef, return to the boil, then reduce the heat and simmer gently for about 2½–2¾ hours. This is going to vary a little depending on your taste, but the meat will be succulent and juicy if it is cooked through but not overcooked. If you pass the optimum time, corned beef becomes fibrous, and when cut, gives off stringy lengths rather than clean slices.

The vegetables all require different cooking times — the carrots need 40 minutes, the parsnips and turnips need 25–30 minutes, the leeks need about 20 minutes, the baby onions and the cabbage wedges need about 15 minutes. Add them to the stew at the appropriate time so that they are cooked to perfection by the time the meat is ready.

The onion sauce: (can be prepared in advance). Place the onions and a knob of butter in a small saucepan, and half fill with boiling water. Cook slowly, covered, until really soft, then drain and purée in a food processor. Set aside.

To make the white sauce, first scald the milk. In a second saucepan heat the remaining butter, add the flour and stir until cooked, then add the hot milk. Stir to the boil to thicken the sauce, add the onion purée, and season with salt, pepper and nutmeg.

If the sauce is made in advance, cover with plastic wrap, pressed down onto the sauce so it doesn't form a skin. Stir with a whisk when reheating.

To serve: Transfer the stew to a large platter, the vegetables arranged attractively around the meat. Spread the top of the meat with marmalade. Serve the onion sauce in a sauceboat. If you need potatoes, boil separately.

THAI BEEF SALAD

This is the best way I know to dress cold roast beef, though it must be rare. The tangy chilli and spices of the traditional Thai sauce are magnificently offset by the cool, refreshing fragrance of mint.

Serves 6

750 g (1½ lb) piece beef fillet, well trimmed
a little peanut oil
2 cloves garlic, crushed
2 tablespoons soy sauce
2 tablespoons Thai fish sauce (nam pla)
2 tablespoons lime juice
50 g (1½ oz) sugar
2 shallots, finely chopped
½ cup fresh mint leaves, shredded
1 cup fresh coriander (cilantro) leaves
4 small hot red chillies, sliced
about 12 water chestnuts, sliced
1 bunch snake beans

The garnish
12–15 cherry tomatoes
3 small hot red chillies, cut into 'flowers'
6 cloves garlic, thinly sliced and deep-fried

Rub the fillet with oil and roast in the oven at 220°C (425°F) until rare or medium rare (about 20 minutes, depending on thickness). Set aside to cool.

Meanwhile, make a paste of the garlic, soy sauce, fish sauce, lime juice, sugar and shallots. Add half the mint and coriander leaves, then the chillies and water chestnuts.

When ready, slice the beef very finely, place in a bowl and toss with the mixture. Blanch the snake beans for 30 seconds, then take 4 per person and make them into a nest on the base of each plate; alternatively, chop the beans and mix through the salad, along with the cherry tomatoes.

To serve, place a pile of beef on each plate, pour the rest of the sauce over all, and arrange the garnish ingredients as desired. Top with the remaining mint and coriander leaves.

Note: to cut a chilli into a 'flower', slice it into quarters from tip to stalk, ensuring you don't cut all the way through. Place the chilli in cold water until it opens like a flower.

HONEYED PORK WITH SOUR CREAM SAUCE

A pan-fry method.

<u>Serves 4</u>

500 g (1 lb) pork fillet
2 tablespoons honey
30 g (1 oz) butter
1 large onion, finely sliced
125 ml (4 fl oz) water
¹/₂ teaspoon turmeric
1 scant teaspoon powdered ginger
pinch of mace
strip of orange rind
1 clove garlic, finely chopped
salt and pepper
250 ml (8 fl oz) sour cream

Cut the pork into medallions about 2 cm (³/₄ in) thick. If the fillets are not wide, cut at 4 cm (1¹/₂ in) and butterfly open. Warm the honey gently in a frying pan; add the butter and brown the pork. When brown, remove, and sauté the onion until lightly caramelised. Return the pork to the pan, add the water, then cover and simmer for 10 minutes, or until the meat is tender. When cooked, add the spices, orange rind, and garlic; season with salt and pepper. Add the sour cream, bring to the boil, and reduce to sauce consistency. Check seasoning and remove the orange peel. Spoon the sauced meat onto plates, and serve with rice and a mango chutney.

BONED LEG OF LAMB WITH BLACK OLIVES

A roast with a Provençal touch.

<u>Serves 6</u>

2 kg (4 lb) leg of lamb, tunnel-boned by the butcher

The stuffing
20 large fleshy black olives (preferably Kalamata), pitted and chopped
1 slice bread, crusts removed, crumbled
3 tablespoons chopped parsley
1 tablespoon chopped chervil
leaves from a sprig of fresh thyme
30 g (1 oz) butter
1 small onion, diced
2 cloves garlic, very finely chopped
salt and freshly ground black pepper

The stuffing: Place the roughly chopped olives in a bowl with the bread and herbs. Heat the butter and fry the onion until softened, but not coloured. Add the garlic for the last 20–30 seconds. Spoon into the bowl with the grease that comes with it, and stir to bind the stuffing. Season with a little salt and plenty of freshly ground black pepper.

The lamb: With the aid of a wooden spoon, push the stuffing into the bone cavity. Using skewers or a stuffing needle and string, loosely sew the ends into shape to prevent stuffing escaping. Rub the lamb with salt, place in a baking dish without fat, and bake in a 230°C (440°F) oven for 65 minutes (if you don't like the lamb to be pink, roast it at 200°C (400°F) for 1¹/₂ hours.

To serve: Carve the lamb into thicker than usual slices, across the stuffing. If you can buy bottled (Italian) black olive paste or tapenade, make small *quennelles* (rissoles) of this on the side as a garnish, and perhaps serve a ratatouille as the accompanying vegetable.

LAMB FILLETS WITH CALVADOS AND APPLE

A pan fry. Currently the darling of good restaurants and the gourmet cook, lamb fillet goes well with everything flavoursome — Mediterranean combinations such as ratatouille or grilled capsicums (bell peppers), a decorative plating of mesclun *salad, the very 'in' hot waxy (yellow) potato salad with bacon and chives, any number of creamy presentations with wild mushrooms (particularly morels) or, like the recipe below, apple pieces and a good dash of Calvados.*

The true lamb fillet is very tiny, and rarely sold separately from the T-bone of the loin chop in which it nestles. On a menu, expect a fillet of lamb to mean the boned out larger part of the lamb chop, sometimes known as the 'eye'. It may also apply to the backstrap, or meat of the cutlet, which is marginally further along the bone. In recipes, the three are interchangeable, with only slight changes in cooking time, but the larger pieces — the backstrap and the loin — can be sliced and fanned over the plate for a snazzier presentation.

Serves 4

45 g (1¹/₂ oz) butter
1 tablespoon oil
12 'true' lamb fillets or 4 backstraps or 'eyes' of the loin (see above)
1 dessertspoon brown sugar
2 tablespoons Calvados (apple brandy) or brandy
250 ml (8 fl oz) cream
salt and freshly ground black pepper

The garnish
2 Granny Smith apples, peeled, cored, and cut into thick slices
seasoned flour for dredging
50 g (1¹/₂ oz) butter

Heat the butter and oil in a frying pan large enough to take the meat in one layer. Fry the lamb to an appetising brown all over — this will take 5–6 minutes for larger cuts (remaining pink inside), while the 'true' fillet takes only 2–3 minutes. When the meat is almost done, sprinkle in the sugar and turn the meat to add colour and caramelisation. Add the Calvados or brandy immediately to stop the caramel burning, then set a match to it or dip the pan to flambé the alcohol. When the flame dies, add the cream and stir up the rich colour from the base of the pan. Season with salt and pepper, and reduce to sauce consistency.

Serve 3 'true' fillets per person, or slice the larger backstrap or 'eyes' diagonally and serve the slices fanned out prettily on the plates. Place the apples alongside the meat; they may be tossed in the sauce to add a sheen.

The garnish: Dredge the apple slices in the flour; pat off the excess. Heat the butter and fry the slices in batches. This can be done either at the same time as the meat or, earlier. If fried earlier, keep the apple slices warm in the oven.

Variations
Try this dish with veal or pork chops, or pork medallions. Adjust the cooking time to the chosen meat.

LOIN OF LAMB WITH HAZELNUT SAUCE
A pan-fry method, using caul to hold the stuffing in place. See the variation below for a roasted method that does not need the caul.

Serves 6
1 bunch spinach, deveined, washed and dried
30 g (1 oz) butter
4 boned loins of lamb, the larger 'eye' sections only (see preceding recipe)
35 g (1¹/₂ oz) champignons, finely sliced
35 hazelnuts, roasted and skinned, then roughly chopped
salt and pepper
grated nutmeg
caul fat to cover the meat (optional), or string to tie the meat
60 g (2 oz) butter, for roasting

The sauce
250 ml (8 fl oz) very well reduced lamb or beef stock
salt and pepper
200 ml (7 fl oz) cream
1 teaspoon brandy

Toss the spinach quickly in a very hot pan with the butter. Transfer to paper towelling to absorb any excess moisture. Lay one piece of lamb on a board and spread over half the spinach. Place half of the champignons here, too, and one-third of the hazelnuts. Salt and pepper lightly, and sprinkle with nutmeg. Lay a second piece of meat across the top and hold the 'sandwich' together by rolling it in caul fat, or tying it together. Make up the second pair of lamb pieces in the same way. Roast the loins in a 230°C (440°F) oven for 14 minutes if in caul; 12 minutes if tied. When cooked, rest for 4–5 minutes while making the sauce, before carving or untying.

The sauce: Deglaze the dish with the lamb stock and reduce to half, stirring up the sediment in the base of the pan. Add the remaining hazelnuts and stir in the cream. Reduce to sauce consistency, season with salt and pepper, and add the brandy.

To serve: Carefully slice the loins into 3 medallions per piece. Serve 2 medallions per person on a bed of sauce, with potatoes or chosen garnish.

Variations

Use this caul-bound method to hold any stuffing that is likely to break up in place — from grated zucchini (courgette), Parmesan cheese and pinenut stuffing, to chopped prunes, bacon and onion stuffing.

Compare this method with a roasted loin on the bone, where you slide a knife along the bone on the meat side to create a pocket into which you push cooked hazelnut and spinach stuffing. No need for caul, and the roast can be oven-cooked at 220°C (425°F) like any full-length rack (about 18 minutes for rare). The choice is yours . . .

COUSCOUS — A TOUCH OF MOROCCO

Couscous is the 'in' grain. All over the world it is being steamed over stews in much the same way as it is in the small tiled kitchens of northern Africa where it has long been the staple grain. In other countries, however, it is being used in much the same way as rice — sitting alongside casseroles and stews, as a cold salad with chopped vegetables such as capsicum (bell pepper) and spring onion (scallion) tossed through it, as a base on which to serve a roasted pigeon or quail (with the typical dark brown saucing of a French *demi-glace*), and even refried with a good sprinkling of traditional Asian ingredients as the modern buff's answer to Chinese fried rice.

Not so in Morocco. Couscous the grain is still served up most often as the base for the traditional lamb stew that shares its name. This simple stew was based on the meats the north Africans most commonly had on hand — the less prime cuts of lamb and the scrawny but flavoursome free range chickens. These, together with root vegetables, zucchini (courgette) and capsicum (bell pepper), are boiled in a coriander and tomato flavoured water in the traditional large pear-shaped aluminium pot called the 'couscousier'. While the stew cooks, the grain is prepared.

Outside north Africa, the grain sold in supermarkets is mostly pre-steamed couscous, which requires little but a soaking in cold water drizzled with a small amount of oil, and then steaming. But the most haunting sight in north Africa is to see the young housewives crouching on the floor outside their houses, chatting to friends while running their fingers through the swollen grain — letting it fall through the air and onto the large round glazed terracotta plate at their feet, and pulling apart the small lumps that stop the couscous running free. The supple grain is then transferred to the colander-like vessel that sits over the top of the coucousier, to be steamed over the reheating stew.

Throughout Morocco, Tunisia and Algeria, the word 'couscous' describes not only the grain, but the traditional dish. Served on colourful pottery and washed down with the traditional mint tea, it is followed with fresh fruits and syrupy-sweet honey pastries, spiced with cinnamon and cardamom.

The recipe is fairly long, but simple, and can be made in advance. It will bring to your table a taste of the medinas of Fez, the souks of Marrakesh, of Tangiers, and Ouarzazat on the fringe of the Sahara . . .

COUSCOUS — THE CLASSIC MOROCCAN WAY

<u>Serves 10–12</u>

200–250 ml (7–8 fl oz) olive oil
1 kg (2 lb) lamb, usually taken from cutlets, pieces of neck and ribs
8–10 chicken pieces
3 large turnips, peeled and quartered
10 small carrots, peeled
2 teaspoons sweet paprika
1 tablespoon tomato paste
salt and pepper
$^1/_2$ teaspoon ground coriander
1 clove garlic
2 cloves
3 onions, peeled and quartered
2 green and 2 red capsicums (bell peppers), cut into chunks
4 zucchini (courgettes), cut in half
500 g (1 lb) chick peas (canned will do as they don't need soaking)

The meat balls
700 g (1$^1/_2$ lb) minced beef
1 small onion, very finely chopped
2 tablespoons chopped parsley
salt and pepper
1 egg
12 merguez (spicy lamb) sausages

The couscous
500 g (1 lb) couscous
about 500 ml (16 fl oz) boiling water
1 teaspoon salt
3 tablespoons olive oil

Heat the oil in a large casserole dish. Brown the meat well, lamb pieces first, then the chicken. Empty out some of the oil, return meat to the pan, cover well with water, then add the turnips and carrots. Bring to the boil, then stir in the paprika and tomato paste. Season with salt and pepper, add the coriander, garlic and cloves, and cook for about 2 hours on a slow simmer.

After this time, add the onion, capsicum and zucchini, and cook for a further 20 minutes. Add the chick peas at the end to heat through. Remove from the stove. The stew can be made in advance and reheated.

The meatballs: Place the mincemeat in a bowl and add the onion, parsley, salt, pepper and egg. Blend well with your fingers and roll into about 22–25 small meatballs. When ready to reheat the stew, heat some the stock in a saucepan and cook the meatballs; alternatively, they can be deep-fried. Pan-fry the merguez sausages as you would any sausages; keep warm.

The couscous: Place the couscous in a bowl. Cover with the boiling water, wait 2 minutes for it to be absorbed, then add salt and the oil. Run your fingers through the grain to break up any large lumps. Then transfer the swollen couscous to the top of a couscousier, or a colander with holes in the base as well as the sides. Cover the colander with foil. Place over the stew to steam while the stew is reheating. The couscous will be ready after about 15 minutes. (Note, if the couscous is hot enough to serve after adding the boiling water, it can be spooned out immediately. An even simpler method is to cover the bowl with plastic wrap and quickly heat the couscous in the microwave.)

To serve: Spoon the couscous grain onto plates, preferably old-fashioned wide soup bowls. Serve the stew, meatballs and sausages separately. Each guest ladles the meats, vegetables and some liquid over the grain. Serve with harissa (a hot sauce available in tubes from gourmet delicatessens, or see page 147 for recipe). Minced chilli is a good substitute, but it is unheard of in North Africa not to serve the dish with liberal amounts of harissa.

BARBECUED FILLET OF LAMB WITH COUSCOUS

A modern application of the traditional Moroccan grain.

<u>Serves 6</u>

¹/₂ bunch each of parsley, mint and coriander (cilantro) leaves, chopped
2 cloves garlic, finely chopped
¹/₂ teaspoon cumin powder
*4 fillets of lamb, taken from the loin or the cutlets (also known as
'backstraps' — see page 140)*
olive oil, for the grill or pan

The salsa
6 very red tomatoes, peeled and diced into small, neat cubes
¹/₂ onion, finely chopped
6 spring onions (scallions), including green part, sliced
1 small hot red chilli, shredded
¹/₂ bunch coriander (cilantro)
salt and pepper
dash of oil and vinegar
4 tablespoons plain yoghurt

The couscous
500 g (1 lb) couscous, prepared using the method above

Mix the parsley, mint and coriander in a bowl with the garlic and cumin. Roll the fillets in the mixture and allow to stand for about 1 hour.

When ready, pan-fry the lamb in a film of oil. Alternatively, heat a barbecue, a cast-iron grill or a hotplate, and brush a thin layer of olive oil over the surface. Grill the fillets, preferably keeping them pink in the middle, for about 3 minutes on each side (cook them for longer if you like the meat well done). Transfer the fillets to a wooden board and rest for 3 minutes, covered with a bowl.

The salsa: Place the tomatoes in a bowl and add the onion, spring onions, chilli and plucked (rather than chopped) leaves of coriander. Season with salt and pepper, and the oil and vinegar. This part can be prepared in advance, but stir in the yoghurt only as you serve, or it falls through and becomes a watery liquid.

To serve: Carve the lamb fillets into thin diagonal slices. Fan the slices of lamb over a large bed of couscous placed on the serving plates. Place the salsa on the side.

LAMB KEBABS

Strictly for the barbecue or to cook on a corrugated cast-iron grill. Although it is possible to pan-fry kebabs, the heat is rarely intense enough to brown these marinade-moistened meats.

Serves 6

1 kg (2 lb) boned leg of lamb, or boned shoulder, cut into 2 cm (³/₄ in) cubes
60 ml (2 fl oz) olive oil
60 g (2 oz) natural yoghurt, mixed with 1 teaspoon harissa
leaves of a rosemary sprig
salt
1 firm, red tomato, cut into wedges
¹/₂ onion, cut into wedges
1 red capsicum (bell pepper), cut into 18 strips

Place the lamb in a bowl or oven bag and add the oil, yoghurt and harissa, and rosemary leaves. Season lightly with salt. Cover the bowl with plastic wrap and place in the refrigerator overnight, or for a minimum of 2 hours.

Thread skewers with the lamb cubes, tomato wedges, onion wedges and capsicum strips alternately, then barbecue or pan-fry until cooked. Serve on a bed of couscous.

MOROCCAN PRESERVED LEMONS

There are two main methods to preserve lemons, Moroccan style.

Method 1: This is the easier. Stick 3–4 cloves into each lemon, then pack the lemons into a jar and cover with olive oil. With this method, it is essential that the lemons are maintained beneath the level of oil or they will start to ferment, but providing they are covered, they will last up to 3 months before the lemon flesh starts to disintegrate. Lemons preserved this way yield softer flesh, and do not have the salty, strong taste of the method below. They are well suited to the famous Moroccan Chicken and Lemon Tagine (casserole), because the whole lemon can be used, flesh included. After two or three weeks, the oil itself is also useful — it can be added to a salad dressing or drizzled over fish, barbecued chicken, and so on.

Method 2: This way is more traditional. Cut the lemons lengthways into four. Pour 3 tablespoons coarse cooking salt into the base of a preserving jar, then pack the lemon wedges tightly into the jar, pressing down firmly so they release their juice. Pour at least 2–3 tablespoons more salt between the wedges as you proceed up the jar. Top up the juice with the juice of two more lemons and fill the rest of the jar with warm, pre-boiled water.

Seal the lid of the jar and shake well. Stand the jar upside down overnight, then shake and invert again two or three times during the next week. Set aside for a month before using. The lemons will last at least a year, although the colour may darken considerably.

When using salted lemons, discard the flesh, rinse under the tap and use the peel only in recipes. The peel is excellent sliced over fish as a garnish, diced and mixed through couscous when served with fish, in the chicken stuffing on page 120, or as a condiment for curries.

See also Seafood Couscous (page 78) and Chicken Stuffed with Couscous (page 120).

HARISSA

Makes about 2–3 cups

3 tablespoons coriander seed
5 tablespoons cumin seed
1 scant tablespoon salt
2 tablespoons chilli flakes, or to taste, but should be very spicy
4 large red capsicums (bell peppers), roasted, skinned and chopped
250 ml (8 fl oz) olive oil

Place the coriander and cumin in a dry pan and roast until they begin to give off a pungent smell. Place in a food processor with the salt and chilli flakes and grind as finely as possible. Add the capsicum and a little oil, and purée everything together to as fine a paste as possible, then pour the olive oil down the funnel. Process until well blended. Transfer to a bottle and cover with a fine layer of olive oil. Harissa will keep in the refrigerator for months as long as the top is covered with oil. Use it as a condiment with grilled meats; it is traditionally served alongside Couscous (the dish).

OLD MOTHER HOLUIGUE'S FOOLPROOF FORMULA FOR CASSEROLES

For some reason, making casseroles does not seem to come naturally to those of us living in warmer climates. We tend to stick to baking and frying, with an occasional weekend barbecue, particularly in summer. In winter, however, we have to look further. Out come the cookery books for something warm and filling . . .

A logical look at the stages involved in creating a good casserole shows, however, that they're all made in somewhat the same way. Whatever the meat, whatever the garnish, we have in fact gone through the same steps to cook it. Be it a chicken dish with cream and champignons, a beef casserole with red wine sauce and a garnish of baby onions and bacon pieces, or cubed pieces of lamb with a tomatoey sauce garnished with chopped zucchini (courgette), capsicum (bell pepper), eggplant (aubergine) and black olives, the format is the same.

Let's construct a six-point formula, and take another look at the dishes in a moment.

1. **Brown** the meat, whatever it may be. For six people, you'll need: 1.5 kg (3 lb) veal, beef, lamb or pork, cut into 2 cm / $^3/_4$ in) cubes; 8–12 chicken pieces; 2 small pheasants or wild duck, quartered; or 2 rabbits, cut into segments. Brown in oil, butter, margarine, or butter mixed with oil, depending on the desired result (butter goes with cream sauces, oil gives a Mediterranean feel). Brown well — the colour of the meat and the sediment on the base of the pan is crucial as the raw material for a rich brown sauce.

   If you want an onion in the casserole, it is often fried with the meat, thus enriching the sediment on the base of the pan.

2. **Thicken**, by spooning a heaped tablespoon of plain (all-purpose) flour over everything, then working it down into the base of the casserole, where it fries a moment to pick up colour, and then sticks to the bottom of the pan, lifting off gently during the simmering time to thicken the sauce without lumping. Some people toss the meat in flour before frying. Don't — it prevents the meat from searing, and often forms a crust which falls off in lumpy sheets in the casserole later. Rather, brown the meat very well first, then use the flour to make a *roux* in the bottom of the casserole — you will see a much better result.

3. **Add the liquids**, whatever they may be. Choose from red or white wine, chicken or beef stock, beer or water, or combinations of these. Red wine makes a great Boeuf Bourguignonne, but this classic also appreciates the gutsinesss of a bit of beef stock to fill out the sauce. White wine is often too acidic for chicken pieces; try 'cutting' it with half wine, half chicken stock. Chicken stock is viscous and gelatinous; the more of it you use, the richer and more 'velvety' the sauce.

4. **Add the flavourings**, whatever they may be. There are many things that can be used to make a flavoursome and sophisticated sauce. Those most frequently used in good casserole cookery are finely chopped garlic and shallots (not spring onions), and a bouquet garni (3 stalks parsley, 1 sprig thyme, and a bay leaf, tied together for easy removal).

    Choose the other additions depending on the effect you want — tomato paste, Worcester sauce, salt, pepper, a piece of celery, carrot or orange peel to enhance flavour, a peeled chopped tomato, beef or chicken cubes, mustard, soy sauce or mirin, spices, and any particular herb you like (particularly tarragon, sage or oregano; basil and the very pungent ones tend to go in at the end).

5. **The cooking time**. Bring the casserole to the boil, turn it down so that it is just simmering, place the lid on to minimise evaporation, and simmer the casserole for the time it takes to cook through. This will depend on the type and size of the chosen meat, but must also take into account the time it took to brown the meat (probably up to 15 minutes if you wanted a good dark brown for a gutsy brown sauce; less for chicken being served in white wine, cream and champignons). As a guide, the simmering time is about 35 minutes for chicken pieces, 1¼ hours for veal and lamb cubes, 1½ hours for pheasant and wild duck, 2 hours for oyster blade, chuck topside and less hefty beef cuts, and 2½ hours for gravy beef (beef cut from the shank) and rabbit pieces.

6. **The garnish** ingredients are so varied it is impossible to list them all. Most common are tomato pieces (if they are to remain intact, they should be quartered and not peeled; compare with those going in as a flavouring ingredient), small onions (which should be boiled for white sauces, or boiled then fried in sugar and butter to caramelise them for darker sauces), crisped bacon pieces, black or green olives, prunes, orange zest and orange segments, and vegetable pieces ranging from broccoli, asparagus or carrot to any of the Mediterranean combinations, or champignons (or other mushrooms), and so on.

The main thing to remember about the garnish is that you need to decide how long it should be cooked in the sauce, and add it to the casserole at the appropriate time. Bacon and fried champignons, pan-fried Mediterranean vegetables such as eggplant (aubergine), zucchini (courgette) and capsicum (bell pepper), or even green vegetables that look best keeping their colour or shape, should go in at the very last minute before serving. Prunes swell in the sauce and enrich its colour, so are best dropped in about half an hour before the end of cooking time. Chopped parsley, or the chopped lemon peel and parsley that are the traditional *gremolata* garnish for osso buco, go directly on the meat on the serving platter.

With a formula such as this, chances are you can now forget the recipe books on casseroles and make up your own delicious varieties using the best of what is available at the market, or the remnants in your fridge. Of course there are traditional casseroles, and you may want to consult a cookbook if you want to make a traditional osso buco, for example. But there is no reason why you can't serve an excellent veal shank dish with a tomato sauce by simply choosing to fry the veal in olive oil, thicken, pour on white wine and chicken stock, flavour with shallot, garlic, bouquet garni, a tomato and tomato paste, simmer for 1³/₄ hours (shank pieces are larger than veal cubes, so take longer to cook) and finish with chunky pieces of tomato garnishing the dish.

Using the same formula, you can make a chicken dish with champignons and cream: brown the chicken in butter, add shallots, white wine and a little chicken stock, bearing in mind that you will be adding cream to further liquefy the sauce a little later. No strong flavourings this time — no onion (which overpowers creamy sauces) and no garlic (it doesn't suit the cream) — just salt, pepper and shallots. Cook through and finish by boiling down the sauce when you have removed the chicken pieces, stirring in the cream and adding the champignons.

Spooned over the chicken, the result will be totally different from a lamb casserole with olive oil, garlic, white wine and tomato in a sauce that is strong in thyme and herbs. Why? Because this time you'd finish with fried pieces of eggplant (aubergine), fresh quarters of tomato and fried zucchini (courgette), capsicum (bell pepper) and black olives, Mediterranean style.

Same technique . . . different ingredients. Gosh cooking's simple!

VEAL PAPRIKA

This classic Middle European casserole is an example of the above formula, as are those that follow.
See also Chicken à la Niçoise on page 114.

See also Chicken à la Niçoise on page 114.

Serves 6–8

60 g (2 oz) butter or margarine
1.5 kg (3 lb) boned veal, from the leg or shoulder, cut into 3 cm (1¼ in) cubes
1 onion, diced
1 heaped tablespoon plain (all-purpose) flour
300 ml (10 fl oz) dry white wine
300 ml (10 fl oz) chicken stock or water
1 tablespoon finely chopped shallots
2 cloves garlic, finely chopped
2 tomatoes, peeled, seeded and roughly chopped
1 heaped tablespoon tomato paste
1 tablespoon sweet paprika
bouquet garni
salt and pepper
250 g (8 oz) small white champignons, sliced
a knob of butter
pinch of cayenne pepper (optional)

Heat the butter or margarine in a thick-based casserole dish (try using enamelled cast iron — nothing makes greater casseroles). Sauté the veal in batches until well browned, then the onion. Add the flour and brown that, too, adding a little more butter if needed. Add the white wine and stock or water, shallot, garlic, tomatoes, tomato paste, paprika and bouquet garni, as well as a little salt and pepper. Bring to the boil, then reduce the heat, cover, and simmer slowly for 1½ hours.

When cooked, remove the meat to a bowl with a slotted spoon. Quickly pan-fry the champignons in a film of butter, then add to the sauce. Raise the heat and boil down the liquid to sauce consistency (it should lightly coat the back of the spoon), then check the seasoning, adding salt, pepper and tomato paste if necessary, and perhaps a dash of cayenne or hot paprika. Return the meat to the sauce, and serve with rice or large, whole potatoes, oven-baked in their skins.

VEAL SHANKS WITH SUN-DRIED TOMATOES

A casserole in the modern style — it combines the comfort of the traditional with flavoursome modern ingredients.

Serves 4

75 ml (2¹/₂ fl oz) olive oil
4 veal shanks cut from white (baby) veal
1 heaped tablespoon plain (all-purpose) flour
400 g (12 oz) can peeled Italian tomatoes
500 ml (16 fl oz) dry white wine
300 ml (10 fl oz) water
bouquet garni
1 carrot, sliced
¹/₂ stalk celery, sliced
2 cloves garlic, finely chopped
1 heaped tablespoon tomato paste
salt and pepper

The garnish
2 small onions, finely sliced
2 tablespoons olive oil
6 sun-dried tomatoes, finely sliced
freshly ground black pepper

Equipment: 30 cm (12 in) diameter, large, deep frying pan, or large casserole dish

Heat the olive oil in the frying pan or casserole dish. Fry the veal shanks until deep brown (about 15 minutes) — on this depends the depth of colour of your sauce. If the saucepan is not wide enough, brown the meat in two batches. Sprinkle in the flour and cook until it is chocolate-coloured and stuck on the base of the pan, then stir in the tomatoes plus their juice, and the wine and water. Add the bouquet garni, carrot, celery, garlic and tomato paste; season with salt and pepper. Bring to the boil, then reduce the heat, cover, and simmer very slowly for 3 hours, turning the shanks at least once.

When cooked, remove the shanks and bouquet garni and pass the sauce through a *mouli* or a blender. Return the sauce to the pan, add the veal shanks, and correct the seasoning. If possible, rest the casserole overnight, covered. Next day, remove any fat that has risen to the top and reheat.

To serve: While heating the shanks, sauté the onion slices in the oil. Cook slowly until softened, without colouring, then add the sun-dried tomatoes. Spoon this garnish over the shanks, and season with the pepper. Serve with rice or oven-baked potatoes.

CARBONNADE A LA FLAMANDE

A classic Flemish casserole cooked with beer.

<u>Serves 6–8</u>

50 g (1¹/₂ oz) margarine or butter
1.3 kg (2¹/₂ lb) gravy beef (beef from the shank),
cut into 3 cm (1¹/₄ in) cubes
2 large onions, sliced
500 ml (16 fl oz) beer
3 tablespoons tomato paste
1 clove garlic, finely chopped
bouquet garni
salt and pepper
6 potatoes, cut into quarters
125 g (4 oz) champignons
a knob of butter
2 tablespoons chopped parsley

In a large casserole dish, heat the margarine or butter and brown the beef cubes. When well browned, add the onions and fry until lightly browned. Add the beer, tomato paste, garlic and bouquet garni; season with salt and pepper. Bring to the boil, then reduce heat and simmer, covered, for about 2–2¹/₂ hours. Add the potatoes about 45 minutes before the end of cooking time; not only will they absorb the flavour of the sauce, but their starch will act as a natural thickener.

When the casserole is nearly ready, sauté the champignons in butter, and add to the casserole for the last 5 minutes. Transfer the meat, potatoes and champignons to a serving plate, and reduce the liquid to sauce consistency. Check the seasoning, then spoon the sauce over the meat and potatoes. Sprinkle with chopped parsley.

Variation

If you prefer, cook and serve the potatoes separately. In this case, the casserole will need to be thickened with 1 tablespoon plain (all-purpose) flour. Simply sprinkle the flour over the browned meat and onions, and toss so the flour mixes with the butter at the base of the casserole dish.

OX TAIL (OR GRAVY BEEF) WITH PICKLED WALNUTS

A classic British recipe. Try this with lamb shanks, too. And if you can't find pickled walnuts, substitute prunes or semi-dried figs.

<u>Serves 6</u>

60 g (2 oz) margarine
2 ox tails or 1.6 kg (3¹/₄ lb) gravy beef (beef from the shank),
cut into 5 cm (2 in) cubes
3 onions, sliced
1 heaped tablespoon plain (all-purpose) flour
600 ml (1 pt) red wine
300 ml (10 fl oz) water
2 bay leaves
4 juniper berries, lightly crushed
2 cloves
¹/₂ small cinnamon stick
salt and freshly ground black pepper

The garnish
9 pickled walnuts, cut in half lengthways
1 tablespoon chopped parsley

Heat the margarine in a cast-iron casserole dish, and brown the meat until it is as dark as possible. Add the onions and fry until they brown a little. Sprinkle in the flour, stir to the base of the pan, and allow to caramelise slightly. Add extra margarine if necessary (the ox tail renders fat, the gravy beef does not; the flour will scorch without grease). Add the wine, water, bay leaves, juniper berries, cloves and cinnamon; season with salt and pepper. Bring to the boil, then reduce the heat and simmer for 3¹/₂–4 hours for the ox-tail, or 2¹/₂ hours for the gravy beef.

For the last 30 minutes, add the pickled walnuts (they add colour and flavour to the sauce). When ready, remove the meat and walnuts with a slotted spoon, raise the heat and boil the liquid down to sauce consistency, stirring occasionally. Check the seasoning, return the meat to the sauce, and serve sprinkled with chopped parsley. Although not traditional, the dish suits the classic osso bucco accompaniment of *gremolata* (chopped parsley mixed with grated lemon peel).

VEGETABLES, RICE AND OTHER GRAINS

VERSATILE VEGETABLES

You do not have to be a vegetarian to like vegetable dishes. A good cook highlights vegetables for their own intrinsic beauty. This can mean cooking them simply but perfectly, or it can mean cooking them in interesting, different ways.

Take a tip from the Chinese — stir-fry vegetables and keep them crisp. Or from the Italians, who mix vegetables with pasta as if the two were made for each other. Try pumpkin ravioli with crispy-fried sage leaves; spring vegetables tossed through fettuccine and finished with cream; red radicchio or winter witlof (chicory) stirred through a pasta with walnuts; spaghetti with tomato, chilli and capsicum (bell pepper) sauces; or tortellini with spinach and mozzarella. Broccoli florets do a fine job too — not with cream, just loads of butter, Parmesan cheese and freshly ground black pepper.

Don't disregard vegetables as interesting appetisers, either. Try char-grilled baby leeks with Parmesan oil; a roast of baby vegetables with aïoli; or boiled baby vegetables offset with a *vitello tonnato* (a mayonnaise with puréed cooked tuna folded through).

Take a hint from Serge Dansereau, executive chef at the Regent Hotel, Sydney. Sear some scallops and place them decoratively around a large nest of spaghetti-cut yellow and green zucchini (courgette) enhanced with a julienne of red and yellow capsicum (bell pepper). Serge's oh-so-healthy sauce rejects butter in favour of a reduction of fish stock and carrot juice. The sauce combines 5 finely chopped shallots, 100 ml (3½ fl oz) white wine, 50 ml (1½ fl oz) white wine vinegar, 400 ml (12 fl oz) fish stock, 100 ml (3½ fl oz) carrot juice, and a few saffron threads, brought to the boil and reduced by half. After boiling, Serge finishes with a dash of lemon juice, salt and pepper and a touch of cayenne pepper. Having spooned a ladleful of this brightly coloured, wondrous mixture over the scallops and vegetables, he tops off the colour and the flavour with a dob here and there of pesto, made by feeding about half a cupful of basil leaves down the chute of a food processor with a couple of small cloves of garlic, a little extra virgin olive oil and salt and pepper to taste.

To tantalise you further . . . years ago at the Howqua Dale Gourmet Retreat in Victoria, I thrilled to the taste of Marieke Brugman's rösti that was made not of potatoes, in the traditional way, but of shredded celeriac fried into a pancake shape with broken-up (pre-boiled) fresh chestnuts. Marieke has also served me wild mushrooms held together in layers in a terrine which she sliced and served sauced with a fresh pea purée. On another occasion, Marieke brought out pea purée again — this time as a dipping sauce for yabbies (crawfish or écrevisses).

I make puréed red capsicum (bell pepper) enriched with cream as a sauce for fish (try it with skate or blue eye). I cook brussels sprouts in stock, drain them and toss with fried bacon and chestnuts; braised lentils with bacon under a rack of lamb scattered with rocket leaves (lentils and black-eyed beans make a great soup too; try finishing them with a few chilli flakes and a drizzling of cream); a Pithiviers (a puff pastry torte) filled with winter vegetables and served with a basil cream sauce; and a 'sandwich' of summer vegetables stacked high and held together with two wafer-thin pieces of fried eggplant (aubergine), and sauced with pesto.

In the last weeks of the Jerusalem artichoke season, I mix boiled, quartered globe artichokes with slices of boiled Jerusalem artichokes, tossing them in a little extra virgin olive oil after draining, and finishing with black pepper and chopped parsley. When globe artichokes are in season, try serving one as an entrée with a simple vinaigrette. For it to taste good, remove the outer, tougher leaves, rub it with lemon juice so it doesn't discolour, boil until tender, then drain upside down until cool. This European classic is simply plucked leaf by leaf with the fingers, dipped into the vinaigrette, the fleshy part dragged over the front teeth, the rest discarded . . . and on to the next leaf. When you reach the 'base', or fleshy centre part, pluck off the hairy 'choke' (it nips off readily with your thumb and first two fingers), and use a knife and fork to eat the base.

The Italians prefer to pluck more leaves off before cooking, and cut the tops from the leaves by slicing the 'globe' part in two and discarding the top half. Then they acidulate it well (i.e. souse with lemon juice) and boil the rest, which for the most part is tender enough to eat whole with a knife and fork. Their saucing varies from simple oil and vinegar dressings (try balsamic vinegar) to the typical tomato sauce or *salsa verde* that can be found in any Italian cookbook.

In summer, when our thoughts turn to salads, colourful *mesclun* blends can be nested into the centre of a plate, and topped with slivers of roasted red capsicum (bell pepper), with pyramids of goat cheese, with smoked chicken or trout, with yabbies (crawfish or écrevisses) and bugs (slipper or hammer-head lobsters), and with a myriad of other ingredients.

Try my vegetable tartlet with black butter sauce suggestion which dresses summer vegetables in a tart base (page 16).

And remember, for great vegetable cookery, there are only three rules — don't boil them to death so they end up as mouthfuls of water, don't serve them in three little piles around the meat, and for goodness' sake, don't overcook them. Cook them with imagination, and eat them aplenty — your health, your waistline and your appetite simply cannot ask for more.

GRILLED VEGETABLES WITH ROASTED GARLIC AND BASIL MAYONNAISES

Inspired by a display at California's famous Highlands Inn at Monterey. This dish must look colourful. Here, eggplant (aubergine), zucchini (courgette) and capsicum (bell pepper) are the stars, though you can mix and match vegetables, use more or less, and vary the sauces, even using the rich home-bottled chutneys now found in the better delicatessens.

Serves 6–8

The vegetables
2 large red capsicums (bell peppers), cored and cut into natural segments
2 yellow capsicums (bell peppers), cut as above
1 green capsicum (bell pepper), cut as above
2 large eggplants (aubergines), unpeeled, stalk removed
salt
3 large zucchini (courgettes), unpeeled, topped and tailed
24 asparagus, tender part only, peeled
5 hard-boiled eggs, cut into quarters lengthways

The mayonnaises
4 egg yolks
1 teaspoon French mustard
about 600–700 ml (20–24 fl oz) olive oil
salt and pepper
a little vinegar
1 small head garlic, unpeeled, plus 3 extra cloves
1 bunch basil (about 1 cup leaves)

The vegetables: Place the segments of capsicum on a foil-lined baking tray and grill until the skin blisters and blackens; remove from the oven and peel off the skin. Slice the eggplant lengthways, place on a tray, salt lightly and leave for 1 hour to degorge. Rinse well and pat dry with paper towelling. Slice the zucchinis lengthways.

Several hours before dinner, drop the asparagus into boiling, salted water and cook until just tender; drain and set aside. Brush the eggplant and zucchini slices with oil and cook on a corrugated cast-iron grill or barbecue hotplate, or in a pan. If using a grill, rotate the slices to imprint them with a criss-cross pattern. Slice into long bite-size strips, then transfer to separate serving bowls. Quickly cook the capsicum and asparagus, too, and transfer to other bowls. Place the egg quarters in yet another bowl.

Serve the vegetables with two mayonnaises — one flavoured with garlic purée, the other with garlic basil paste.

The mayonnaises: (made in advance). In a small bowl, using an electric mixer, whisk the egg yolks and mustard together, then slowly incorporate the oil in a thin steady stream, until it combines to form a thick mayonnaise. Season with salt, pepper and vinegar to taste.

Slice the top off the head of garlic so that only the tips of the garlic cloves are exposed. Rub with oil, wrap in foil and bake in a 175°C (350°F) oven for about 45 minutes. Remove from the foil, press the softened garlic out of the peel, and mash the pulp.

Meanwhile, place the 3 cloves of garlic and the basil leaves in a mortar and pestle or in a blender, and process to as fine a pulp as you can, adding about 3 tablespoons oil to help make an emulsion.

When ready, divide the mayonnaise mixture in half; flavour one half with roasted garlic, the other with the garlic basil paste.

RED CAPSICUM SALAD

Serves 6

6 red capsicums (bell peppers), cored, seeded and cut into lobes
2 onions, finely sliced
2–3 tablespoons olive oil
1 scant tablespoon best (smallest) capers
a few black olives, pitted and chopped
salt and freshly ground black pepper

Place the capsicum pieces on a foil-lined rack and grill until well blistered and blackened. Remove, cover the rack with a tea towel, then remove one piece at a time to peel off the skin. Place in a covered dish in the fridge until ready to use. You can even prepare them a day in advance: they will drop their juices, so use less oil.

Sauté the onions in the oil until soft, but not more than lightly coloured. When softened completely (about 15 minutes), place the onions and the oil in which they were fried into a bowl with the capsicum pieces, capers and olives. Toss well, season with salt and pepper, and drizzle in enough oil to moisten as a salad.

CARAMELISED WITLOF

Serves 6

4 large or 6 small witlof (chicory)
8–10 spring onions (scallions)
55 g (2 oz) butter
1 teaspoon sugar
salt and pepper
2 teaspoons lemon juice
2 teaspoons chopped parsley

Peel the leaves of witlof whole from the plant. Trim the spring onions, but leave whole. Heat the butter in a frying pan and add the sugar. When it starts to caramelise lightly, add the spring onions and sauté briefly, then add the witlof leaves. Stir until coated with grease (adding more if needed), then cover, reduce heat and cook until softened (about 4–5 minutes). Season with salt and pepper, and add the lemon juice. Serve topped with chopped parsley.

RED CABBAGE

Serves 6

35 g (1¹/₂ oz) butter
1 onion, chopped
¹/₂ red cabbage, finely shredded
5–6 cloves
1 large Granny Smith apple, peeled and cubed
3 tablespoons malt vinegar
1 tablespoon sugar
salt and pepper

Heat the butter in a large saucepan and sauté the onion until well greased, then add the cabbage. Stir until it starts to soften, then add the cloves, apple, malt vinegar and sugar; season to taste with salt and pepper. Place the lid on the saucepan and cook on a low heat, stirring from time to time, for about 35–40 minutes. If the heat is too high and dries out the moisture, add a couple of tablespoons water, but on a low heat the cabbage should render enough liquid to prevent scorching. To finish, test for the sharpness of the vinegar, adding more if necessary.

OKRA WITH CHILLI

Working alongside wonderful cookbook writer Sarah Belk, from Carolina, inspired me to develop this okra recipe. Cooks unused to okra are not pleased with the slime it produces when boiled. When fried, however, there is no such problem, particularly when the stalk is removed without piercing the 'cap' at the top of the vegetable.

40 small or 25 medium okra, trimmed
olive oil, for frying
2–3 small hot red chillies, seeded and sliced
a dash of soy sauce, or salt

Rinse the okra and dry well. Slice larger ones (only into two or three slices) on the diagonal. Heat the olive oil in a pan and shallow-fry the okra in much the same way as you would mushrooms, glazing well in the oil. Add the chillies, to taste, towards the end of the cooking time. The okra pods are cooked when they wilt, but I prefer them somewhat crisp (about 5–6 minutes). Season with soy sauce or salt, but no pepper.

GLAZED PARSNIPS WITH ALMONDS

Serves 4

4 parsnips
40 g (1¹/₂ oz) butter
1 scant teaspoon sugar
2 tablespoons flaked almonds
coarsely ground black pepper
1 tablespoon chopped parsley

Peel the parsnips and cut across the thin tail end to obtain a piece about 20 cm (8 in) long, then halve or quarter the thicker part to get similar sized pieces. Boil in salted water until soft but not mushy; drain. In the empty saucepan, heat the butter, then add the sugar and flaked almonds. Sauté until golden brown, then add the parsnips to glaze. Season with the pepper and garnish with chopped parsley.

Variation

If you don't like almonds, you can glaze in sugar only. To glaze vegetables successfully, particularly those that need browning a little (e.g. turnips and parsnips), the trick is to cook the sugar in the butter until it just begins to brown, and then the vegetable. The result is caramelised, and tastes less sweet.

MUSHROOMS BORDELAISE

Serves 6

1–1.5 kg (2–3 lb) large capped field mushrooms
150 g (5 oz) continental bacon, bought in one piece
120 ml (4 fl oz) olive oil
2 cloves garlic, finely chopped
1 heaped tablespoon dried breadcrumbs
salt and freshly ground black pepper
4–5 tablespoons chopped parsley

Peel only the mushrooms you deem tougher (the larger ones); trim tails. Cut large mushrooms into 3 or 4 pieces, cut medium-sized mushrooms in half, and leave smaller ones whole. Remove the rind from the bacon and cut into bite-size pieces. Heat a large frying pan to very hot and cook the bacon until crisp. Add about 4 tablespoons oil to the rendered fat, then sauté the mushrooms on high heat for about 3 minutes. Halfway through the cooking time, add the garlic, stirring continually so it cannot scorch. Add more oil as the pan dries. When the mushrooms start to sweat, sprinkle with the breadcrumbs and continue to fry in enough oil to colour the breadcrumbs. Working very fast and on high heat, the water loss can be kept to a minimum and the mushrooms served fleshy, without diminishing much in size. Sprinkle with the salt and pepper, stir through the parsley and serve immediately.

GREEN PEAS, FRENCH STYLE

Serves 6

50 g (1½ oz) butter
1 kg (2 lb) peas (shelled weight)
10 tiny onions, enlarged summer spring onions (scallions), or shallots
salt and pepper
2 teaspoons sugar
4 large lettuce leaves, washed

Melt the butter in a shallow thick-based saucepan with a tight-fitting lid. Stir-fry the peas and onions until shiny and well greased. Add the salt, pepper and sugar. Place the lettuce leaves on top of the peas to cover the entire surface area. Cover with the lid, reduce to a low heat and simmer for 25–30 minutes, depending on the quality of peas. Avoid opening the saucepan, as steam escapes. Discard the lettuce leaves before serving.

GREEN BEANS (OR PEAS) WITH TOMATO AND ONION

Serves 6

60 ml (2 fl oz) olive oil
1/2 small onion, diced or sliced
1 clove garlic, finely chopped (if using beans)
1 large tomato, peeled and coarsely chopped
500 g (1 lb) stringless beans, as small as possible, or
350 g (11 oz) peas (shelled weight)
salt and pepper
pinch of sugar (if using peas)

Heat the olive oil in a thick-based saucepan. Add the onion and garlic (if using) and sauté for a moment, then add the tomato and sauté until it softens. Add the beans or peas, stirring to bring out the colour, then season with salt and pepper (and sugar, if using peas). Cover the pan, reduce the heat and simmer the beans for about 10 minutes (depending on size), or the peas for 20–25 minutes (depending on quality). Stir once or twice during cooking.

BRAISED LENTILS

Serves 6

250–300 g (8–9 1/2 oz) dried brown lentils
4 tablespoons olive oil
1 small onion, diced very finely and evenly (brunoise)
1 small carrot, diced very finely and evenly (brunoise)
1–2 cloves garlic, finely diced
2 tomatoes, peeled and chopped
500 ml (16 fl oz) chicken or veal stock
salt and pepper
1 teaspoon tomato paste
2 teaspoons fresh thyme leaves
2 tablespoons chopped parsley (optional)

Soak the lentils in cold water and leave to swell for 1 hour, then drain.

When ready, heat the oil and sauté the onion, carrot and garlic for a moment. Add the lentils, stir once or twice to grease them, then add the tomatoes and stock. Bring to the boil, season with salt, pepper, tomato paste and thyme, then reduce the heat and simmer for 25–30 minutes, partially covered. By the time the lentils are softened, but not mushy, the liquid should be all but evaporated. Finish this dish by stirring through plenty of chopped parsley (if using).

Variation

I have made many variations of this recipe. Using haricot or cannellini beans requires no change in method except soaking the beans in two changes of water for about 4 hours before cooking. Drain and proceed as above. Chick peas require even longer soaking (about 24 hours in 3–4 changes of water), so sometimes I use drained, canned chick peas and cook only enough for the tomatoes and other ingredients to form a good sauce.

For those of you who are fans of tripe, try this simple, flavoursome dish. Fry the carrot, onion and some strips of tripe, add the tomatoes, stock, tomato paste and thyme, then simmer for 1 hour. Season liberally with pepper, and garnish with plenty of chopped parsley.

VEGETABLE CURRY, NORTHERN THAI STYLE

This recipe is from my favourite Isthmus of Kra chef, Beh Kim Un.

<u>Serves 6</u>

The sauce
90 ml (3 fl oz) vegetable oil
$^1/_2$ onion, thinly sliced
3 cloves garlic, finely chopped
1 heaped tablespoon Thai yellow curry paste
OR the following 11 ingredients to make your own:
6 coriander (cilantro) roots, very finely chopped
2 tablespoons dark mustard seed
10 cardamom pods
10 cloves
1 cinnamon stick
1 teaspoon powdered turmeric
1 tablespoon ground coriander seed
$^1/_2$ tablespoon ground cumin
1 teaspoon chilli powder
2 scant tablespoons palm or raw sugar
1 tablespoon curry leaves
400 ml (12 fl oz) coconut milk
1 teaspoon salt
2 tablespoons natural yoghurt

The vegetables
(all cut into 2 cm ($^3/_4$ in) chunks)
6–8 cups mixed cooked vegetables, tender but not overcooked.
Choose from tomato, carrot, potato, butternut pumpkin, zucchini (courgette),
yellow squash, okra, mixed colour capsicums (bell peppers), green beans,
and eggplant (aubergine)

Heat the oil in a thick-based saucepan or casserole dish. Sauté the onion and garlic until golden, then add the curry paste or follow the method below to make your own paste. Stir for a moment, then add the coconut milk, a little at a time. Stir until an oily sheen appears. Add the salt, bring to the boil, and simmer gently for 5 minutes. When ready to serve, add the vegetables to the curry sauce to heat through. Serve with Chinese-style rice (page 172).

Method for making curry paste: Sauté the onions and garlic, add the coriander root, mustard seed, cardamom pods and cloves. Fry until fragrant (30–40 seconds), then add the cinnamon stick, ground herbs, sugar and curry leaves, and continue frying until fragrant. Reduce the heat and add the coconut milk, then proceed as above.

Variation

The sauce is excellent with fish or small chicken pieces, too. These pieces may be added raw and simmered slowly in the sauce until they cook.

CHIPS — 'FRENCH FRIES' STYLE

Old-fashioned recipes called for chips to be plunged in very hot oil — the term used was 'when a "haze of blue smoke" can be seen'. The heat was kept on high until the chips were well-browned and cooked through. Dark brown chips, however, do not stay crisp, and modern methods take their cue from the technique of 'French fries', where the chips are plunged into oil twice, but at a lower temperature. The second fry dries them out and they stay crisp for much longer. Every French family has a deep fryer (friteuse), but a large saucepan with a frying basket will suffice. Kept only for this purpose, the oil can be set aside for re-use. Change the oil when the starch from the potatoes makes it heavy (indicated by white froth on the surface when cooking) or if the oil burns. A deep-fry thermometer will help guard against this.

Allow 1 large potato per person and enough oil to reach a depth of 10 cm (4 in) minimum in the saucepan (about ¹/₃ full). Peel the potatoes and cut into chips of 7.5 mm (¹/₄ in) width. Soak the chips in water for a minimum of 1 hour, preferably 2. Heat the oil to 165°C (330°F). If you are without a thermometer, test with one chip. As soon as the oil sizzles around the chip, it is hot enough. Lower the well-dried chips into the hot oil in the basket slowly, as the oil will rise and bubble, then subside.

The purpose of the first frying is to cook the chips, not to brown them. When they have softened, lift the basket out and allow the oil to reheat to the same temperature or perhaps a little higher — 170°C (335°F), but no more. Lower the basket into the oil once more until the chips are golden brown. This may take 4–5 minutes at this temperature, but it will serve to dry them out and help lock in the crispness. When ready, drain the chips, season with salt, and serve immediately.

PERFECT PUREE POTATOES

The modern style puréed potatoes made famous in Paris by Joël Robuchon. This recipe works best with yellow 'waxy' potatoes such as Padrone, Desirée or Bintge. Mash will never be the same!

Serves 6

1.2 kg (2½ lb) waxy potatoes, peeled and cubed
125–150 ml (4–5 fl oz) milk
125 g (4 oz) unsalted butter
100 ml (3½ fl oz) cream
salt and pepper

Boil the potatoes until soft, then drain and pass through a *mouli* or any other masher, making sure you leave no lumps (never use a food processor, which whirrs up a glutinous mess).

Bring the milk to the boil. Place the puréed potatoes in a separate saucepan, and stir in first the butter, then the cream, and finally the hot milk. Season with salt and pepper. The result should be wetter but more unctuous than traditional mashed potato.

Variation

Boil 3 cloves peeled garlic with the potatoes and include them in the mashing.

POTATOES SAUTEED WITH GARLIC AND ROSEMARY

Serves 6

4 potatoes, peeled and cubed (make them about 2 cm (¾ in) square, but not too even)
olive oil, for frying
12 cloves garlic, unpeeled
2 scant teaspoons fresh rosemary leaves
salt and freshly ground black pepper

Blanch the cubed potatoes in a large saucepan of boiling, salted water for 4 minutes; drain and pat dry.

In a large frying pan, heat enough olive oil to cover the base, and fry the potatoes. Allow them to colour and crisp a little on one side before turning — turning them too frequently prevents them crisping. Add the garlic cloves and sauté with the potatoes, tossing often so they do not catch on the base of the pan. Toss the rosemary through when the potatoes begin to look golden. Add olive oil as necessary. Season with salt and pepper before serving. To eat the garlic, simply press the softened flesh from its skin.

SLICED POTATOES IN THE OVEN WITH BLUE CHEESE

This dish is a flavoured variation of the classic Dauphinoise.

Serves 6–8

6 large potatoes, peeled and finely sliced
salt and pepper
50 g (1¹/₂ oz) blue cheese
300 ml (10 fl oz) cream

Arrange the potato slices in layers in a shallow oval or rectangular ovenproof dish, lightly seasoning with salt and pepper between layers. From time to time, crumble in some of the blue cheese. Ensure the top layer is smooth and neatly arranged in an overlapping pattern (do not use cheese on this layer). Pour the cream over the top.

Cook in the oven at 160°C (325°) for 50–60 minutes, and test with a knife to check they are tender. These potatoes are served without a gratinéed look on top. If they colour, the cream evaporates and risks curdling — with this method, they come out with the cream remaining as a sauce.

JANSEN'S POTATOES

Serves 8

35 g (1¹/₂ oz) butter
3 medium onions, finely sliced
6 medium potatoes, cut into thin chips
12 anchovy fillets
salt and pepper
150 ml (5 fl oz) milk
220 ml (7¹/₂ fl oz) cream
3 tablespoons breadcrumbs
a few knobs of butter

Butter a 26–28 cm (10–11 in) white porcelain dish (round or rectangular). Sauté the onions in butter until softened, but not browned. In the base of the dish, make a layer of half the potatoes, then spread half the onions over them and scatter with anchovy fillets. Cover with the rest of the potatoes, then the remaining onions. Season with pepper and a minimum of salt, as the anchovies are quite salty. Mix the cream and milk and pour over the potatoes, then top with the breadcrumbs and dot with the butter. Cook in a preheated oven at 160°C (325°F) for 50–60 minutes, or until the potatoes are tender.

POLENTA

Polenta (cornmeal) is traditionally used in the Mediterranean as a soft-textured, porridge-consistency accompaniment, served in much the same way as mashed potato. There are two grain sizes on the market, fine and coarse, and there is an instant one that cooks in 5 minutes, but which I find unsatisfactory. It has much less texture because the base product is pre-steamed and thus broken down.

Soft polenta:

For 6 serves, pour 300 g (9^1/$_2$ oz) polenta into 1.25 L (2 pt) water or light stock, salted. Cook for 25–30 minutes over low heat, stirring often, until the grain has broken down and softened.

English vegetarian food writer Colin Spencer uses a quicker method. He brings 750 ml (25 fl oz) water to a rolling boil, combines 250 ml (8 fl oz) cold water with 250 g (8 oz) polenta, then pours this into the salted water and stirs for 10 minutes.

Soft-textured polenta is used for the veal shank recipe on page 152.

Baked (dried) and pan-fried polenta:

Cook the polenta using the method above, then pour onto a greased, flat baking dish and spread to a smooth, thick layer of about 1–1.25 cm (^{1}/$_3$ – ^{1}/$_2$ in). Brush the top with oil, then place in the oven at 150°C (300°F) to dry out, for about 15–20 minutes.

Cut this dried-out polenta into portions. In Italy it is common to cut it into 4–5 cm (1^1/$_2$ –2 in) squares and stack, after reheating, with a meat sauce, and then top with Parmesan cheese.

As a crispy accompaniment, polenta is usually cut into squares or rectangles and placed in the oven to reheat and crisp with Parmesan on top . . . or brush it with olive oil and pan-fry; better still, cook it on a corrugated cast-iron grill so that the criss-cross markings are imprinted. Like this, it makes a great accompaniment to almost anything, notably with something like mushroom ragoût, Mediterranean fish and roasted capsicum (bell pepper), or goat or braised meat casseroles (particularly goat), and as a base for finger food, topped with seafood morsels, roasted Mediterranean vegetables, tapenade, *pasta d'oliva* (black olive paste), fresh tomato and shredded basil, or almost any other savoury item.

. . . AND ALL THINGS RICE

When cooking rice, even simple boiled rice, people tell tales of gluggy messes and claggy masses stuck to the base of their pot — all sorts of horrors. Boiled rice must be cooked in hot water, never cold, and in at least eight times its own volume of water. The reason is simple: there must be enough water for the starch to be absorbed, otherwise as soon as the water becomes laden with starch, it is likely to impart the stickiness back onto the rice. (You will have noticed the white claggy look that the water gets when there is too little). No washing, no panicking — all you need do is make sure you have enough salted water to drown the rice, bring it to the boil, then add the rice.

However, there are many other interesting ways to cook rice. All yield a slightly different flavour, and most often a different texture. The Indians toss rice in oil and use a greased absorption method, as do people in many of the Asian nations and some in the North African and Mediterranean regions. The liquid rice cooks in need not always be water, and a lot of rice dishes are improved by being cooked in chicken or seafood stock. The great masters of this method are the Italians, who use their famed Arborio rice from the Po valley. This rice has a very different consistency from the more ubiquitous long-grain and short-grain rice, and is now widely available from delicatessens and better supermarkets.

The Italians cook the stock out of their rice only partially, and an Italian risotto is served unctuous and *al onde* (swirling like an ocean wave) so that the flavoursome liquid enhances the texture of the finished dish. Great Italian risotti are made with chicken livers, prawns, seafood or mushrooms embedded in the rice.

The Chinese and Japanese however, use an absorption method with very little water — some even call it steamed rice. Their method yields a slightly stickier rice — not claggy, for it's always well-washed to rid it of most of the starch before the cooking is started, but definitely sticky. Perhaps it makes using chopsticks easier if the grains of rice stick together. For the making of sushi, the rice must hold well in firm little pads on which to nestle the fish. The Thais also use an absorption method, and often use coconut milk instead of water.

There are millions of rice recipes, but only a few truly different methods. The recipes below cover the three main ones. They are all successful even though they seem contradictory — for example, the Chinese cover the pot, but my recipe for plain boiled rice says you must never cover the pot; some recipes wash the rice, my boiled one (for which I typically use long-grain rice, but which also works with short-grain) says never wash the rice. The purpose of washing rice is to wash off some of the starch; cooking in a large volume of water will do the same. However, poorer quality rice is not devoid of small stones, remnants of husk or blemishes. Wash if you would rather, and always wash the rice when making Asian recipes.

BOILED RICE

No need to measure the water — simply make sure there is plenty in a large pot, bring it to a rolling boil, and add the rice. Using such a large volume of water means that there is absolutely no need to wash the rice first. Salt is the only necessary accompaniment, but you may like to add a bay leaf, or a couple of pieces of lemon, or some saffron to the water.

When you have added the rice, return to the boil, stir once to lift the rice from the bottom, and simmer until tender. This will take approximately 10–11 minutes, but depends on the type and quality of rice. Don't put the lid on the pot when cooking, as starchy water will drip over the stove!

To test whether the rice is cooked, taste one of the grains — it should be *al dente*: with a firm bite but no crunch. When ready, drain through a large colander. Never run water through it, unless you want to cool it instantly for making a rice salad. In this one case, cool it quickly to make sure its own heat doesn't cook it any further.

To make in advance and reheat: Rice can be made in advance if you wish and either left to reheat in the colander over a pot of steaming water, or placed in the oven with a couple of nobs of butter on top, maybe some freshly ground black pepper and lemon zest or parsley, and covered with foil. Never leave too long in the oven or it will dry on top. Really cold or refrigerated left-over rice reheats well covered with plastic wrap in the microwave.

RIZ PILAF

Serves 6

40 g (1¹/₂ oz) butter
1 small or ¹/₂ large onion, diced
375 g (12 oz) long-grain rice
750 ml (25 fl oz) hot water
salt and pepper
pinch of nutmeg

Melt the butter in a thick-based, ovenproof saucepan. Fry the onion until transparent. Add the rice and stir for a moment until it has taken on a greased look, then add the hot water. Bring to the boil, stirring. Add the salt and pepper and nutmeg. Cover with the lid and place the saucepan in a 200°C (400°F) oven for 16–18 minutes, depending on the quality of the rice.

When the rice is cooked, remove from the oven and rest for 5 minutes before taking the lid off and forking through the rice.

Note: There is no need to wash the rice here, even though it is an evaporation-style recipe, because the grains have been well-greased before starting (compare it with the Chinese-style Rice on page 172). Neither, incidentally, does the rice stick to the bottom of the pan, because the heat of the oven comes from all round, not just the base, as in the Chinese style.

Variation

Many ingredients can be added to this recipe to enhance the flavour — spices and saffron, as well as garnish-like ingredients such as chicken livers, peas, or other vegetable pieces that are fried with the rice at the beginning.

One of the most successful I have found is to add a couple of pods of green cardamom, 2–3 sprigs curry leaves and 3 cloves to the water after stirring; they impart a wonderful fragrance. A more sophisticated Indian-style recipe is below.

PILAU OF BASMATI RICE, INDIAN STYLE

Serves 6

125 g (4 oz) butter
1 onion, grated
¼ teaspoon saffron or saffron stamens
500 g (1 lb) long-grain Basmati rice
¾ cup curry leaves
1 onion, sliced
oil, for deep frying
125 g (4 oz) seeded raisins
125 g (4 oz) whole blanched almonds

Sauté the onion and saffron in the butter and then almost immediately add the rice. Keep stirring until the rice is well coated with butter. Remove from the heat and add enough boiling water to cover the rice by 5 cm (2 in). Add the curry leaves and bring to the boil. Boil for two minutes, then stretch a small piece of towelling over the top of the pot and cover with the lid to keep the towelling in place (this keeps the steam in). Cook very slowly until tender — that is, until the water is evaporated.

To serve: Deep-fry the slices of onion and scatter on either side of the rice. Pan-fry the raisins and almonds and scatter over the top of the rice.

CHINESE-STYLE RICE

*This recipe is from my friend, international award-winning
Chinese cookbook author, Elizabeth Chong.*

<u>Serves 6</u>

750 g (1¹/₂ lb) long- or short-grain rice

To prepare the rice: Place the rice in a saucepan and wash in cold water. Swill the rice around the saucepan in a circular movement until the water becomes cloudy and milky. Strain, add fresh water and repeat until water is clear; at least five washes will be needed.

To cook the rice: Add enough water to cover the rice by 1 cm (¹/₃ in), and bring to a rapid boil over high heat, preferably with the pot covered. Reduce to medium heat and continue until the water is absorbed. At this stage, the rice will look moist, with little 'craters', but there must be little visible water in the pot before you reduce the heat to a low simmer.

When the water is absorbed, simmer the rice for 15–20 minutes. You must keep the lid on the pot during this simmering time. Longer simmering will not harm the rice, but you will probably get a crust on the bottom of the pot, and if you are cooking a very small amount of rice, then you will end up with only a little to eat.

JAPANESE VINEGARED RICE (FOR SUSHI)

<u>Serves 6</u>

*500 g (1 lb) short-grain rice
cold water, for soaking
500 ml (16 fl oz) cold water plus an extra 4 tablespoons
a dash vinegar
salt and pepper*

Rinse the rice thoroughly, then soak in cold water for up to 15 minutes. Drain well and place in a pot with the cold water. (As a guide, use 1 cup plus 2 tablespoons water per cup of rice.) Cover with a tight-fitting lid and bring to the boil quickly, then reduce the heat and simmer for about 10 minutes, or until all visible water has been absorbed. Turn off the heat and let the rice rest for a further 15 minutes to allow any remaining water to evaporate.

When ready, remove the lid and transfer the rice to a large wooden bowl. While still tepid, stir in a little vinegar flavoured with salt and pepper — just enough to slightly flavour the rice. Leave the rice to cool. Once cooled, the rice can be formed into a wad with the fingers and, when correctly made, will hold its shape for sushi-making.

See also Risotto with Prawns (page 30), Risotto Nero (page 31) and Paella (page 80).

DESSERTS,
CAKES,
BISCUITS
AND BREAD

FRUITFUL DESSERTS

For a maximum of eye-appeal, a minimum of cooking and just the right balance to finish a meal without feeling over-full, the clever cook need look no further than a fruit dessert. Here are some ideas . . .

- Peeled and seeded pawpaw or melon halves look great as 'baskets' for fresh berries. While in season, add some cherries, leaving their stalks on so your guests can lift them with their fingers. The berries can be drizzled with port or rolled in redcurrant jelly, but stay away from the sugar pot — they shouldn't need it.

- Purists say that strawberries should be served naked, in all their glory. True . . . for the first of the season. If not, try adding a dash of Kirsch, Maraschino or Framboise liqueur and castor sugar to the strawberries and allowing them to macerate in a bowl for an hour before dinner. A variation on this theme would be Grand Marnier and orange peel. If using blackberries, change the liqueur to Crème de Cassis.

- Perhaps you've heard of the old horticulturist's trick of sprinkling pepper on strawberries. Learn, too, from central Italy, where they splash a little balsamic vinegar on them with the sugar — see even a paltry or wilted strawberry come alive and shiny again, rich in flavour.

- Substitute the cream you serve with the berries with mascarpone, or whipped sour cream with orange peel. You can even serve ricotta or mascarpone with chopped glacéed fruit mixed through it. The effect can be dressed up a little by presenting them in a brandy snap or biscuit basket.

- Fancy your cherries poached? Try 250 g (8 oz) sugar per 2 kg (4 lb) cherries, along with 750 ml (25 fl oz) water and 3 star anise pods. Bring these to the boil with 1 tablespoon orange peel 'threads' (i.e. cut with a marmalade shredder rather than grated), simmer for 5 minutes to dissolve the sugar and infuse the flavours, then add the stoned cherries. Return to just under the boil for 3 minutes, stirring 2 or 3 times, then turn off the heat and allow to cool without refrigerating. I have a penchant for serving these with yoghurt; in summer it seems more refreshing than cream.

- Rockmelon (cantaloupe) should be rich and flavoursome, but sometimes, despite all the sniffing in the world, we get one without any richness. Learn from Jim Dodge, master baker and teacher at The American Culinary Institute, and try stirring 300 g ($9^1/_2$ oz) honey with 300 g ($9^1/_2$ oz) sugar and 500 ml (16 fl oz) water to the boil. Skim off the foam, transfer to a container and refrigerate the syrup until cool.

Quarter the melon, seed and peel it, then cut each quarter crossways into 1 cm (⅓ in) slices. Arrange the slices on a shallow soup plate or dessert dish starting with the largest slice near one edge of the plate, matching the curve of the plate. Centre each slice, in descending order of size, overlapping the one before. The final shape will resemble a fan. Pour about 125 ml (4 fl oz) of the chilled syrup over each portion just before serving. One rockmelon (cantaloupe) cut this way serves 8.

- Try serving raspberries with the segments of 4 medium grapefruit (preferably pink) or 2 pomelos. A punnet will be enough for 8 people. First, make a fine julienne of the peel of half a grapefruit, removing all the pith before you cut it into strips. Peel the grapefruits as you would an orange, then, with a very sharp knife, cut the segments between their membranes so that you end up with whole segments without any pith. Place in a bowl.

  Make a syrup of 375 g (12 oz) sugar and 750 ml (25 fl oz) water, stirring to the boil and dissolving the sugar, then pour the syrup, still hot, over the segments and the julienne of peel. Wait 5 minutes, then add the raspberries. Allow to cool before serving. To dress it up, pile on plates and top with sabayon (page 197), or decorate with piped meringue and brown until golden under the grill.

- Or try poached peaches. Make up a poaching liquor of 400 g (12 oz) sugar and 500 ml (16 fl oz) water to which you add 300 ml (10 fl oz) Champagne or dry white wine. Cut a cross in the base of the skin of each peach before you poach, so they can be skinned after poaching. Poaching them with their skins on allows a lovely pink colour to infuse from the skin and tint the poaching liquor. And how long do you poach them for? As with all fruit, it depends on how ripe the peaches are. It can be for as little as 5–6 minutes, but up to 18. All poached fruit should be allowed to cool in the syrup.

  Serve the peaches in the syrup, or drained and placed beside a red wine granita (based on the white wine one on page 177). Or make Peach Melba with home-made vanilla ice cream, the perfectly poached peach, and a raspberry coulis made by puréeing a punnet of raspberries in the blender with some sugar and a dash of Kirsch or Crème de Cassis. Strain it for the true silky texture.

- Pears can be poached in a simple syrup, or one spiced with juniper, cinnamon and a piece of orange peel, or even a few green peppercorns. Try also fresh basil leaves thrown in just as you turn off the heat. When poaching in red wine, choose the shapely Beurre Bosc, but for poaching in white wine, the Williams, Sensation or Corella. For a special treat, make the wine a Sauternes-style and serve simply — fanned over a small plate with a little of their juice, or sauced with a sabayon (page 197).

- With any fruit, the poaching liquor can be used to make a jelly that is so much better than any packet jelly on the market. To make the jelly, simply measure the liquor and add gelatine. Most often I count on 3–4 teaspoons gelatine per 600 ml (1 pt) poaching liquor, but unfortunately this varies depending on the amount of pectin and acidity in the fruit (and the enzymes — don't try to make one with pineapple or kiwi, they are gelatine's natural enemies). If by chance you have miscalculated and it doesn't set, don't despair. Gelatine is reversible; simply remelt and add a little more. Place some of the poached fruit pieces in a bowl, then pour the matching jelly over the top and refrigerate until set.

- Fresh lychees make a pretty dessert when you peel the top half only, then set a few per person into a dish piled with crushed ice. When cherries are in season, dot a few, stalks up, into the ice too — but don't leave them there long enough to get icy. A few mint leaves make a nice garnish.

- Though ice cream is difficult to make smooth and creamy without a churn, granita recipes work with ease in the home kitchen. The mixture is simply spilled into a wide dish, such as a lamington (Swiss roll) tray, placed in the freezer, and stirred from time to time until it sets. When ready, it is chunky and textured, and makes a refreshing dessert. Serve it alone, piled high into a martini glass with a mint sprig for decoration, or serve in a bowl with either one perfectly chosen companion piece — a poached peach or a halved, poached pear, or half a fresh mango, cubed on its skin and turned inside out — or a mixture of fresh fruits or berries. Two granita recipes follow, from which you can springboard to others, along with a few slightly more complicated, but wonderfully inviting other 'fruitful' desserts.

Watermelon granita

Take 500 g (1 lb) pulp from a watermelon, measured after the rind and seeds are removed. Purée in a blender or food processor, adding 90 g (3 oz) sugar and the juice of half a lemon. This is not particularly sweet, because sugar content gives a 'syrupiness' that prevents the icy granules forming. Pour into a tray and place in the freezer, stirring with a fork at least twice to break up the mixture into soft ice particles. When finally broken up, the granita is better served the next day. It must be served in icy-cold glasses, or it will melt immediately. For added sophistication, I like to drizzle a little Crème de Cassis (or blackcurrant juice for the kids) over it as I serve.

White wine and cassis granita

First, you need to make a basic sugar syrup. Bring 500 g (1 lb) sugar and 500 ml (16 fl oz) water to the boil, stirring to dissolve the sugar, then cool. Measure the amount needed for the granita, and store the remaining syrup in a cool place. The syrup will keep indefinitely.

Mix together 450 ml (15 fl oz) sugar syrup and 750 ml (25 fl oz) fruity white wine (e.g. Frontignac, Chablis, Sauvignon Blanc), 2 tablespoons Crème de Cassis, the juice of an orange and the juice of either 4 green limes or 2 lemons. Pour into a tray and place in the freezer, stirring with a fork several times as it freezes.

Piled into the centre of a wide Old English-style soup bowl, this granita looks great surrounded by attractively arranged fresh fruit.

CARAMELISED FRESH PEACHES

Serves 4

8 medium or 6 large ripe free-stone peaches (or nectarines)
90 g (3 oz) light brown sugar
4 x 12 cm (5 in) round discs puff pastry, thin shortbread
or brandy snaps (optional)

The Amaretti butter
100 g (3¹/₂ oz) unsalted butter
3 tablespoons light brown sugar
2 tablespoons Amaretti di Saronno (Italian bitter almond liqueur), or to taste
(if unavailable, use Marsala or brandy)

Halve the peaches and remove the stones. Peel each half, then cut into thick slices.

Make a spiral of peach slices on 4 small heatproof plates, or on the discs of puff or shortbread pastry. Daub with about 1¹/₂ tablespoons of the Amaretti butter, sprinkle with the pouring sugar, then place under a very well preheated griller for 2–3 minutes, or until the sugar caramelises. If you do not have a good griller, place in a hot oven for 2 minutes only, then caramelise the pouring sugar with a handyman's blow torch.

The Amaretti butter: Soften the butter, then cream with the soft sugar until fluffy. Flavour with the chosen liqueur.

Variation

Add 4 tablespoons of crushed bitter almond macaroons to the Amaretti butter, and spoon the mixture into unpeeled peach halves lying in an ovenproof dish. Drizzle some Amaretti liqueur over all, and a little melted butter, then bake the peaches at 160°C (325°F) for 18–20 minutes. Serve warm, with whipped cream.

SUMMER BERRIES IN APPLE JELLY

Makes 10–12 slices

250 g (8 oz) strawberries
125 g (4 oz) youngberries, blackberries or raspberries,
depending on availability
125 g (4 oz) blueberries
10 leaves gelatine, or 9 rounded teaspoons powdered gelatine
750 ml (25 fl oz) apple juice
Equipment: 1 L (1³/₄ pt) pâté mould, nut loaf or bread tin

Hull the strawberries. Place the youngberries, blackberries or raspberries on paper towelling to blot up any moisture. Place the mould in a large baking dish filled with water and lots of ice cubes.

Add the gelatine to 500 ml (16 fl oz) apple juice, and stir over heat until melted. Pour into a jug with the remaining apple juice, stir, then allow to cool.

When ready, pour the apple juice mixture into the base of the mould to a depth of about 1 cm (¹/₃ in). When it is nearly set, scatter some of the mixed berries over it and pour in a little more apple juice mixture to hold the layer in place. Continue placing the berries and topping up with the juice until all is used. Make an effort to stand some of the berries so the layered effect is not only of fruit that is lying down. Wait until each layer is nearly set before continuing, otherwise you will have little control over the placing of the fruit. Make sure the top layer of fruit is not too high in the mould; there should be as much apple jelly above the fruit as there is on the base (i.e. about 1 cm). Refrigerate for 3–4 hours before serving, or overnight.

To unmould, run a knife around the edge, place a serving dish or board on top, and invert. If it doesn't unmould, wet a tea towel with very hot water, wring out well, and hold around the edge of the mould for a moment, then try again.

To serve, cut into 1 cm (¹/₃ in) thick slices and serve with a small salad of mixed berries on the side.

GRATINEE OF SUMMER FRUITS

Serves 4

The custard (crème pâtissière)
300 ml (10 fl oz) milk
2 egg yolks
4 tablespoons castor sugar
1 heaped tablespoon cornflour (cornstarch)
dash of Grand Marnier
grated zest of 1 orange
200 ml (7 fl oz) cream, whipped

The fruit

500 g (1 lb) fresh seasonal fruit, cut into wedges and slices
225 g (7¹/₂ oz) mixed summer berries
75–90 g (2¹/₂–3 oz) castor sugar

The custard (crème pâtissière): Scald the milk. Place the egg yolks in a bowl with 4 tablespoons castor sugar, then blend in the cornflour and a little of the hot milk. Place this mixture in the saucepan with the rest of the milk and stir with a whisk until the mixture comes to the boil and thickens. Remove and transfer the custard back to the original bowl, then stir in the Grand Marnier and orange zest. When cool enough not to melt the whipped cream, fold the cream through carefully, to lighten the mixture.

The fruit: Arrange the mixed fruit on small serving plates. Top with the custard, leaving some fruit exposed. Sprinkle the castor sugar over the top and gratinée. The fruit will gratinée best under a very well-heated griller, but if your domestic griller does not give enough heat, a handyman's blow torch does the job brilliantly.

Variation

Try this dish with a mixture of peeled and attractively cut fruits when berries are not in season. In this case, try substituting passionfruit for the orange peel. You can also substitute a sabayon (page 197) for the custard.

THE FRENCH KITCHEN'S COLD LEMON SOUFFLE

Serves 6—8

juice and grated zest of 3 small or 2 large lemons
200 g (7 oz) castor sugar
4 eggs, separated
3 teaspoons powdered gelatine
300 ml (10 fl oz) cream
toasted flaked almonds, to decorate
Equipment: 1.2 L (2 pt) soufflé bowl or 6 small ramekins

Place the lemon juice, sugar and egg yolks into a bowl over a saucepan of hot water. Whisk with a hand-held electric beater over heat until the mixture thickens and triples in volume. In a small saucepan, soften the gelatine in a little water, then shake over heat until it melts. Drizzle into the lemon mixture, still beating, then remove from heat and continue beating until cool, adding the grated zest only at the end. Stand the mixture on ice until it begins to thicken, stirring occasionally so that it cools evenly.

Meanwhile, whip the cream, and then whip the egg whites to a firm snow. When the texture of the lemon mixture is approximately the same as the whipped cream, fold in first the cream, then the egg whites. Pour into the ungreased soufflé bowl (or 6 small ramekins), which should be prepared with a false border of oiled greasproof paper so that the mixture may be poured to at least 3–4 cm (1–1½ in) above the top of the bowl. Refrigerate until set — about 4 hours, or overnight.

To serve: Peel, don't pull, the paper off. Decorate the exposed wall of the soufflé with toasted flaked almonds by pressing them against the sides.

Note: To prepare a false border for the soufflé bowl, tie grease proof paper around the mould to exceed the height by about 15 cm (6 in). If using ramekins, the border should exceed the height by about 5 cm (2 in).

RHUBARB MACADAMIA CRUMBLE

Serves 4

400 ml (12 fl oz) water
90 g (3 oz) sugar
½ lemon, cut into small wedges
1 kg (2 lb) rhubarb, trimmed, lightly scraped and sliced

The crumble
65 g (2½ oz) plain (all-purpose) flour
40 g (1½ oz) sugar
½ teaspoon baking powder
45 g (1½ oz) unsalted butter, chopped, plus about 20 g (½ oz) butter, melted, to brush on the top
35 g (1½ oz) macadamia nuts, roughly chopped
½ egg (beat one in a cup and use half)

The garnish
cream or crème fraîche
a little lemon peel cut from the cooking lemons

Equipment: 4 x 8 cm (3 in) round scone or bisuit cutters. My be cooked and served in small ramekins, if preferred.

Bring the water to the boil with the sugar and lemon, add the sliced rhubarb, reduce to a simmer and cook until tender (3–4 minutes). Drain in a sieve, retaining the juice. Place the biscuit cutters on a tray lined with baking parchment and pack each with the well-drained rhubarb. Reduce the cooking liquid to a thickened syrup.

The crumble: (can be prepared in advance). In a small bowl, place the flour, sugar, baking powder and chopped butter; blend together with your fingers. Add the macadamias and pour in the egg, again blending with your fingers.

To cook and serve: Disperse the crumble mixture in fairly coarse pieces over the top of the rhubarb. Drizzle with the melted butter and bake at 200°C (400°F) until warmed through and golden (about 6–8 minutes). Transfer each to a plate, add a large daub of cream or crème fraîche decorated with a little lemon peel, and spoon around some of the warmed cooking syrup.

THE CREME DE LA CREME

While all custards are made of egg and milk, their texture and richness can vary enormously when these two ingredients are combined in different ratios. Some custards, notably those that bake in the oven until set, are made with whole eggs (e.g. crème caramel, or the custard which sets rice, queen or bread and butter pudding). Others, notably those served at sauce consistency to pour over steamed puddings and the like, are made with yolks only. Some are thickened by the binding power of the eggs only, some with flour. Some use cream combined with the milk to give a more unctuous, richer result.

CUSTARDS MADE WITH YOLKS ONLY

There are two major basic custards made with yolks only: the *crème anglaise* (literally 'English cream'), bound only with yolks, and the *crème pâtissière* (pastry cream) thickened with flour. Both can be used as a sauce, but they also have a role to play as a basic ingredient on which to build other, more complicated desserts. Since the clever cook will call on them often, I have placed both recipes on page 182 so that you can compare the differences in ingredients, balance and method.

The *crème anglaise* is the base of Bavarian cream (*bavarois*), and the traditional base for ice cream. The *crème pâtissière* is most often used as a tart filling. Pour it directly into the tart while still hot, so it forms its own level. It is both the cream used in a pre-cooked tart under cooked fruit or meringue, and the cream that can be used in an unbaked tart, topped with, say, sliced apple, and then baked. It is also a filling for any kind of choux pastry, cream horns, or, mixed with whipped egg white, the filling for the famous Gâteau St Honoré. It binds fillings for a variety of sweet crêpes. And it needs only flavouring and the addition of whipped egg whites to be transformed into a sweet soufflé.

The sabayon on page 197 is an example of a whisked (aerated) custard made over heat so as to lightly poach the egg and set the custard.

CREME ANGLAISE

500 ml (16 fl oz) milk
1 vanilla bean, cut in half lengthways
4, 5 or 6 eggs, depending on 'binding' power (thickness) required
3 tablespoons sugar

Scald the milk with the vanilla bean. Place the eggs in a bowl and blend with the sugar. Pour on a little of the hot milk, blend well, then return all to the saucepan. Using a whisk, not a wooden spoon, stir over heat until it thickens. Take care not to boil the custard, as it will curdle — as a guide, curdling point is 84°C (183°F). To avoid continued cooking, transfer to a jug immediately; strain through a sieve if you suspect light curdling. If serving cold, cover with plastic wrap and refrigerate until needed.

CREME PATISSIERE

500 ml (16 fl oz) milk
50 g (1½ oz) each of vanilla sugar and sugar, mixed together
3 egg yolks
50 g (1½ oz) plain (all-purpose) flour or cornflour (cornstarch) —
the latter is lighter

Bring the milk and half the sugar to the boil. Remove from heat. Meanwhile, whisk the yolks and the remaining sugar together in a bowl, gradually stirring in the flour or cornflour to form a pale yellow paste. Carefully pour a small amount of the boiled milk onto the yolks, whisking it to incorporate the hot milk. Continue until you have mixed in half the milk, then return the remaining milk to the heat and carefully stir in the egg yolk and milk mixture.

At this point the mixture must be stirred briskly, as it will quickly thicken. Continue stirring until the thickened sauce reaches boiling point. Transfer to a clean bowl, cover with plastic wrap and place in the refrigerator. Prior to use, beat the mixture until it is smooth and creamy.

Variation

The above is an average thickness *crème pâtissière* — on occasions, thickness will need to vary; reduce the flour according to your requirements.

WALNUT (OR PECAN) CREME BRULEE

<u>Serves 4</u>

400 ml (12 fl oz) cream
1 vanilla bean, cut in half lengthways
4 egg yolks (use large eggs)
40 g (1½ oz) castor sugar
4 tablespoons walnuts (or pecans), roughly broken into pieces
castor sugar, for dusting

Equipment: 4 small, eared ovenproof dishes or ramekins; bain-marie (baking tray) filled with hot water

Place the cream in a saucepan with the vanilla bean and bring to the boil. Meanwhile, blend the egg yolks and sugar in a bowl with a whisk. Whisk in a little of the hot cream, then return this mixture to the rest of the cream in the saucepan. Whisk until it thickens like a light custard, but do not boil, as it will curdle.

Pour the custard into the ovenproof dishes or ramekins. Drop in the walnut or pecan pieces. Stand the dishes in a bain-marie of hot water and bake in the oven at 175°C (350°F) for 8 minutes, until the custards have a light skin on top. Remove and cool.

To serve: No more than 2 hours before serving, dust the tops with a layer of castor sugar. Place under a very well preheated griller to 'burn' the tops, or use a brûlée iron or blow torch.

Note: To make larger quantities, the basic custard recipe is easily multiplied in the ratio of 100 ml (3½ fl oz) cream, 10 g (⅓ oz) sugar and 1 egg yolk per person.

Variations

The above is already a variation on the classic *crème brûlée,* which is normally made with only a strong dose of vanilla infused from a bean and then scraped from its pod into the custard (this 'peppering' shows the vanilla has come from a real pod).

I have seen variations in which fruit — strawberries, kiwi slices or segments of orange — float through the custard. The fruit must not be cooked, for it wilts and loses water, so it is best placed in the dishes before pouring on the custard; this way it is heated only lightly during the short cooking period in the oven.

Personally, I like very few additions other than the nuts. I do, however, admit to changing the flavouring by the infusion of 5 small green cardamom pods, for example, or the infusion of some raw grated ginger (later strained out), some lime juice, or some chopped glacé ginger.

CUSTARDS MADE FROM WHOLE EGGS

When whole eggs are combined with milk, the result is less rich, but the setting ability, boosted by the albumen in the egg white, is greater. Most baked custards are a combination of milk and whole eggs. For added richness, a portion of cream can be mixed with the milk. Crème caramel is the classic French baked custard; bread and butter pudding the most traditional of English varieties.

When baking custards, a bain-marie is used to stop direct heat causing the milk to rise and thus aerate the mixture. Use hot water in a bain-marie, as cold water slows the cooking time. Ensure it is deep enough to act upon the whole custard or air holes will form.

The following three recipes are all variations on this same method.

CLASSIC CREME CARAMEL

Recipes for crème caramel vary, and I have seen them made with up to 9 eggs for the quantity of milk below. My recipe is light on eggs and therefore fairly 'junkety', a texture I much prefer. What this means, though, is that you must not unmould it too long before serving, or it may crack and divide. Add more eggs as a lesson in textures, and settle on the amount you prefer.

Serves 8

The caramel
180 g (6 oz) sugar
about 250 ml (8 fl oz) water, to cover

The custard
900 ml (1½ pt) milk
1 vanilla bean, cut in half
90 g (3 oz) sugar
6 eggs

Equipment: 23 cm (9 in) cake tin of 1.2 L (2 pt) capacity; bain-marie (baking dish) large enough to hold the cake tin, filled with hot water.

The caramel: Spoon the sugar into the cake tin and cover with 1 cm (⅓ in) water. Place on the heat, stirring gently until the sugar is dissolved (to prevent granules forming, dissolve the sugar before the water comes to the boil). Stop stirring and allow the water to boil down until the sugar syrup is so dense that it starts to caramelise. Swirl the dish from time to time from when the syrup starts to turn beige until it reaches a medium brown (this is to even the colour, and cannot be done by stirring since the sugar will attach to the spoon). Stop the heat darkening the caramel any further by placing the base of the tin in a pan of cold water.

When the caramel has cooled a little, roll it around the walls of the tin to coat the base and sides. Keep rolling until it has cooled completely, then set the mould aside and make the custard.

The custard: Scald the milk with the vanilla bean and sugar. Break the eggs into a bowl and pour in the milk, whisking well. Strain the custard to remove any coagulated albumen and pour it into the caramel-coated mould.

Place the mould in a bain-marie of hot water and cook in the oven at 200°C (400°F) for 35 minutes, or until it firms and draws away from the sides of the mould. When the custard is cooked, remove and leave to cool, then refrigerate for at least 6 hours. Just before serving, invert carefully onto a platter with enough depth to catch the caramel.

Note: If you prefer, divide the mixture into 8 small (150 ml/5 fl oz) ramekins, making the caramel in a saucepan and dropping a little into the base of each ramekin to set before adding the custard.

LITTLE POTS OF ORANGE CREAM

Serves 6–8

4 large pieces orange peel, pith removed
500 ml (16 fl oz) milk
1 vanilla bean
4 tablespoons sugar
4 eggs

The garnish
300 ml (10 fl oz) cream, whipped and slightly sweetened
julienne of orange peel, boiled in sugar syrup for 5 minutes and drained
Equipment: 8 small *crème pots*, moulds or 100 ml (3¹/₂ fl oz) soufflé ramekins; bain-marie, filled with hot water

Infuse the orange peel in the milk for 4 hours, then scald the milk with the vanilla bean, peel and sugar. In a bowl, whisk the eggs, then pour on the scalded milk, whisking well. Strain the liquid into the *crème pots*. Stand the pots in the bain-marie filled with hot water, cover them with a sheet of baking parchment, and bake at 190°C (375°F) for 20 minutes. Remove and cool.

To serve, decorate with piped whipped cream and top with 2 or 3 pieces of the julienne of candied orange peel.

Variation

Substitute mandarin for orange. You may choose to serve this dish with a small salad of orange segments and peel. For a special occasion, place the pots around the edge of a large salver, and in the centre place a large pile of peeled navel orange slices. Just before serving, make a caramel of 75 g (2¹/₂ oz) sugar and water to cover, and pour over the oranges, where it will set immediately as a light toffee. Crack the toffee and serve a pot to each guest with a toffeed orange slice.

ALMOND BREAD AND BUTTER PUDDING WITH BISCOTTI

Serves 6

1 tablespoon glacé ginger

1 tablespoon glacé cedrat (sometimes called citron, and available from better Italian delicatessens or specialty cheese shops)

1¹/₂ tablespoons mixed peel, or 1 tablespoon mixed peel and 1 tablespoon glacé orange

4 tablespoons unblanched almonds, roughly chopped

10–15 Italian almond biscuits (biscotti), depending on size. Try to choose the largest. (Biscotti are available dried or semi-dried from Italian delicatessens and most supermarkets)

butter, to spread over the biscotti

125 g (4 oz) sugar

6 eggs

500 ml (16 fl oz) milk

500 ml (16 fl oz) cream

pinch of cinnamon

3 tablespoons Amaretto di Saronno (Italian bitter almond liqueur)

icing (confectioners') sugar, for dredging

spun sugar to decorate (optional)

Equipment: 1.5 L (2¹/₂ pt) rectangular ovenproof dish (deep, not shallow), or a large round soufflé bowl

Place all the chopped fruit and peel in the base of the dish, along with about 1 heaped tablespoon almond. Butter the biscotti as you would bread, and place a layer of biscotti, butter side up and not too tightly packed, on top of the fruit, peel and almonds in the base of the dish.

Whisk the sugar and eggs in a bowl until blended, then whisk in the milk, cream and cinnamon. Pour over the biscuits, and bake in the oven at 180°C (350°F) for 30 minutes.

Remove from the oven and scatter the remaining almonds over the top, drizzle with Amaretto di Saronno and dredge with icing sugar. At the same time, test with a skewer to see if the custard has set; if it has, the skewer will come out dry and hot, not milky.

Return to the oven and cook for 5 minutes until the almonds have coloured, or until the custard is fully set. Decorate with spun sugar (if using).

RICE PUDDING

Some cooks make their rice pudding with eggs, as in the typical whole egg custard of the preceding recipe; this one relies solely on the starch of the rice to bind it together.

<u>Serves 6</u>

2 tablespoons rice
600 ml (1 pt) milk
25 g (1 oz) sugar
1/2 tablespoon vanilla essence
1 teaspoon nutmeg

Wash the rice and place it in a pie dish with the milk, sugar and vanilla. Sprinkle nutmeg over the top. Bake at 130°C (265°F) for 2 hours, or until thick and creamy.

Variations

The classic English rice pudding is made with milk and rice only. Richer variations can be made by substituting up to 250 ml (8 fl oz) of the milk with cream. Sultanas (golden raisins) can be added, as can glacé fruit mixtures or even fresh, hardy fruit such as peaches, apricots and pears. Do not add berry fruits or cherries, as they wilt and lose water during cooking, emitting little ponds of water that ruin the custardy texture.

ORANGE PUDDING WITH CARAMEL–ORANGE SAUCE

<u>Serves 6–8</u>

4 navel oranges (other types tend to slice less evenly)
about 2 tablespoons light brown sugar

The pudding
140 g (4¹/₂ oz) butter
140 g (4¹/₂ oz) sugar
3 x 55 g (2 oz) eggs
140 g (4¹/₂ oz) plain (all-purpose) flour mixed with 1 heaped teaspoon baking powder, or 140 g (4¹/₂ oz) self-raising flour

The caramel–orange sauce
4 tablespoons sugar
90 ml (3 fl oz) water
fine julienne of peel of 1 orange
100 ml (3¹/₂ fl oz) orange juice diluted with 50 ml (1¹/₂ fl oz) water
Equipment: 1.5 L (2¹/₂ pt) steamed pudding or charlotte mould

DESSERTS, CAKES, BISCUITS AND BREAD

To prepare the mould: Grate the rind of 1 orange and set aside, then squeeze the juice from this orange and set aside. Peel and cut the other 3 oranges into medium thin slices. Grease the mould well with butter, then sprinkle with brown sugar, rolling it around so that it lightly coats the base and sides. Arrange the orange slices decoratively on the base and sides, pressing into the butter and sugar to hold them in place.

The pudding: Cream the butter and sugar until light and fluffy. Add 1 egg at a time, stirring well, and blot up excess moisture by adding about 1 tablespoon flour/baking powder mixture between egg additions. Add the rest of the flour and enough orange juice to bring the batter to 'dropping' consistency (usually about 3–4 tablespoons). Add the grated orange zest.

Pour the batter into the prepared mould and tap it on a bench so that the batter fills in around the oranges. If using a steamed pudding mould, cover with greaseproof or brown paper tied in place, then cover with the lid and cook in a large saucepan of simmering water for 1 hour. If using a charlotte mould, bake the pudding in the oven at 190°C (375°F) for 35–45 minutes, or until a cake tester comes out dry.

Unmould the pudding onto a serving plate and serve with either caramel–orange sauce or heated marmalade.

The caramel–orange sauce: Dissolve the sugar in the water and bring to the boil. As it boils, drop in the julienne of orange peel until it softens (45 seconds); remove with a slotted spoon and set aside.

Reduce the syrup until it caramelises. When the caramel is a fairly deep golden, add the orange juice and water mix to stop the cooking at the colour you want — a fairly deep brown is the nicest; too pale and the result is too sweet. Make sure there is not a burnt or bitter edge to the taste, which results when the syrup is cooked for too long.

Return the mixture to the boil, shaking to melt down the caramel. Reduce the sauce by one-third, then cool and refrigerate. Return the julienne of orange peel before placing in a sauce boat to serve.

Variations

The basic recipe of a steamed pudding is the classic *quatre quarts* cake or Victoria Sandwich (page 204). To make a more traditional steamed pudding, omit the orange peel, flavour with vanilla, and use water rather than orange juice to make the batter 'dropping' consistency. You'll note that I unbalance the egg measurement a little. This is because I prefer the base mixture a little richer in egg. I also use plain (all-purpose) flour, not self-raising, so I need to add a teaspoon of baking powder, but use self-raising flour, which already has the raising agent built in, if you prefer.

PINA COLADA BAVAROIS

*A tropical-flavoured version of the classic Bavarian cream in which
a crème anglaise is set into a mould with the addition of gelatine.
Make up more flavours as you wish — coffee, mandarin, puréed
strawberry or raspberry — remembering that you will need more
gelatine the more liquid you use.*

<u>Serves 8</u>

*1¹/₂ packets sponge finger biscuits (approx. 15, depending on size)
3 mm (¹/₈ in) thick layer of sponge cake the diameter of your mould (optional)
2–3 tablespoons white rum*

The filling
*3¹/₂ teaspoons gelatine
4 tablespoons white rum
425 g (13¹/₂ oz) can crushed pineapple, drained, with
1 tablespoon juice reserved
300 ml (10 fl oz) milk
4 tablespoons castor sugar
4 egg yolks
grated zest of 3 green limes
3 tablespoons shredded coconut
350 ml (11 fl oz) cream, whipped*

Equipment: 22 cm (9 in) round cake circle or springform mould without a base.

Cut the sponge fingers to the height of the mould. If possible, place the mould directly in the centre of a serving plate, as the bavarois will not be easy to transfer later (or make on a circular cardboard base as do pastry shops). Drizzle the unsugared side of the biscuits with some rum and place around the inside walls of the mould, cut end at the bottom and sugared side facing out. Place the sponge cake base (if using) in the base of the mould, thus wedging the biscuits into place. Drizzle with a little more rum.

The filling: In a small bowl, soften the gelatine with the white rum and pine-apple juice. In a saucepan, scald the milk with 2 tablespoons castor sugar. Place the egg yolks in a bowl and break them up with a whisk, adding the other 2 tablespoons sugar. Pour in the scalded milk, return the mixture to the saucepan and whisk until the mixture has lightly thickened, but not come to the boil.

Remove and quickly strain into a bowl. Add the softened gelatine mix-ture and stir until dissolved by the heat, then add the lime zest, pineapple and coconut. Place over ice and stirr occasionally. When the texture of the cooled filling is about the same thickness as the whipped cream, fold the two together and pour into the biscuit-lined mould. Refrigerate for at least 4 hours to set.

To serve: Carefully lift off the mould and finish by tying a lemon- or lime-coloured ribbon around the circumference. This is removed at the table before cutting the dessert into portions.

TART BUT SWEET

In France, where apple tart is on everyone's Sunday table, pastry-making is a skill learned from mother; flour on a bench, eggs and sugar added, sleeves rolled up, and hands into the dough. I still prefer to make pastry by hand. I love to feel the dough and judge its springiness. Only then do I know exactly when to stop kneading, and how to keep it light and airy.

When good shortcrust pastry comes together beneath your hands, there is a moment when you feel the first tendency of the dough to spring back a little. When it does, stop right then; your dough will never be over-kneaded, never tough.

However, the food processor has made pastry-making so easy that even those unwilling to try before have added pastry-making to their repertoire. Simply place the ingredients in the bowl, process with a pulse action until the dough is kneaded into a ball, and *voilà!* Both methods are described in the Shortcrust Pastry recipe on page 191.

The simplest of the sweet tarts is undoubtedly the apple tart. All you need to do is peel, core, quarter and slice about 6 apples, then spiral the slices around the edge and centre of a 26–28 cm (10–11 in) tart mould. Sprinkle with 1 tablespoon sugar and bake in the oven at 200°C (400°F) for about 35 minutes, or until tender. This easiest and most commonplace of tarts — don't underestimate its flavour because of that!— is finished with a glaze of smooth apricot jam which has been heated until it is soft enough to spread with a pastry brush.

Once you know how to make pastry, your choice of filling is limited only by your imagination. When stone fruits are in season they can be halved and pitted, then placed in the tart base (cut-side upwards so their juices don't make the pastry soggy). After baking, the fruit should be glazed — an apricot or pale-coloured fruit with apricot jam, a plum or dark-coloured fruit tart with redcurrant jelly.

If a tart is baked blind (i.e. without filling) a custard (*crème pâtissière*, see page 182) may be spread in its base and topped with any canned fruit (e.g. apricot or pear halves), or a layer of fresh, hulled strawberries or mixed berries. Again, the top is glazed with jam. To bake blind, first roll out the pastry to fit the mould, then prick the base at regular intervals with a knife to prevent the pastry blistering. The tart floor should be covered with foil to allow only the exposed sides to brown during cooking. Bake in the oven at about 180°C (350°F) for 30 minutes.

These, of course, are some of the least sophisticated tarts. The clever cook will make up many others.

SHORTCRUST PASTRY

The following recipe describes both hand and machine methods for making shortcrust pastry to fit a 26–28 cm (10–11 in) tart mould.

<u>Serves 8</u>

200 g (7 oz) plain (all-purpose) flour
100 g (3¹/₂ oz) unsalted butter, softened
3 tablespoons sugar
1 egg yolk
3 tablespoons water

Method by hand: Place the flour on a slab of marble or other cool surface. Make a well (hole) in the centre and add the egg yolk, sugar and softened butter. Add 2 tablespoons water and mix the ingredients in the well together, then start blending with the flour. Rub the flour and butter together between your fingertips, letting it fall through the air to keep it light. When it all seems to be one colour — that is, no specks of white flour separate from the butter — add another tablespoon of water and continue to blend until the pastry starts to come together in a ball. Taking care not to knead too much, push the ball of pastry towards and away from you on the bench with the heel of your hand, and re-roll into a ball two or three times. Stop as soon as there is a slight springiness in the pastry. Refrigerate for 20 minutes, covered with plastic wrap or a tea towel, then roll out the pastry and line the tart mould.

Method by food processor: Place the flour, butter and sugar in the processor bowl and use a pulse action repeatedly until chopped enough to resemble sand. Add the egg yolk and pulse again two or three times, then add 2 tablespoons water (usually the processor demands less water than the hand-made method, but this depends on the texture of the butter). Continue to process until the pastry forms balls and sits above the blades of the machine. It is possible to increase the butter in the food processor method to 125 g (4 oz) and omit the water. Refrigerate for 20 minutes and finish as above.

CITRUS FRUIT TART

If in doubt as to how 'sweet-toothed' your guests are, the first rule is to set aside the cloying and pick a dessert with a bit of a tang to it.

<u>Serves 8</u>

The shortcrust pastry
1 quantity of shortcrust pastry (see recipe above)

The filling
3 eggs
1 egg yolk
juice of 3 lemons and 1 orange
150 ml (5 fl oz) cream
150 g (5 oz) sugar

The garnish (optional)
2 lemons
2 oranges
200 ml (7 fl oz) orange juice, strained
2 tablespoons lemon juice
120 g (4 oz) sugar
Equipment: 26–28 cm (10–11 in) tart mould with removable base

The pastry: Make the pastry following the recipe on page 191. Rest it for 20 minutes. When ready, roll out the pastry and line the tart mould with a removable base. Bake blind for 20 minutes at 200°C (400°F), the centre protected with foil.

The filling: Beat all the filling ingredients together until light and fluffy. Pour into the par-baked pastry base and bake at 180°C (350°F) for 30–35 minutes. Remove and cool. The tart may be served without the fruit garnish but, if using, proceed as below while the flan is cooking.

The garnish: (optional). Slice the oranges and lemons as finely and evenly as possible, keeping the slices together but slightly fanned out like a deck of cards. In a large but shallow saucepan, melt the sugar in the orange and lemon juice and, with an egg lift, place the fanned out fruit in the mixture to poach. The fanning should expose mostly peel, and protect the pulp from fraying. Poach until the peel is glazed and tender, usually about 20 minutes. Transfer the slices to a cake rack to cool. When ready, decorate the top of the tart with alternate slices of lemon and orange, arranged ina spiral pattern. Boil down the juice to a light syrup and glaze the top of the tart.

ROSE-PATTERNED STRAWBERRY TART

<u>Serves 8</u>

The shortcrust pastry
1 quantity of shortcrust pastry (page 191)

The crème pâtissière
300 ml (10 fl oz) milk
3 tablespoons sugar
1 heaped tablespoon plain (all-purpose) flour
vanilla essence, or the grated zest of one orange and
a dash of Grand Marnier

The garnish
500 g (1 lb) large strawberries (preferably pointed ones, not those with
a double crown)
Equipment: 28 cm (11 in) tart mould with removable base

The pastry: Make the pastry following the recipe on page 191. Rest it for 20 minutes. When ready, roll out the pastry and line the tart mould. Bake blind for 20 minutes at 200°C (400°F), the centre protected with foil.

The crème pâtissière: Make up the *crème pâtissière* using the method on page 182. Fill the cooked tart base with the *crème pâtissière*.

The garnish: Hull the strawberries and cut into slices. Set aside the outer slices and keep only the long pointed ones (there should be 2 per strawberry, sometimes 3). Starting from the outside edge of the cream-filled tart, arrange the strawberry slices in a spiral pattern, and finish neatly with one whole strawberry in the centre. To serve, cut the tart into wedges.

The remaining strawberry pieces can be puréed, sweetened and used for a coulis. This can be served with the tart, or frozen for later use.

Variation

Instead of the *crème pâtissière* fill the cooked tart base with 400 ml (12 fl oz) cream, whipped, sweetened, and enriched with a dash of vanilla.

LORETTA'S NUSSTORTE

*A favourite Swiss classic of Loretta Sartori, pastry-smith at
The French Kitchen.*

Serves 8–10

750 g (1½ lb) shortcrust dough (a double amount of the recipe on page 191)
450 g (14½ oz) castor sugar
400 g (12 oz) cream (35 per cent milk fat)
4 tablespoons honey
80 g (2½ oz) cornflour (cornstarch)
400 g (12 oz) walnuts, roughly chopped
icing (confectioners') sugar, for dredging
Equipment: 28–30 cm (11–12 in) tart mould

In a copper, stainless steel or enamelled saucepan, stir a small quantity of sugar over a moderate heat until it dissolves, then add a little more sugar. Continue in this manner, waiting until each addition of sugar has dissolved before adding more. This way, there should be no lumps or sugar crystals.

Continue cooking the sugar to a light brown caramel, then slowly add the cream. The mixture will bubble up high in the saucepan, so stir to ensure it doesn't spill over. At this point, the caramelised sugar will sink to the bottom in lumps, because it is not yet combined with the cream. Lower the heat and continue to stir until the sugar and cream are well blended, then transfer to a clean, metal or high heatproof bowl. Allow the caramel to cool completely before stirring in the honey, then the cornflour.

Roll out two-thirds of the shortcrust pastry and line the base of the tart mould. Pour in the thick caramel. Sprinkle the walnut pieces over the caramel, then roll out the remaining pastry and make a top for the tart. Pinch the edges together well to seal the tart. Bake in the oven at 180°C (350°F) for about 40 minutes, or until crisp and golden. Cool on a cake rack, and dredge with icing sugar before serving.

PUFF, THE MAGIC . . .

How people shy away from making puff pastry! They blame the butter, the heat of the day, the time it takes — anything and everything. But the fact is, puff pastry requires only one 7-minute working period and two 3-minute periods. That's less time than it takes to drive to the shop and buy it — and few shops sell good quality butter-based puff.

The more you practice, the more skilled you will become. You'll learn to judge how warm the pastry should be to have more 'plasticity', and you'll roll more neatly and have squarer edges. But a few simple hints are all that is needed to help you make puff pastry like an old 'pro' from your very first time.

Two points are important before you start. First, I suggest a beginner start with a good-sized amount of flour, say 500 g (1 lb) rather than a small quantity. It is easy to vary this amount later, because the ratio of ingredients is simple to adapt. Second, honour the rest periods — they allow elasticity to abate. After resting, return the pastry to room temperature before trying to roll it. The important notion behind this is again 'plasticity'— the pastry's ability to roll without cracking, and to roll smoothly, with a minimum of pressure from the roller. If the pastry cracks at the edges, and butter escapes from the all-important alternate layering that allows the pastry to rise, all is lost. Understand this, and you have understood all. Now to the detail . . .

CLASSIC PUFF PASTRY

In a classic puff pastry the weight of butter is the same as the weight of the flour, and the water is half that weight. This allows you to alter the quantity with ease, and make as little or as much as you like. However, beginners should not start with less than 300 g (9¹/₂ oz) of flour and butter. Smaller quantities are harder to work successfully. Most recipes use the butter in one piece in the middle of the ball of dough (called the détrempe*). I prefer to incorporate some butter in the* détrempe *itself, to 'soften' and enrich this flour and water layer. Both methods are valid. The best puff pastry is made with unsalted butter, but stay away from farm butter, which often 'bleeds' water.*

500 g (1 lb) butter
500 g (1 lb) plain (all-purpose) or baker's flour
pinch of salt
250 ml (8 fl oz) water
To glaze the pastry before use: 1 whole egg, beaten

Soften 75 g (2¹/₂ oz) butter (keep the remaining butter cold), and place in a mixing bowl with the flour and salt; blend together, pouring in the water in a thin stream. You may do this by hand or in an electric mixer fitted with either a dough hook or a 'paddle'. When the pastry is lightly mixed together, transfer to a board and 'ball' with the heel of your hands. Rest the pastry for 1 hour (optional).

Sprinkle a little flour over both the work surface and rolling pin, and roll this ball of dough to a disc approximately 28 cm (11 in) in diameter. Pound the remaining butter into the centre of the dough and fold the edges in from four sides, enveloping the butter completely. Give it a couple of taps with the rolling pin to ensure the parcel stays together.

Roll the pastry into a long rectangle of about 55 x 22 cm (22 x 9 in). Apply pressure evenly and take care not squeeze butter from the mixture; keep the ends as square as possible. Fold the pastry into three, first folding towards you to a central point, then folding the bottom third over the rest. Grip this rectangle of pastry firmly and turn it 90 degrees so the folds run right to left in front of you.

Once again, roll the pastry into a long rectangle, to the same dimensions as before. This rolling technique has now worked the pastry in a different direction. Fold again in three as above; you have now completed two 'turns'. Cover the well-floured pastry with foil or greaseproof paper, tucking the ends in so they don't dehydrate, and rest it in the refrigerator for 2 hours. Then complete two more turns, rest again, then complete the final two turns. Well covered, the pastry can rest overnight before the final two turns.

A six-turn pastry is a completed pastry. It can be used immediately or stored in the refrigerator, well wrapped, for up to 3 days. Puff pastry can be frozen, but is better frozen after four turns so that the two final turns are completed after thawing, thus negating any tendency to 'scab'. Remember never to disturb the layers when thawing or rolling.

Use this pastry for any recipe requiring puff, remembering that any surfaces to be stuck together require brushing with egg wash, as does the top layer for a final sheen when baking.

TARTE TATIN

Serves 8

90 g (3 oz) unsalted butter
180 g (6 oz) sugar
9 pears or apples (preferably Golden Delicious or Red Delicious)
peeled, halved and cored
250 g (8 oz) puff pastry (see recipe above)
Equipment: 24 cm (9¹/₂ in) heavy frying pan, ovenproof

In the frying pan, melt the butter and sugar. Expect the sugar to 'mass' — that is, the sugar does not dissolve fully. When the sugar turns into a light brown caramel, remove the pan from the stove immediately, and quickly dip the base into a tray of water to avoid further darkening.

Place the halved apples or pears in a spiral pattern around the pan, each slightly overlapping the next. Fill the entire area with two circles of fruit. Bake in the oven at 200°C (400°F) for 30 minutes.

Meanwhile, roll out the pastry to a thickness of about 4 mm ($^1/_6$ in) in a circle a little larger than the diameter of the pan. Place on a baking tray and freeze for about 20 minutes; this will help minimise shrinkage in the oven.

After 30 minutes, remove the pan from the oven. The fruit will have softened a little, and before adding the pastry top, you should push each half apple or pear a little to slant the rounded edge to the base of the mould (otherwise when unmoulded, the finished cake will show fruit standing on their side). Place the frozen disc of pastry directly over the fruit, and, using a knife, quickly pierce about 4 slits in the pastry as steam vents. With the pastry still stiff and frozen, return the pan to the oven for a further 25–30 minutes, or until puffed and golden.

Remove from the oven, wait 5 minutes, then place a serving platter over the pan and carefully invert the tart onto the plate. Watch out for any hot caramel falling — don't burn yourself.

Serve hot, warm or room temperature, with whipped cream. Never refrigerate.

Variations

There are now many small, modern versions of Tarte Tatin with fresh fruit such as mango, kiwifruit, peaches or even strawberries. Bake a puff pastry disc of about 12 cm (5 in) diameter, add the raw fruit, sprinkle with sugar, and caramelise under a hot griller or with a blowtorch (a little like the method for Caramelised Peaches on page 177).

TARTE FINE AUX POMMES

Compare the following apple tart recipe, known as the 'fine' apple tart, with the traditional French apple tart on page 190. This light version, which uses puff pastry, and a minimal amount at that, became a favourite of restaurants during the landmark days of nouvelle cuisine.

Serves 6

350 g (11 oz) puff pastry (see page 194)
4 Granny Smith apples, peeled, cored and cut into slices
6 teaspoons sugar
3 tablespoons butter, melted
200 ml (7 fl oz) cream, whipped and sweetened with Calvados
or orange marmalade

Roll out a very thin layer of puff pastry per person, and cut into a round disc of about 12–15 cm (5–6 in) diameter. Rest the discs in the freezer for 20 minutes, so that there will be a minimum of shrinkage during cooking. Just before putting each tart into the oven, spiral a layer of very thinly sliced pieces of apple around each disc, and sprinkle each lightly with 1 scant teaspoon sugar. Bake in the oven at 220–230°C (425–440°F) for about 10 minutes.

When ready, brush with melted butter or, if preferred, warmed smooth apricot jam. Serve with whipped cream, flavoured with Calvados or a little orange marmalade.

FEUILLETEE DE POIRES, SAUCE SABAYON

Serves 6

500 g (1 lb) sugar
1 L (1³/₄ pt) water
dash of sweet white wine
1 vanilla bean
3 pears, peeled, with stalks left on
6 dates, prunes or pieces of almond marzipan (optional)
350 g (11 oz) puff pastry
egg wash: 1 whole egg plus 1 yolk and 1 tablespoon milk, beaten with a fork

The sabayon
4 egg yolks (one of the eggs may be added whole to give
extra volume and firmness)
4 heaped tablespoons sugar
pulp of 2 passionfruit (optional)
3 tablespoons Kirsch or dry Marsala

To poach the pears: Place the sugar, water, wine and vanilla bean in a casserole dish large enough to hold the pears snugly. Bring to the boil, stirring to dissolve the sugar. Add the pears, reduce to a simmer and poach until tender — usually about 15–20 minutes, depending on ripeness. Allow the pears to cool in the liquor. When needed, drain well on paper towelling and split each pear in two, halving the stalk as well, if possible. Remove the core gently, without disturbing the stalk.

To assemble the pears: (can be made in advance and reheated). Make a template for the pastry by tracing the halved pear shape, with its stalk, onto thick cardboard. The outline should be about 1.5 cm (¹/₂ in) larger than the pear to allow for shrinkage, and to allow the pastry to frame the pear. Roll out the puff pastry, then cut out six pear-shaped pieces of pastry using the template. Transfer the six shapes to a baking tray, dry the pear halves well, and place them, cut side down, in the centre of the pastry shapes. Place a date, prune or piece of almond marzipan (if using) in the centre of each pear to replace the core. Brush well with the egg wash. Bake in the oven at 200°C

(400°F) for 20 minutes, turning the tray once — and only after 15 minutes — if there is any sign of patchy cooking. Serve warm, not hot, with the sabayon sauce.

The sabayon: Place the egg yolks in a bowl, preferably metal, or one that can take the heat (I use a copper egg-white bowl). Using a hand-held mixer, mix well, and add the sugar and the Kirsch or Marsala. Place the bowl over a pan of steaming water on the stove and whisk until the mixture doubles or trebles in volume and poaches just enough to thicken; take care not to overheat and scramble the egg. When thickened, take off the heat and continue to whisk, to reduce the heat just a little. Serve immediately; spoon some over one edge of the pear, and place the rest in a sauceboat.

Note: A true sabayon is served warm, and must not be made too long in advance, or reheated. A cold version can be made by whisking 2 leaves softened gelatine with 200 ml (7 fl oz) cream (whipped), and pouring into glasses to set. If the sabayon is too difficult to make at the last minute for this dessert, use warm *crème anglaise* (page 182) or a large dob of thick cream.

Variation

My friend, chef Barry Meiklejohn, serves a warm pear dish similar to this as a starter or as a finale to a short meal. Barry places a small knob of Roquefort or another strong blue cheese and a small piece of smoked salmon in the hole under the pear where the core was removed. The baked pear is served with a sauce made of boiled cream flavoured with mashed Roquefort and nutmeg. As a starter it looks great placed on a bed of watercress; as a cheese course, serve with the sauce spilling over one side of the pear onto the plate.

CHOCOHOLICA

Whether making chocolate crackles, licking the wooden spoon from Mum's chocolate sponge, or beating up our first-ever attempt at baking a packet cake, most people's childhood food memories include chocolate. Many of us carry a soft spot for chocolate right into adulthood. Set aside regional biases — the pavlova in Australia, the *pie à la mode* in the US, the *crème caramel* in France — and I'd bet my bottom dollar that the two desserts highest on everyone's preferred list, worldwide, are ice cream with chocolate sauce and chocolate mousse.

But just how many of us make a great job of either?

Neither the sauce nor the mousse are fraught with danger when you understand what you are getting into. Chocolate is temperamental when subjected to either heat or cold. At one end of the scale it has to be melted slowly and not stirred too much in case it becomes pasty; at the other, it has to be quickly and thoroughly blended with the cold ingredient to prevent it setting. When melted, it has to be removed from the heat immediately, or the 'grease' particles will separate out as oil and the sugar and cocoa will crystalise into sugary particles.

It is not coincidental that some chocolates melt better than others. You only have to compare a velvety chocolate with one with a high degree of 'snap' to understand that much of the difference in taste and texture has to do with how much oil and fat the chocolate has in it. The type of chocolate used for cooking is different from chocolate that is designed for eating at the cinema. Melt some chocolate and it will 'ball' around the spoon; try a 'couverture' style which is high in cocoa butter and the melt will be much smoother and more moist. To guide you, some brands have 'cooking chocolate' or 'couverture' on the label. Compare them, though. Some are better-tasting than others, mostly depending on the percentage of cocoa butter compared with other fats such as palm oil and copha. If you try melting an eating chocolate and compare it to a great cooking chocolate like Belgium's Callebaut or Switzerland's Carma or Felschlin, you will spot the difference immediately. When making and coating your own chocolates, the viscosity and 'flow' that these latter brands guarantee is even more essential.

Although there are many ways of melting chocolate — including pouring boiling water on and off broken-up cubes without disturbing or stirring them, or by using a microwave — most methods have drawbacks. You can only use the water trick if the water won't ruin the chocolate for whatever you intend to do with it. For example, if you are melting chocolate to transfer to baking paper to cut out shapes, cover leaves or pipe butterflies, you will have broken its texture and it won't reset. But it is an excellent method for making chocolate mousse.

If you use the microwave, you must work in stages, with rest periods in between to equalise the heat, and you must watch for overheating, as the chocolate will crystallise. These methods work, but they seem to require the patience of Job, or perfect timing. If you doubt yourself or your recipe, you can avoid all these problems simply by placing the chocolate in a bowl over steaming water. Stir only from time to time (if you stir too much, it will become pasty and lose sheen), and remove before overheating.

At the lower end of the temperature scale, chocolate sets almost at room temperature, so when we add something cold to it, such as a large volume of whipped cream, if we don't blend it in quickly and throughly, we 'seize up' the tiny particles of chocolate. These particles set immediately on contact with the cream and remain as rough, gritty morsels on the tongue rather than blending smoothly with the mixture.

Therein lies half the problem in making a chocolate mousse, and if you understand that alcohol also 'seizes up' the chocolate, many of you will quickly recognise a major trap people fall into when making chocolate sauce. The chocolate must be first melted with a plain liquid, such as water, milk or cream (or even a similar-viscosity grease like butter), and the alcohol should be added only once the chocolate has been diluted.

I hope I haven't made this sound difficult just because I have given so much detail. The problems are non-existent when the method is understood.

Now to the recipes . . .

MY PREFERRED CHOCOLATE SAUCE

Serves 4–6

100 g (3¹/₂ oz) good quality dark chocolate
1 heaped tablespoon butter
1 heaped tablespoon icing (confectioners') sugar, sifted
100–200 ml (3¹/₂ – 7 fl oz) cream
dash of Grand Marnier, rum or brandy

Melt the chocolate with the butter and sugar, then stir in enough cream to make a smooth, silky textured sauce, without drowning the strength of the chocolate. Add a dash of Grand Marnier, rum or brandy, depending on what the sauce is to be served with.

CHOCOLATE MOUSSE

<u>Serves 4</u>

120 g (4 oz) good quality dark chocolate, broken into squares
4 teaspoons unsalted butter, softened
4 eggs, separated

Place the chocolate in a bowl and cover with boiling water. When the chocolate is soft enough for the point of a knife to pass through the pieces, pour off the water. While the chocolate is still warm, quickly stir in the butter so it melts easily into the mixture. (If by chance you are not quick enough, hold the bowl over hot water a moment and continue stirring.) Stir in the egg yolks, one at a time. Leave to cool.

Whip the egg whites as firmly as possible — preferably by hand in a copper bowl. The better whipped the egg whites, the creamier the mousse. Egg whites beaten by hand are firm and dense; those beaten by machine are full of airholes, rather like shaving cream compared to beer froth. The traditional French mousse has no cream in it — and it doesn't need it if you beat the whites to a firm, stiff snow. If you do not beat your eggs by hand, add a teaspoon of sugar halfway through whipping.

Fold the egg whites into the cooled chocolate mixture, then pour into individual dishes or one large bowl. Place in the refrigerator to set for at least 4 hours before serving.

Note: This recipe is easily adapted to cater for more people. Multiply in the ratio of 30 g (1 oz) chocolate, 1 egg and 1 teaspoon butter per person.

Variations

Almost everyone but the purist French cook thinks chocolate mousse is better with a touch of whipped cream. You can make a richer mousse by adding 150 ml (5 fl oz) whipped cream. In French, the classical name then becomes Mayonnaise au Chocolat. Fold it in before the egg whites — to keep the whole effect light and fluffy, the lighter ingredients must always go in last.

Vary the flavour by adding 1 tablespoon of instant coffee diluted with as little water as possible. It is now Mocha Mousse. Try pouring the mousse over a bed of prunes marinated in tea or Marsala before placing it in the refrigerator to set, or add grated zest of orange peel and a touch of Grand Marnier or Cointreau. You can even fold melted marshmallows through the mousse — use 100 g (3½ oz) vanilla marshmallows, semi-melted in 20-second pulses in the microwave, or melted in a bowl over boiling water. If you fold the marshmallows through only partially, the mousse will have an attractive marbled look. Finish this one with piped cream and nuts.

TRUFFES AU CHOCOLAT

Makes 25–30 truffles, depending on size

300 g (9½ oz) good quality dark chocolate
2 tablespoons brown rum
1 tablespoon milk
100 g (3½ oz) unsalted butter
3 egg yolks
cocoa, for dredging

In a double-boiler, melt the chocolate with the rum and milk. When three-quarters melted, add the butter and stir until melted. Off the stove, stir in the egg yolks and place in the refrigerator until firm. Stir once or twice while cooling or the butter will rise to the top and form a line of grease.

When the chocolate is firm but still workable, shape into rough-edged balls and roll in cocoa. Dust off excess cocoa and store in refrigerator. Because this is not rich in cream, it lasts longer than the more traditional ganache-based truffle (see below), and is perhaps the handiest for domestic cookery.

GANACHE TRUFFLES

Makes 25–30 truffles, depending on size

100 ml (3½ fl oz) cream
100 g (3½ oz) good quality dark chocolate, grated or finely chopped
in a food processor
2 tablespoons very soft butter (but not melted)
2 tablespoons rum
cocoa for dredging

Heat the cream in a saucepan and, while hot, pour it over the chocolate in a bowl. Stir until the chocolate is dissolved. Allow to cool enough so the butter cannot melt, and so the mixture firms. Stir in the butter until there is no trace of it, then add the rum. Ball as above and roll in cocoa.

BITTER CHOCOLATE SOUFFLE

A recipe from Robert Lynx of Maison de Chocolat, Paris. Robert serves
his soufflé with Bitter Chocolate Sorbet (see opposite),
but if you prefer, serve it with vanilla ice cream.

Serves 4–8

4 egg yolks
4 tablespoons sugar
35 g (1 oz) plain (all-purpose) flour

250 ml (8 fl oz) milk
180 g (6 oz) good quality dark chocolate, finely grated
3 tablespoons bitter cocoa (any Dutch brand)
5 egg whites
butter and sugar to line the ramekins
cocoa or icing (confectioners') sugar, for dredging

Equipment: 8 x 150 ml (5 fl oz) ramekins, 9 cm (3½ in) in diameter, or 4 x 275 ml (9 fl oz) ramekins, 12 cm (5 in) in diameter

In a bowl, cream 2 egg yolks and the sugar, then stir in the flour. Scald the milk and stir it into this mixture; return to the saucepan and bring to the boil, stirring constantly.

Remove from the heat and stir in the remaining egg yolks, 150 g (5 oz) chocolate, and the cocoa. Blend well.

Whip the egg whites to a firm snow. Whipping the egg whites in a copper bowl with a balloon whisk definitely gives the best results. With a machine, you end up with larger air holes (thus allowing the air to escape later), but you can help tighten these by whisking in a tablespoon of sugar just before you finish. You will see the air holes diminish before your eyes.

Fold the egg whites into the egg and chocolate mixture, then fold in the remaining chocolate. Butter and sugar the ramekins; divide the mixture among them and bake at 220°C (425°F) for 12 minutes.

When ready, dredge with cocoa; if this is too bitter, dredge with icing sugar. Serve immediately.

BITTER CHOCOLATE SORBET

Serves 6–8

500 ml (16 fl oz) milk
125 g (4 oz) castor sugar
125 g (4 oz) good quality dark chocolate, roughly chopped
65 g (2½ oz) bitter cocoa (any Dutch brand)

Equipment: Ice cream churn

Bring the milk and castor sugar to the boil, then pour over the chocolate pieces. Stir in the cocoa powder. When the mixture has cooled, place in an ice cream machine and churn according to the instructions on the machine. Store in a sealed container in the freezer for up to 5 days.

HAVE YOUR CAKE
AND EAT IT TOO

Some people are cake-makers by nature, but I have found a great standby for the home baker without a range of recipes at their fingertips — the *quatre quarts*. Known in English recipes as the Victoria sandwich, the *quatre quarts* is a simple butter cake recipe, so named because it is made from only four ingredients, combined in equal parts.

It's easy to remember and so many variations can stem from this simple formula that even those only moderately interested will be surprised at the number of great cakes they can turn out to wow their guests. Meet the one cake that is many . . .

THE BASIC RECIPE

For a 20 cm (8 in) cake tin:
*2 eggs, and their weight in sugar, butter and flour. Use either plain (all-purpose) flour with baking powder in it, or self-raising flour (see **Note**)*

For a 23 cm (9 in) cake tin:
Weigh 3 eggs instead of two.

Note: Plain flour is better than self-raising flour since the cream of tartar in the latter tends to leave a bitter taste, particularly if it has been sitting on the shelves for too long. Refer to the packet for the exact quantity of baking powder to add; generally 1 rounded teaspoon for the 2 egg mixture, 2 scant or level teaspoons for the 3 egg mixture.

To make the cake: Cream the butter and sugar until light and fluffy. Add 1 egg at a time, stirring well, and blot up any excess moisture by adding 1 tablespoon flour between additions. Add the rest of the flour, enough water to make the batter of 'dropping' consistency (usually 2–3 tablespoons), and a little vanilla essence. Spread evenly into a well-greased cake tin and bake in the oven at 190°C (375°F) for 30–35 minutes for the 2-egg cake, 35–45 minutes for the 3-egg cake.

THE VARIATIONS

The variations are obtained by changing the recipe in two major areas. These, plus the final icings and garnishes, will make possible an infinite variety of cakes from this one basic recipe.
1. The water that is added to give 'dropping' consistency can be changed to other liquids — for example, instant coffee (blended to a paste with a little water), rum or orange juice.
2. The flour can be mixed with other compatible ingredients — for

example, almond meal, ground hazelnuts or walnuts, cocoa or instant coffee. Note that the flour proportion in the cake can be expanded by up to 35 g (1½ oz) to help accentuate these ingredients.

THE POSSIBILITIES

Orange cake

Change the water to orange juice, add the grated peel of an orange, and you have a very acceptable orange cake recipe. Ice with icing (confectioners') sugar softened with orange juice, or egg white and orange juice, with the addition of some more grated peel and a little Grand Marnier or Cointreau if you so desire.

Tea cake

This is readily prepared using the basic vanilla-flavoured quatre quarts. Slice the cake horizontally into two equal layers. Sprinkle the bottom layer with melted butter, cinnamon and castor sugar. Reassemble the cake and garnish the top in the same way, also using a few large, spreadable dollops of butter. Place under a very hot griller for a few moments to caramelise the sugar and make the cake crunchy on top.

Hazelnut or walnut coffee cake

Replace the water with instant coffee dissolved in a small amount of boiling water. Make it strong enough to impart a good flavour. Use 1 tablespoon less flour, and add 30–35 g (1–1½ oz) hazelnut meal or ground walnuts. The ground nuts give the cake a lovely texture, and the moisture from the oil of the nuts helps the cake last longer. Ice with a coffee *crème au beurre* (see butter creams in your better cookbooks). Create a simple decoration is achieved by patting the edge of the cake with ground nuts after spreading with the coffee butter cream. You can make it dressier by piping eight rosettes of butter cream around the top of the cake and filling each rosette with a nut.

Chocolate cake

Although there are richer chocolate cakes, the *quatre quarts* can have a chocolate variation. Melt 60 g (2 oz) dark chocolate in 2 tablespoons hot water, rum or coffee. Cool, then add the chocolate to the cake mixture with about 1 level tablespoon cocoa sifted into the flour. With the melted chocolate, no further 'water to dropping consistency' is necessary, but 2 tablespoons milk can be added to give it the heavier, richer consistency of a continental cake.

The simplest decoration is to put either whipped cream or raspberry jam in the centre of the cake and cover with a chocolate icing made from 120 g (4 oz) melted chocolate combined with 40g (1½ oz) unsalted butter. Spread the icing evenly over the top and sides while still warm and runny. Do this over a cake rack so the excess can drop away. Alternatively, melt 200 g (7 oz) dark chocolate and, still over the heat, stir in 250 ml (8 fl oz) cream. Stir until it blends well, then use it as a filling or as a spreadable icing (ganache). Top the cake with whole caramelised unblanched almonds. Drop the almonds into caramelised sugar. When coated with the hot caramel, remove them one by one with a fork and place on an oiled baking rack to cool.

Mock black forest cake

This can be made with a chocolate *quatre quarts* sliced horizontally into three equal layers. Spread the bottom layer with whipped cream, the middle one with ganache and top with cherry cream and shredded chocolate.

Cherry cake

Slice a vanilla-flavoured *quatre quarts* in half horizontally and spread redcurrant jelly in the centre and on top. Decorate the top with a tin of drained pitted cherries. Mask the sides with cream piped vertically around the edge with the star nozzle of a piping bag.

Fruit-glazed cake

This cake is similar to those used in German pastry shops. Spread the centre of a *quatre quarts*, as well as the top and sides, with apricot jam. Decorate the top with a ring of pineapple in the centre, a ring of apricot halves around, and fill any spaces between the fruit with pineapple pieces, grapes or strawberries. Glaze with more apricot jam, or with an arrowroot-thickened combination of boiled juices from the tins. Place a strawberry on top of the central ring to finish, and pat almond meal or toasted flaked almonds around the edge.

A novel checkerboard cake

Use white icing on a square cake and then place little squares of chocolate in chessboard fashion across the top. Finish with an edging of toasted almonds stuck on with apricot jam.

MY FAVOURITE 'FLOURLESS' CHOCOLATE CAKE — WITH FLOUR!

So named because it has the beautiful, fudge-like texture of the flourless chocolate cake, with just a little flour to guarantee it slices easily.

Serves 8–10

320 g (10¹/₂ oz) good quality dark chocolate
160 g (5¹/₂ oz) castor sugar
160 g (5¹/₂ oz) unsalted butter
5 eggs, separated
2 tablespoons plain (all-purpose) flour, sifted
icing (confectioners') sugar, for dredging

Raspberry coulis
250 g (8 oz) raspberries
3–4 tablespoons sugar
1 tablespoon Kirsh (optional)

Equipment: 23 cm (9 in) round springform cake tin

Melt the chocolate, sugar and butter in a bowl over a saucepan of hot water. Remove from the heat, stir to blend, then add the egg yolks, one by one.

Whip the egg whites to a firm snow. Fold the flour into the chocolate mixture with half the egg whites, then, more carefully, fold in the second half of the egg whites. Pour into a greased cake tin and bake in the oven at 180°C (350°F) for 45 minutes. Expect the cake to firm on top; even to crack when it falls. This is not strange to this style of recipe.

Allow the cake to cool completely in the mould before carefully unbuckling the sides. Dredge with icing sugar and serve with whipped or clotted cream. As a dessert, I prefer to serve it also with a few spoonfuls of raspberry coulis.

The raspberry coulis: In a food processor or blender, purée the raspberries with 3–4 tablepoons sugar and, if desired, 1 tablespoon Kirsch. It is best served sieved to rid it of the seeds, but this is not essential.

RICH CHOCOLATE TORTE

Makes 12 slices

200 g (7 oz) unsalted butter
150 g (5 oz) castor sugar
6 eggs, separated
250 g (8 oz) ground almonds
150 g (5 oz) good quality dark chocolate, melted

The ganache
150 ml (5 fl oz) cream
2 teaspoons instant coffee
225 g (7¹/₂ oz) good quality dark chocolate, grated or melted
cocoa for dusting
Equipment: 30 x 20 cm (12 x 8 in) lamington (Swiss roll) tin

To prepare the torte: Cream the butter and sugar in an electric mixer or food processor. Add the egg yolks, one by one. Remove and stir in the ground almonds and chocolate, which must still be fluid, but cool enough not to melt the butter.

Whip the egg whites to a firm snow, fold carefully into the mixture, and spread into the greased lamington tin. Bake in the oven at 180°C (350°F) oven for 15 minutes. Cool on a cake rack, then cut the cake into three long rectangles of equal size.

The ganache icing: Heat the cream and instant coffee, stirring until well blended. Cool until the mixture thickens slightly and can be spread. (Note: Ganache is the technical name for the combination of cream and chocolate that forms this icing. It is well-known, too, as the centre filling for truffles and other chocolates.)

To assemble the torte: Wedge the three layers of the torte together with a good 1 cm (¹/₃ in) of ganache between the layers. Refrigerate for a moment so it's easier to deal with, then spread the ganache over the top and sides of the torte. Finish by sifting a layer of cocoa over all.

Note: The torte may be garnished with cocoa-dusted almonds (see below). If the cake is cut horizontally into layers and wedged with ganache, it can be cut into small squares, and each square individually iced with chocolate couverture and served as petit fours.

COCOA-DUSTED ALMONDS FOR GARNISHING CAKES

Makes 40–50 almonds

55–70 g (2–2¹/₂ oz) cocoa
4 tablespoons sugar
4 tablespoons water
4 tablespoons blanched almonds

Sift the cocoa onto greaseproof paper. Place the sugar and water in a saucepan. Bring to the boil, stirring to dissolve the sugar before the water boils (to avoid crystallisation). When boiling, stop stirring and allow the water to evaporate and turn to a pale beige caramel, then immediately add the almonds. Stir with a wooden spoon to coat the almonds well with the caramel, and cook through until they start to crackle slightly (this adds crispness).

Remove from the heat and lift out the almonds a tablespoon at a time, using a fork to knock them one by one onto the cocoa-covered paper (this stops them forming clusters). Turn the almonds until well coated in cocoa, and repeat this procedure until all the almonds are coated. Set aside to cool, then store in a sealed jar. The almonds will keep indefinitely this way.

APPLE AND PECAN NUT CAKE

2 apples, cored and sliced
250 g (8 oz) sugar
2 eggs
125 g (4 oz) pecan nuts
90 g (3 oz) plain (all-purpose) flour
90 g (3 oz) self-raising flour
1 teaspoon bicarbonate of soda
1 teaspoon cinnamon
1 teaspoon allspice
125 g (4 oz) butter
icing (confectioners') sugar, for dusting
chocolate, melted (optional)
Equipment: 1 L (1³/₄ pt) kugelhopf ring mould

Prepare the mould by greasing it with melted butter applied with a pastry brush.

Place the apple slices in a bowl; add the sugar, then the eggs, and mix well. Stir in the nuts and the dry ingredients, then melt the butter and add it. Pour the mixture into the kugelhopf mould and bake at 200°C (400°F) for 10 minutes, then reduce the heat to 180°C (350°F) and bake for a further 50 minutes, or until cooked. Leave to rest for about 10 minutes before unmoulding onto a cake rack. Serve dusted with icing sugar or pour melted chocolate lightly over the top so some drizzles down the sides decoratively.

CLASSIC ALMOND TUILE BISCUITS

Makes 12–15 tuiles

4 tablespoons unsalted butter, softened
4 tablespoons castor sugar
50 g (1¹/₂ oz) plain (all-purpose) flour, sifted
vanilla essence
1¹/₂–2 egg whites
60 g (2 oz) flaked almonds
icing (confectioners') sugar, for dusting

Cream the butter and castor sugar until light and fluffy. Stir in the flour and a few drops of vanilla essence, then add enough egg white to soften the mixture to a fairly thin 'dropping consistency'.

Drop about 2 teaspoons of the mixture onto a greased scone tray for each biscuit, and flatten with a fork or metal spatula dipped in water. Spread each biscuit into a 7.5 cm (3 in) circle (bang the scone tray firmly against the bench to help them spread). Sprinkle with flaked almonds and bake in the oven at 190°C (375°F) for 6–8 minutes, or until firm. The edges should be beige, not brown, the centre white but cooked through.

When ready, remove the biscuits from the tray. Using a metal spatula, quickly place the hot biscuits over the curve of a rolling pin or milk bottle to shape as they cool. When cold, dust with icing sugar.

HONEY MADELEINES

Makes about 12 large or 25 dwarf macaroons

90 g (3 oz) unsalted butter, softened
75 g (2½ oz) castor sugar
2 teaspoons raw sugar
pinch of salt
1 level teaspoon honey
2 eggs
90 g (3 oz) plain (all-purpose) flour mixed with
1 scant teaspoon baking powder and sifted
grated zest of 1 orange
icing (confectioners') sugar, for dusting (optional)
Equipment: Madeleine tins or a non-stick baking tray

Work the butter to a face cream consistency, then cream in the sugar, raw sugar, salt and honey. Add the eggs, one at a time, then the flour/baking powder mixture. Stir in the orange zest, then set aside for 30 minutes.

Spoon the mixture into the well-greased and floured madeleine tins (see Note). If using a non-stick baking tray, butter it well, but there's no need to flour.

Bake at 210°C (410°F) for about 5–7 minutes, or until golden. Wait a few seconds before unmoulding one by one onto a cake rack. The madeleines are at their best eaten soon after baking, though they will keep overnight in a closed biscuit tin. To serve, dust the madeleines with icing sugar (optional).

Note: Since this mixture is magically light and may stick, the best way to butter the moulds is by brushing melted butter onto them once, cooling them well in the refrigerator or freezer, then brushing on a second coat of butter and dusting them with flour before using.

WHITE MAGIC!

A meringue is simply beaten egg whites stiffened with sugar, but the addition of other ingredients, or a change in the way in which the ingredients are combined, creates a quite remarkably different texture in the end result.

In most international cookbooks there are three recognisably different types of meringue — the Swiss (sometimes known as the French), the Japanese, and the Italian. Undoubtedly the soft-centred Australian/New Zealand pavlova is quite distinct from the others, although it is rarely included in international cookbooks. So let's add it here, and review the difference between these four types of meringue.

SWISS MERINGUE

Sometimes known as *Meringue Française*, this mixture is the one to use to spoon or pipe onto baking trays for small patty-pan-sized meringues, for individual firm meringue baskets to hold cream, fruits, ice cream or chocolate sauce, for large piped circular discs for vacherins, or as cake bases. This meringue combines raw egg white beaten with sugar in the ratio of twice the weight of sugar to egg white. In order to dissolve the sugar well, it should be added during the whipping of the whites. Most recipes suggest starting to add the sugar when the whites are half mounted. Better-researched recipes suggest that a firmer result is gained by adding half the weight in icing (confectioners') sugar, which should be folded in after the rest of the sugar has been incorporated and the whipping is over. (Use only pure icing sugar, *not* soft icing sugar, which has cornflour (cornstarch) in it; and never over-stir when adding.) The only other addition to Swiss meringue is vanilla essence.

Vacherin

(Makes a 3-disc 20 cm (8 in) meringue basket, or 6–8 small ones.)
Beat 250 g (8 oz) egg whites to a firm snow with 50 g (1½ oz) sugar at the start, adding 200 g (7 oz) during whipping. After you finish beating, fold in 250 g (8 oz) sifted icing sugar and a few drops of vanilla essence. Pipe into the shape(s) required. Bake at 150°C (300°F) for 25–30 minutes for small meringues, 50–60 minutes for large discs.

JAPANESE MERINGUE

This mixture has a texture similar to nougat, owing to the ground almonds or hazelnuts. Japanese meringue, instead of being slow-cooked to stay white, is cooked faster, at a higher heat, and the external texture is thus firmer than the internal texture, making it chewy and nougat-like. Discs of this meringue, wedged together with flavoured creams or ice cream, make ideal desserts. This meringue is also the basis of Almond Macarons de Nancy and other macaroon-style biscuits.

Strawberry meringue ice-box cake

(Makes a 2-disc 23 cm (9 in) cake.)

Beat 4 egg whites to a firm snow, adding 8 tablespoons sugar, two at a time, but only after the whites are 90 per cent beaten. Whisk the sugar in well until the mixture becomes whiter, sticky and quite thick (and forms a ribbon). Change to a wooden spatula and fold in 125 g (4 oz) ground hazelnut or almonds and ½ teaspoon vinegar. Spread the mixture into two well-greased springform pans and bake at 190°C (375°F) for about 40 minutes. Wedge the meringue discs together with cream or ice cream, top with strawberries or raspberries and glaze with redcurrant jelly; or make up a variation of your own, such as a coffee-flavoured whipped cream centre and chocolate icing on top.

AUSTRALIAN MERINGUE

I add the Pavlova-style meringue here because it is more a variation of the above than of the Italian meringue which follows. It is characterised by a marshmallow centre with a beige, lightly crisped external crust. The texture is created by the addition of vinegar, or sometimes lemon juice. Cornflour (cornstarch) is another ingredient not found in the other meringue recipes, but this is not so much to change the texture as to promote a drier surface and to prevent the sugar weeping.

Traditional pavlova

Beat 4 egg whites to a firm snow, adding 250 g (8 oz) sugar, a third at a time. When stiff, add 1 teaspoon vinegar and a few drops of vanilla. Pile the mixture onto baking parchment sprinkled with cornflour (cornstarch). Bake at 190°C (375°F) for 10 minutes, then turn the temperature down to 150°C (300°F) and bake for a further 30 minutes. Turn off the heat and leave the pavlova in the oven to cool. When ready, transfer gently to a serving dish and garnish with whipped cream and fruit — most typically strawberries, kiwifruit slices or passionfruit pulp.

ITALIAN MERINGUE

This cooked meringue is made by pouring sugar syrup (of a density of 30 Baumé) onto the egg whites as they are being beaten, preferably with an electric mixer fitted with a whisk attachment. The heat poaches the egg whites and yields a glossy, soft-style meringue that is rarely used for baking, but most often used in flummery-like desserts to give them the body and texture of a mousse. It sweetens and lightens desserts and is now often combined as an alternative to the richer and heavier addition of whipped cream in modern bavarois, mousses or pastry fillings. It is also used with fruit purée in sherbets and ice creams, to lighten them. It is not a meringue in the 'cakes and biscuits' sense, but is clearly of the same genre.

To make the meringue, combine 200 g (7 oz) sugar and 60 ml (2 fl oz) water, and stir to the boil. Wait until it reaches a temperature of 120°C (250°F) (use a sugar/deep-fry thermometer to test it), then combine this syrup with the beaten whites.

The technique is to start whipping 100 g (3$^{1}/_{2}$ oz) egg whites, already combined with 40 g (1$^{1}/_{2}$ oz) uncooked sugar, just as the water comes to the boil. This way the whites are par-whipped by the time the syrup is formed. Pour the syrup in a thin stream into the egg whites after they are fully mounted. The heat of the syrup poaches the egg whites into a shape, while sweetening them — giving them a full sheen and making them more stable, and able to 'hold' longer. Continue whipping until the mixture is cool; it is then ready for use.

HINTS FOR SUCCESS

If you have trouble with meringues, here are some hints that will help you make perfect meringues, every time.

- Older egg whites beat better than fresh. Separated whites can be stored in the refrigerator for up to three weeks. They can also be frozen, but watch the containers — no water must get in as they thaw or they will not rise when whipped.
- Utensils must be clean; above all they must not be greasy or wet. Dry well any freshly washed bowl.
- An egg white's aversion to yolk is akin to not liking grease or fat. If badly separated, any yolk particles will inhibit whites from rising.
- Professionals suggest that egg whites without sugar are best beaten in copper bowls with a balloon whisk. Nothing aerates eggs with greater volume or with such a fine texture as a balloon whisk — a machine injects air too quickly and large airholes stress the protein bands of the egg whites, ruining their texture and making them 'furry'. Once sugar is part of the mixture the action required is to cream the egg whites and sugar. The machine does a better job of this as it is more capable of breaking down the sugar particles which bind the protein molecules. Meringues can certainly be made by hand, but relax, machines do a fine job, particularly good ones fitted with a wire 'balloon whisk' attachment.
- Don't ask egg whites to wait when beaten. Once made, the mixture should be formed and baked as soon as possible.
- Regardless of whether the recipe says it or not, meringues benefit from being left to cool in an extinguished oven.

ON BREAD ALONE

There doesn't seem to be a cookbook on bread that doesn't wax lyrical about 'back to nature', 'conjuring up the staff of life', or the earthiness of hands in the dough. Perhaps I'm not a romantic, but not since I made mud pies at age four have I felt poetic about getting my hands elbow deep in messy substances, picking dough out from under my fingernails, scrubbing dried flour off my hands and wiping it from my cheeks, workbench and floor.

The reason you make home-made bread is not mystical at all. You go to the trouble because the smell while it's baking is one of the greatest odours ever to travel through a kitchen and around a house. You make bread because — God help our waistlines — the taste of bread straight from the oven is the best definition I know of the word 'sublime', and you make bread because there just isn't one on the market that tastes as good as the one you make at home.

When we started a new bread course at The French Kitchen, with my bread-baking expert Cathy Gale, I saw an ideal opportunity to demystify the art of baking a great loaf of bread by taking one basic loaf, learning the technical aspects behind making it successfully, then inventing some variations. This one basic loaf became the 'one bread that is many', like my cake technique on page 204.

Bread-making is a world where many home cooks fear to tread, but Cathy's skilful guidance on the following pages can help you discover just how satisfying it can be to master a good basic bread recipe, and turn it into a myriad of magnificent loaves.

CATHY'S BASIC RECIPE FOR WHITE YEAST-RISEN BREAD

Makes 2 large loaves or 4 smaller loaves

600 ml (1 pt) water
35 g (1½ oz) fresh compressed yeast
1 kg (2 lb) baker's flour (i.e. high gluten or 'strong' flour)
20 g (¾ oz) salt
semolina or polenta, to dust the baking tray

To make the dough: Pour the water into the base of an electric mixer, and crumble in the yeast (use the formula below in 'Hints' to determine the temperature of the water). Using the mixer attachment on a low speed, quickly add three-quarters of the flour, then the salt. Knead the dough on the lowest or second lowest speed for 10 minutes, adding the remaining flour if necessary — that is, if the dough appears wet or a little sloppy (see 'Hints'). Respect the kneading time, because the dough must build a little interior heat from the kneading action.

At the end of 10 minutes, check that the blend is smooth and elastic — that is, that the gluten development is good (see 'Hints'). Remove the dough from the machine. Shape it into a mound with both hands, place it in an oiled bowl, then wrap the bowl in a plastic shopping bag. Leave for 1½ –2 hours, or until it doubles in bulk.

When the dough has doubled, 'knock back' (i.e. punch the air out) and return it to the bowl for a further 1 hour. This will give a better textured bread. You may, however, choose to shape the loaves at this stage.

To shape the loaves: Knock back the dough again and roll it into a log. Divide it in half with a sharp knife or pastry scraper. (To make 4 loaves, divide the dough into 4 equal portions.) Roll each portion into a ball, tucking rough edges under the base of the ball as you go. The top of the ball must always remain on top, and the motion should always aim to keep the top of the dough slightly stretched and pulled downward, thus keeping the top round and without wrinkles. You can keep the ball round, or form it into a slight oval with your hands as you go.

At this stage, the portion can be rolled into baguettes (it will make six), or into many small bread rolls. To give baguettes a more French look, brush with the white of an egg which has been lightly beaten with 180 ml (6 fl oz) water.

Place the two loaves on a baking tray sprinkled with semolina or polenta (it's better than fine flour), allow to prove (i.e. rise) for about 40 minutes, then slash three diagonal lines across the top using a sharp blade (it is better to use a Stanley knife or razor blade than an ordinary knife, as there is much less risk of tearing the dough).

To bake the loaves: Place the tray in an oven preheated to 250°C (500°F) or shake the loaves from the tray directly onto a terracotta baking tile, already preheated in the oven (see 'Hints'). Quickly throw a dozen or so ice cubes into a small tray in the oven, to create steam. Alternatively, spray well with a good burst of water from a water spray such as those used for ironing.

Bake the loaves for 30 minutes, or until they sound hollow when tapped; if making baguettes, bake for about 25 minutes. Remove and cool on a cake rack. You may prefer to bake in oiled loaf tins, in which case remove the loaves from the tins at the end of cooking time and bake for a further 5 minutes to improve colouration on the sides and dry out the crust.

HINTS FOR SUCCESS

- Bread proves best when the finished dough has an internal temperature of between 26°C (79°F) and 30°C (86°F) — the optimum temperature being about 28°C (82°F). Under 26°C (79°F) gives a 'sleepy' dough; over 30°C (86°F) gives a quick-rising dough with an under-developed flavour. To ensure the dough is the right temperature, simply vary the temperature of the water you use to make the dough. Try these two formulas to control the internal temperature better.

For machine-made dough: Take the temperature of the room, add the temperature of the flour, then subtract the total you obtain from 64. The resultant figure will be the temperature in Centigrade at which you should add the water — you may even have to add ice to it if you live in a hot climate and take into account the heat gained from the temperature of the machine.

For hand-made dough: Take the optimum temperature (i.e 28°C), double it (i.e. 56°C), then subtract the temperature of the flour to find the ideal temperature of the water.

- By using the mixer paddle first, before changing to the dough hook for kneading, you ensure greater homogeneity of the ingredients. Good mixing is the starting point of good bread.
- Note the 60 per cent moisture content in the recipe above is really the minimum desirable. A wetter dough gives better bread, but it is somewhat more difficult to handle — try increasing the moisture up to 65 per cent. Some Italian breads go up to 70 per cent; French is usually about 63 per cent.
- To test gluten development and ensure you have kneaded enough, pull a little of the dough from the mix and see if it springs back when stretched. If it does, you have brought out the required elasticity.
- To improve the texture, flavour and keeping qualities of bread, lower the yeast content by 5–10 g (¼–⅓ oz). But expect to wait longer for the fermentation process (proving time).
- Baking the bread on a tile rather than an oven tray improves both flavour and crust. You'll need a large, unglazed terracotta tile, a good 2 cm (¾ in) thick. Season before using by placing in a low oven for 3–4 hours, then simply reheat to baking temperature when needed, remembering that tiles need a full hour to heat fully.

THE VARIATIONS

1. The simplest possible variation is to add chopped fresh herbs. Parsley, sage, rosemary, thyme, oregano, dill, basil, or combinations of these can be put in at the very beginning as long as they are finely cut. One tablespoon olive oil gives a lovely silkiness and helps keep the bread longer, too. Finely grated Parmesan or tasty cheese can also be added in this way.
2. Additions such as sun-dried tomatoes, pitted black olives and so

on, are best kneaded in by hand after the dough is finished so they don't get mashed up by the machine (thus ruining their identity and shape, but also changing the colouration of the bread). Similarly, add chopped bacon, salami or prosciutto. Olive oil works with these, too, and the bread can also be brushed with olive oil as soon as it comes out of the oven to give it a pungent flavour and sheen.

3. If using walnuts, try substituting 150 g (5 oz) — about 15 per cent — of the flour with either rye or wholemeal flour. Roast the nuts first, then knead in by hand at the end. A combination of walnuts and sultanas (golden raisins) can be made the same way. Both are excellent breads to serve with cheese.

4. To make the basic recipe into a form of spiced fruit loaf, add currants, mixed peel, raisins, sultanas, singly or in combination. The above recipe will take between 300 g (9$^{1}/_{2}$ oz) and 500 g (1 lb) of fruit. The mixture can be sweetened with 1–2 tablespoons honey or sugar if necessary, and is at its best with a dessertspoon of powdered cinnamon and a pinch of powdered cloves. A touch of pepper is surprisingly good, too.

ON THE PATH TO SOURDOUGH — A BAKER'S TRICK

Although sourdough is technically a bread made without yeast, some of its attributes can be duplicated with this fairly standard bread mixture by using a baker's trick and allowing it to develop flavour through a short fermentation process. Next time you mix up a batch of dough, try using only three-quarters of it. Reserve about 300–400 g (9$^{1}/_{2}$–12 oz), place it in a sealed plastic container and allow it to ferment, at room temperature, for up to two days (not less than one). In this time it will rise, go bubbly and smell slightly sour, then fall back to nearly its original volume. This is called 'ripening'.

When ready, return this ripened dough to your mixer (using the mixing paddle, not the dough hook), and add 250 ml (8 fl oz) water and 3 tablespoons olive oil. Mix until the dough has dissolved back into the water, then add 500 g (1 lb) flour and a teaspoon of salt. When a soft dough forms, change to the dough hook and knead for 6–8 minutes, then place on lightly floured board and shape. Allow the dough to rise until it has doubled in bulk (about 1$^{1}/_{2}$ hours), then slash three diagonal lines across the top. The bread can now be baked in the same way as a white bread, with any of the additions mentioned above. Olive or sun-dried tomatoes make delicious additions to this bread. **Note:** If using sweet additions — currants, raisins, dried pear or apple, etc. — omit the olive oil and use 290 ml (9$^{1}/_{2}$ fl oz) water.

PAIN DE GRUAU

A white French bread, made with strong bakers' flour. I've had the luck to be taught how to make some great breads by a few chefs who are naturals when it comes to baking. One is Meilleur Ouvrier de France pastry-smith Joël Bellouet, who was France's Pâtissier of the Year in 1994. He taught me how to make this basic French cottage loaf, now a staple in our house.

Makes 2 round loaves or
1 larger oval plus 1 smaller round loaf

600 ml (1 pt) water
20 g (³/₄ oz) compressed yeast
2 teaspoons gluten flour (available from bread or health food shops)
25 g (1 oz) salt
1 kg (2 lb) bakers' flour

Equipment: thermometer; electric mixer with dough hook or food processor; large greased baking tray or pizza stone

Using the formula on page 216, determine what temperature the water should be. In some cases you will be adding warm water, in others you may need to add iced water. Use the thermometer to ensure the water is the correct temperature.

In the base of an electric mixer fitted with a dough hook, or a food processor, put 60 ml (2 fl oz) water and the crumbled yeast. Mix the gluten and salt with the flour, then place the mixture in the mixing.

Beat at medium speed for about 8–9 minutes; 4 if using a food processor. The texture of the ball of dough should be fairly firm. Remove the dough and form it into a rounded shape. Lightly flour the base of the bowl, replace the dough, cover with a damp tea towel, and leave for 3 hours to prove (rise). (If you prefer the dough to prove in 2 hours, increase the yeast to 25 g (1 oz), but longer proving gives a more flavoursome bread.)

After 3 hours, the dough should have doubled in size. Divide it into two and form round or oval loaves by balling the dough on a floured board, always stretching the dough from the top downwards, and tucking all ragged edges underneath the ball. This will give a smooth finish to the top of the loaf.

Place the loaves on a greased baking tray or pizza stone. Brush the top with water, then spread a thickly heaped layer of flour on top. Slash diamond patterns on top with a razor blade or Stanley knife, then leave to rise for a further 30 minutes. Place the bread and a small bowl of water (or a few ice cubes) in an oven preheated to 250°C (500°F) and bake for 30–35 minutes.

For the best crust, spray inside the oven twice with a mist of water (page 214) — at the start, then near the end of cooking time. The bread is cooked when it sounds hollow when you tap it, but you must leave it for a little longer if you prefer it a darker brown. Allow it to cool on a cake rack before serving.

ROSEMARY, BLACK OLIVE AND SUN-DRIED TOMATO BREAD

One chef definitely inclined to wax lyrical about being close to nature as you knead bread is Danish chef Mogens Bay Esbensen. In the many years of our friendship I have never seen Mogens write bread on a shopping list — only yeast. One night he produced this magic combination of flavours in this simple yeasted bread. As always, he was happy that I pass it on.

<u>Makes 1 x 28 cm (11 in) oval loaf</u>

500 g (1 lb) plain flour
2 tablespoons fresh yeast dissolved in a little lukewarm water
1 tablespoon sugar
300 ml (10 fl oz) tepid water
1 tablespoon coarsely chopped black olives
2 tablespoons coarsely chopped sun-dried tomatoes
1 scant tablespoon fresh rosemary leaves
1 tablespoon Maldon or other flaked sea salt
1 tablespoon olive oil

Place about 450 g (15 oz) flour in a bowl. Make a well (hole) in the centre and stir in the dissolved yeast, then the sugar, then the tepid water. Blend well, then upturn onto a floured board and start to knead, gradually adding more flour as necessary so that the dough becomes a light, elastic, not-too-sticky ball. As you knead, incorporate the olives, sun-dried tomatoes, rosemary leaves and 1 teaspoon salt. Lightly oil the bowl, then return the kneaded ball to the bowl, cover with a cloth and allow to rise until doubled in size. This should take about 1–1¹/₂ hours, depending on the warmth of the room.

When the dough has doubled in size, transfer it to a floured board and punch it down to rid it of air bubbles. Shape it into a ball and place it on a greased oven tray (or pizza stone). With a Stanley knife or a sharp razor blade, score a widely spaced criss-cross pattern on the top and sprinkle the remaining Maldon salt over. Wait a further 15 minutes before baking.

Bake in a preheated oven at 200°C (400°F) for 25–30 minutes, or until the cooked loaf sounds hollow when you knock on it. To accentuate the crispness of the crust, spray the oven with a mist of water as you put the loaf in, then again 5 minutes later (open and shut the oven door only for a moment, and never bang it shut), and, finally about 3–5 minutes before the end.

Variation

This recipe is very versatile. If you want to change this bread to a black olive bread, simply delete the sun-dried tomato and rosemary, and instead use about 350 g (11 oz) black olives, chopped free from their stones. Or sauté a chopped onion (1 large or 2 medium) slowly in olive oil until it is glassy and compôte-like, and fold this through the basic dough.

FOCCACIA

A simple version of Italy's famous flatbread, derived from a recipe of my friend and mentor in all things Italian, Giuliano Bugialli.

20 g (³/₄ oz) compressed yeast
250 ml (8 fl oz) warm water
450 g (15 oz) plain (all-purpose) flour
2 teaspoons salt
2 tablespoons rosemary leaves
1 tablespoon Maldon or other flaked sea salt
3 tablespoons olive oil, plus a little extra, for serving
freshly ground black pepper
Equipment: 30 x 40 cm (12 x 16 in) baking tray

Dissolve the yeast in the water. Place the flour on a board, make a well (hole) in the centre, then add the yeast water. Sprinkle the salt over the flour rather than on top of the yeast, as salt kills the yeast action. Slowly incorporate all but 3–4 tablespoons of the flour from the inside of the well. At this point the dough should be firm. Knead it for a further 15 minutes.

Sprinkle a bowl with some of the remaining flour, place the ball of dough in the bowl, then cover and rest the dough for 1¹/₂ hours, or until it has doubled in bulk.

When risen, use a rolling pin to shape the dough to a large rectangle. Place it on the greased baking tray and spread it to cover most of the tray (it will only be about 4 mm (¹/₄ in) thick). Sprinkle the rosemary leaves on top, as well as the Maldon salt and the olive oil. Allow the dough to swell for a further 30–40 minutes, then bake at 225°C (430°F) for 15–20 minutes, or until golden and crisp.

Cut into squares, drizzle with the extra olive oil, and serve immediately.

THE LAST
WORD ON . . .

STOCKS IN TRADE

People who do not understand why stocks are the basis of good sauces, soups and casseroles need only understand the meaning of one simple word — viscosity.

Stocks give richness to a sauce in the form of body and gelatinous quality, not in terms of flavour. A stock cube diluted with water is high on chicken flavour, but low on gelatinous quality and body; true chicken stock is high in natural 'gel' and a certain fatty thickness, and low on chicken flavour. Just remember that no cook asks his or her asparagus soup to taste of chicken — but to have the richness and velvety quality that is directly attributed to high quality, well reduced stock . . .

Here are the basic stock recipes I make in my own home — on rainy days and in large quantities so that they are always on hand. If a cook has to start a casserole recipe by spending hours making stock — even I would cheat. It's best to make them in advance and get them into the freezer in cartons of 300 ml (10 fl oz) and 1 L (1¾ pt).

FUMET DE POISSON

Also known as fish fumet, or fish stock.

1 onion, finely chopped
1 medium carrot, diced
1 shallot, finely sliced
a few champignons, or their parings
2 tablespoons butter
about 1 kg (2 lb) fish bones and heads (as little as the bones, heads and skins of 4 whiting will do. If the fishmonger suggests one large head, make sure that you wash it well to reduce the blood content around the gills.)
3 sprigs parsley
½ leek, well cleaned and finely sliced
a little celery, finely sliced (optional — some argue against its sweetness)
5 peppercorns
about 1.5 L (2½ pt) water, to cover
125 ml (4 fl oz) dry white wine (optional, but the acidity of a little wine helps in fish sauces)

Sweat the onion, carrot and shallot in the butter. Pile the fish bones on top, pressing a little to see how much space they really take up, then the mushrooms, parsley, leek, celery (if using) and peppercorns, and cover them by *only* 2–3 cm (¾–1 in) of water. Add the wine, if using. Bring to the boil, then reduce the heat and simmer slowly for about 20–30 minutes, skimming off any scum that comes to the surface.

Long cooking does not help fish stock, as the bones quickly give a bitter, almost steely taste to this delicate liquid. Because the stock does not cook for long, it is best to cut all the vegetables very small so that they give up their flavour in a minimum time.

Strain, then reduce the stock to the desired consistency. Fish stock can be quite gelatinous — it is good practice to have some containers stored as 'fish stock' and some as 'jellied fish stock' so you can choose according to how it will affect the recipe that it is to go into.

FOND DE VOLAILLE

The chicken stock is also known as fond blanc — white stock.
It is possible to make chicken stock with whole chickens — and indeed the Chinese and Italian methods prefer this. This method, however, is somewhat greasier and more chicken-flavoured. In keeping with the fact that the French use stocks for body viscosity (velvetiness) rather than for chicken flavour, it is more typical in France to see them made with carcasses. If you joint chickens regularly, you can save the carcass offcuts (neck, wingtip, etc) until you have three on hand — or buy them from one of the specialist chicken shops common in produce markets. Carcasses are high in gelatin, which gives a good, velvety texture to chicken stock for soups and sauces.

3 chicken carcasses, plus their wingtips and necks
2 onions, sliced
2 carrots, sliced
1/2 small turnip, studded with 2 cloves
1 stalk celery, finely chopped (optional, as it adds sweetness)
1 leek (including green part), well cleaned
3 sprigs parsley, stalks included
6 peppercorns (no salt)
1/2 bay leaf (optional)
mushroom parings (optional)
3 L (5 1/4 pt) water

Place all the ingredients in a stockpot. Bring to the boil, then reduce to a simmer and cook, uncovered, for a minimum of 3 hours. Skim off any scum that rises, particularly in the first 30 minutes.

When ready, strain through a colander into a bowl. Rest the stock overnight, then skim off the fat that has risen to the top. Reheat and strain through a fine sieve, then decant into suitably sized containers for storage.

FOND DE BOEUF/VEAU

Beef or veal stock, also known as bouillon de boeuf or fond brun — brown stock.

60–90 g (2–3 oz) margarine (not butter or oil)
3.5 kg (7 lb) beef shin bones plus at least 1 veal shank
1 kg (2 lb) gravy beef or other gelatinous cut (in the case of a veal stock, this would be veal flap belly, plus the veal shank), cut into cubes
2 large onions (keep their skins), sliced
2 large carrots, sliced
at least 4–5 L (7–8³/₄ pt) water
1 small or ¹/₂ large turnip, studded with 2 cloves
4–5 sprigs parsley, stalks included
8 peppercorns (no salt)
1 stalk celery, sliced
1 leek (including green part), well cleaned
mushroom parings

Note: Beef stock has much less gelatin content than veal, and the modern tendency is to prefer veal. However, adding a pig's trotter, a veal shank or a chicken carcass makes a difference.

Heat the margarine in a large thick-based stockpot or enamel casserole dish and brown the bones very well, but do not brown too many at once. Add the meat and continue browning. When the meat is 90 per cent browned, add the onion and carrot and continue to brown until even the edges of the carrot slices take on a caramel colour. Add enough water to cover the bones, then add all the remaining ingredients, including the onion skins. (Some people add a bay leaf and thyme or a couple of juniper berries. I find the bay leaf musty, but it is acceptable. For the rest, I prefer to make my stocks 'non-specific' so the dish they are added to can be given the desired flavour.)

Bring to the boil, then reduce the heat and simmer very, very slowly for 4 hours. The slower it simmers, the less skimming is necessary, and the clearer the stock will be. However, the stock should be skimmed at least once after the first 20 minutes and at any other time scum appears on the surface.

Strain the stock through a colander into a large bowl. Rest it overnight, preferably in the refrigerator. The next day, remove any grease that has formed on top, reheat and strain through a fine sieve, then decant into suitably sized containers for storage. At the point of reheating you can reduce some or all of the stock so as to have it in the freezer in different strengths.

Variation

Most chefs brown the bones and meat in the oven at maximum heat — about 275°C (525°F) — but if you use this method, transfer the bones and meat to the stockpot after having browned the onion and carrot (called the *mirepoix*), and then deglaze the pan with water so that the stock takes in all the colour from the sediment obtained in the oven.

BROWN SAUCES

Brown sauces are the stock-in-trade of professional chefs. The problem is that in the home they are rarely treated as separate entities that can be prepared in advance to enhance dishes. Generally we see them as gravies made in the meat's roasting tray, or as sauces made in a pan with the meat sediment after frying.

The art of deglazing a pan is not unimportant (page 133). Indeed, great, quick sauces are built this way, but the complex brown sauces are so much more than this — well-simmered, sophisticated sauces with great body and depth. Good, basic stocks with gelatinous consistency are the basis of all good brown sauces, but the clever cook can take one step more up the ladder and have an even more advanced tool on hand in the freezer — a *demi-glace*.

A true *demi-glace,* as the word itself means, is a strong beef stock reduced 'halfway to glace' (a *glace de viande* is a glassy, almost solid 'essence'), and is thickened only by reduction. The drawback of the true *demi-glace* is that it has too much jelly-like material, giving it a 'sticky-lipped' feel that it is not always pleasant. A further drawback is that the gelatine melts when heated, so the apparent thickness disappears, and the sauce does not adhere to the meat it is saucing. So, although the true *demi-glace* has been in fashion for the last two decades (since the nouvelle cuisine era, when flour thickening became unfashionable), there has been a tendency to return to the habit of slightly thickening the *demi-glace* with a touch of flour. Although still referred to as a *demi-glace*, this thickened version is, in fact, simply a lighter version of the classic Escoffier Sauce Espagnole.

DEMI-GLACE

This reinforced beef stock gives better body to sauces than reduced stock. Although strictly called a Sauce Espagnole (not a demi-glace) *when flour is added, I prefer this 'bound' version in which 1 heaped tablespoon of flour per litre is cooked into the sauce after browning meat to make a brown* roux, *but before adding the liquid. Note the parallel to the casserole. The clever cook will quickly see that the* demi-glace *method below is like making an abstract version of the casserole formula without the meat.*

*75 g (2¹/₂ oz) margarine (*not *butter, it burns)*
150 g (5 oz) beef trimmings, including muscle but no fat (These can be the parings of a beef fillet, 3 or 4 cubes of gravy beef, or mince topside. If the demi-glace *is destined to be a duck sauce, substitute the beef with duck neck, wingtips and gizzard.)*

2 onions, chopped
2 medium carrots, sliced
1 tablespoon plain (all-purpose) flour
1 L (1³/₄ pt) beef stock
300 ml (10 fl oz) dry white wine
300 ml (10 fl oz) water
mushroom parings and a little onion skin, to intensify the colour
(optional, but frequently used by chefs)
4 shallots
2 cloves garlic
1 clove
¹/₄ turnip
¹/₂ leek, chopped
1 stalk celery, sliced
2 heaped teaspoons tomato paste
large bouquet garni (parsley, thyme, but no bay leaf)
1 beef cube
salt and pepper

Melt the margarine to very hot and fry the beef trimmings until as brown as possible. Add the onion and carrot and continue to brown. Even the carrot edges must be coloured before you proceed further. The colour obtained at this point is crucial to the success of the sauce.

Add the flour and stir to make a *roux*. Add the beef stock, wine and water, then the remaining vegetables, tomato paste, bouquet garni, beef cube (to reinforce the beef flavour, not as a substitute for the stock).

Bring to the boil, then reduce the heat and simmer, uncovered, for a minimum of 2 hours, but preferably 8–10 hours. During this time evaporation will take place and the loss can be replaced by water. This act is in itself beneficial because the evaporation will have caused solids to caramelise on the edge of the pot. Brushing this down constantly and stirring it through the *demi-glace* increases both the colour and the strength of flavour.

When the *demi-glace* is ready it can be lightly salted and peppered, but for the most part the seasoning is corrected at the stage when it is made into a sauce. Strain it through a *chinois* (conical strainer) or a fine sieve, forcing it through with a whisk, to extract its full strength and all the liquid.

The *demi-glace* can be used immediately, stored for up to 5 days in the refrigerator, or frozen in tightly capped yoghurt or ice cream cartons.

THICKENERS

When a student once asked what I thought was a basic question about a flour and butter *roux*, I realised just how little understanding there is of the nature of the 'thickening' processes used in sauces and/or casserole cookery. So perhaps this rather technical treatise will serve you well, and help you avoid taking a trial and error approach to great sauces and casseroles.

The most obvious thickeners available in our kitchens are flour and starches such as cornflour (cornstarch), arrowroot, potato and rice flour, as well as the less frequently thought of egg yolks and butter.

There is also the simplest of all methods of thickening a sauce — reducing it by boiling and evaporating the moisture content. This in itself is often enough to reduce a meaty, gelatinous sauce, *demi-glace* or casserole liquid to a consistency thick enough to be called a sauce.

All these methods are successful, but they are markedly different and have differing drawbacks. A little knowledge and understanding will help you choose the right one for the right occasion.

FLOUR

Plain (all-purpose) wheat flour, which contains starch, is the most frequently used thickener in sauces and casseroles. Flour is also used in the classical French *roux*, and in *beurre manié* (see page 229).

A *roux* is made by blending more or less equal quantities of flour and melted fat and cooking for a few minutes — forming the base on which a sauce or casserole is built. The modern tendency is to unbalance a *roux* in favour of the fat — using a little more fat (usually butter or margarine) than flour. A *roux* may be cooked to various stages: a white *roux* is cooked only enough to eliminate the raw starch taste (so essential and yet so often forgotten when making simple white sauces such as béchamel or velouté), a 'blonde' *roux* is cooked until it attains a light straw colour, while a brown *roux* is cooked to a hazelnut colour, the colour desired for winter casseroles or brown-sauced dishes.

When dry heat is applied to starch, as is done in making a *roux*, it reduces its thickening power, since some of the starch molecules have been broken down to dextrin, a substance without thickening ability. With this knowledge it becomes obvious that you will require twice as much brown *roux* as white to achieve the same thickening. So rather than relying just on the colour obtained from browning the *roux* itself, most brown *roux* are made by first browning a *mirepoix* (finely diced carrot and onion) or some meat parings in the fat before adding the flour. This enhances the browning so essential to obtaining a good colour in the sauce without drying out the flour too much.

In the case of a casserole, the same effect is gained by browning the cubes of meat or pieces of chicken in the fat before sprinkling in the flour to form the *roux*. Compare this with the British method, in which the meat cubes are tossed in the flour first. There are two problems here: first, the meat itself never sears and seals, nor adds its own brown sediment to the sauce, and second, the flour fries in sheets, often dropping off the meat in small 'wads' that later leave lumps in the sauce. Work with the French method, please!

As mentioned above, when adding the flour for the *roux* after browning ingredients like meat or onion, it is essential to brown the *roux* flour to a light cocoa colour, otherwise the colour of the sauce will lack accordingly. Also remember that in cooking the *roux* you are ridding the flour of its starchy taste by breaking up the gluten particles. An undercooked *roux*, which is common and easily detected (less common in casseroles, where there is drawn-out cooking, but quite apparent in the much shorter cooking times of white sauces), is difficult to eliminate later in the cooking as frying temperatures — around 170° –240°C (335°–465°F)— can break up the gluten far more quickly than boiling temperatures of 100°C (210°F).

For a sauce, my recommendation is to add hot liquid to a hot *roux* — and it should be added in large quantities. By stirring briskly and continuously with a whisk (*never* a wooden spoon, which simply pushes the flour in front of it around and around the saucepan), the sauce comes back to the boil quickly, and there is no risk of lumping. This is in contrast to the frequently taught method of dribbling small quantities of cold liquids (milk from the fridge!) onto a hot *roux*, returning each addition to the boil, and repeating the action several times. Time-consuming and not as foolproof. (The method is quite different from thickening with starches such as cornflour — page 229.)

Another point to remember is that if adding sugar and/or an acid-based ingredient to your sauce, add it after boiling and thickening the mixture. Chefs commonly expect a 'backlash' or thinning action when adding wine or, in the case of desserts, an acidic juice such as pineapple, to a sauce.

As a general guideline, a *roux* based on 60 g (2 oz) butter and 55 g (2 oz) flour will thicken about 600–700 ml (20–24 fl oz) liquid to 'sauce' consistency. In a casserole with around 1.4 kg (3 lb) cubed meat, or 8–10 pieces chicken, it will take about 600 ml (20 fl oz) liquid to cover the meat. In the base of the casserole dish you'll need to start with about 60 g (2 oz) butter, margarine or oil and, after browning, sprinkle in two heaped tablespoons of flour, work it to the bottom and brown until it sticks to the base of the dish, where it will lift off little by little into the sauce. When removing the meat (with a slotted spoon) at the end of cooking, it is usual to reduce the sauce by boiling until it reaches the desired sauce consistency.

BEURRE MANIE

When butter and flour are kneaded together in more or less equal quantities, the result is another effective and popular thickener, the *beurre manié*.

Beurre manié is added to a sauce or stew after the cooking has already taken place. It is essential that the flour be well kneaded into the butter, and the best method of doing this is to knead the two together with the back of a fork in a cup or small bowl. A little is then taken onto the back of the fork, dipped into the hot liquid and shaken gently back and forth until the mixture has reached the required thickness. The *beurre manié* will not lump the sauce if the butter and flour have been reduced to a kneaded fine paste, and if the mixture is agitated until it reaches the boil again when full incorporation has taken place. Always add it in small portions, checking the thickness at boiling point to see if further additions are necessary.

Beurre manié is the ideal thickener when the mixture was better cooked without a thickener — such as when you braise meat in a small amount of liquid and prefer to avoid the possible scorching of a thick mixture in the base of the pan. It is also handy when you misjudge the original thickening and didn't add enough to do the job intended.

Beurre manié can be used to thicken soups, sauces, and so on, when you are in doubt as to how much flour to use at the beginning, or when the vegetable is not starchy enough to do the job naturally, or when further reduction of, say, a casserole sauce will render it too powerful in flavour or too salty. Most people judge the flavour of a *beurre manié* to be less offensive than cornflour (cornstarch), although other feculants, such as potato flour and arrowroot, are also good choices for the job.

COMMON FECULANTS

Cornflour or cornstarch (made from corn and wheat — read the back of the packet, sometimes 'corn' flour is a misnomer), potato flour and rice flour (and ground rice) are the starches most common in our supermarkets. Other starches include tapioca, manioc and taro starch.

These starches thicken as a result of being heated in liquid. The starch granules swell as they absorb liquid, a process known as gelatinisation. The thickening is most apparent after the liquid comes to the boil, so additions should be in small doses, and the mixture should return to the boil for evaluation before any further additions.

All these fine starches 'pack' and lump if added directly into the mixture, so they must be blended, or 'slaked', with a little cold liquid first (usually about twice their volume). The slaking mixture can be water, stock, milk or even fruit juice, as in many dessert recipes. This pasty liquid — called a 'slurry', paste or 'whitewash' — is blended in a cup or small jug, into which a little of the hot liquid to be thickened is also then stirred. It is then poured back into the soup or sauce and stirred to the boil. Be warned that the sauce may still lump if the stirring is not continued until boiling point is reached.

Sometimes, most notably when making a cake glaze from cold fruit juice, a slurry may be used to thicken liquid not yet heated. In this case, the slurry can be made in the base of the pot by using a small quantity of the liquid (or water) for the initial blending, then adding the rest, stirring the starch and the liquid to the boil at the same time. (This is the way I make chocolate soufflés.)

In either of these cases, thickening will only be achieved after boiling point is reached. Boil for 30–60 seconds to eliminate the raw starch taste and to achieve maximum thickening. To further prevent lumping, use a whisk rather than a wooden spoon. In my 25 years as a professional cook, I have never made a sauce without a whisk.

Paradoxically, it is also important not to overcook, because thinning can occur, just like the 'backlash' mentioned above caused by using acidic additions. Compare the effect of arrowroot or potato starch, which weaken at temperatures above 160°–190°C (325°–375°F) on sustained heat, with plain (all-purpose) flour, which can support a temperature of 194°C (380°F) for many minutes without giving up its thickening power.

Note that not all the starches I am grouping together here have the same effect. Cornflour (cornstarch), to me, is stronger in flavour and hence to be avoided, although many cooks use it to thicken cream sauces (I strongly prefer simply reducing the cream). It should also be noted that all starches look milky white as they heat, but potato starch and arrowroot become transparent at boiling point, and therefore are the best choice for thickening fruit juices for, say, a cake glaze.

EGGS

One of the more familiar ways in which eggs are used as a thickener is in the making of a custard (*crème anglaise*). Here the molecules of egg protein are 'de-natured' by heat and unite to form a network which enmeshes the milk and so forms a gel. Heating undiluted eggs also causes a gel to form. However, eggs must never be heated above 84°C (183°F) or yolks above 60°C (140°F), as they will poach and solidify (curdle). Thus sauces using eggs as thickeners should never boil.

When eggs are used primarily to thicken, they should be stirred with a little of the hot mixture, then returned in a stream to the original mixture, stirring all the time until thickening takes place. Remember to always remove from heat before boiling.

Curdling may be prevented by various methods: add a small amount of heated sauce to the mixture, or use a double boiler to slow the risk of scrambling, or add eggs in conjunction with flour (compare a thickened custard — *crème pâtissière* — to the *crème anglaise* spoken of above; the *crème pâtissière,* which has flour in it, does not curdle on boiling).

Note that stirring the eggs to break them up for addition to a sauce or soup should only be done to a smooth paste — if you beat extensively, it will incorporate a considerable amount of air, which results in egg foam floating on the surface of the mixture to be thickened.

An even more beautiful way to thicken sauces and pale (white-sauced) casseroles — and especially soups — is to blend egg yolks with cream. This delays possible curdling. Egg and cream, or egg/butter and cream additions — known as enriching liaisons — are some of the creamiest and richest additions to sauce cookery, but *per se*, must be added at the last minute, and the mixture must not come to the boil.

PUREES

A lesser-known thickening technique used by modern chefs is that of thickening or binding a sauce with the addition of vegetable purées or, to a lesser extent, fruit purées. These are easier to achieve since the introduction of the food processor and, depending on the fruit or vegetable selected, may be purées of either cooked or uncooked produce. Puréed potato is the most classic example of this type of thickener (particularly in soups), but try also puréed garlic to thicken gravy for a roast, or a purée of capsicum (bell pepper), mushroom, or any other vegetables which might add an intensity and depth of flavour to many a soup, stew, sauce or gravy.

REDUCTIONS

Reducing a sauce — that is, boiling it down to reduce the liquid by evaporation — is a somewhat obvious way to thicken it while at the same time intensifying its flavour. Since the advent of nouvelle cuisine, there has been a marked dislike of floury-tasting sauces, so reduction is the choice of most modern cooks, but there are a couple of warnings to be given:

1. Salt does not evaporate, but intensifies during the reduction; test that the mixture is not too salty before using this technique.

2. Some meaty flavourings high in gelatinous richness are simply too strong to be reduced further. When highly reduced, they become incredibly sticky and even impossibly rich. They sometimes even have a salty, bony taste that is almost repulsive — a mistake detectable in many a *demi-glace* in some restaurants. This type of sauce would be better thickened with a *beurre manié*.

Neither extreme is correct, however — perfect sauces should never be gluggy from too much flour, never so thin that they drop to the base of the plate without adhering to (napping) the product they are supposed to sauce, and never, absolutely never, should the flavour of the thickener be obvious.

THE FEAR OF FRYING

Complicated cuisine can make for grand occasions and spectacular dinner parties, but the more I dine the more I believe that the simpler things are the hardest to make. This certainly seems to apply to fish and chips. True fish and chips — when the chips are crispy and the batter on the fish is light, fluffy and crunchy — are undoubtedly a thing of beauty, but oh so hard to do well.

This is typical of the rather homey things that we should be able to cook, but can't always succeed with as we'd like. Another is rice (see pages 169–70 and get better at that). I cannot count the number of students who have asked me how to get rice right. Another, funnily enough, is a hard-boiled egg. And a good cup of coffee . . .

But here we'll tackle the fear of frying.

FISH IN BATTER

Fish has a high water content and is thus almost always coated in flour, even a tiny dusting of it, in order to seal in this moisture and give it a protective coating to fry crisply. Simple, tiny fish like whitebait and sardines are usually only dusted with flour (sometimes shaken in a paper bag with flour), the excess patted off, and then dropped in hot oil. Essentially, the oil should be deep enough to allow them to swim easily in the fat and hot enough to immediately seize the flour to a crisp rather than permeating the fish.

The oil

What temperature exactly should the oil be? 'Hot enough' means a temperature of about 170°C (335°F), slightly higher if you are cooking a large amount of fish because plunging a large quantity of cold ingredients into the fat immediately lowers the heat, and it can take a while to get back to frying temperature again.

Temperature depends also on the thickness of the fish — ideally the batter or flour should not brown too much while waiting for the fish to cook through. Tiny whitebait can be cooked at 180°C (350°F) because they cook instantly; thicker fillets use the more standard 170°C (335°F). You may choose to preheat to a little higher, then standardise to these temperatures during the cooking.

Testing the temperature of the oil is a must. A deep-fry thermometer is a help, but you can also test it by throwing in a couple of drops of water. If the oil is not hot the water sinks and seems to take a moment to get expelled; if it is hot enough, there is instant crackle as the oil evaporates it. Some people prefer to test oil with a chip or piece of fish — if so, the sign to look for is that it doesn't sink before sizzling: the oil should instantly bubble and sizzle around the food.

What kind of coating?

The finest coating is flour only, and it is usually used for tiny fish like whitebait, although it can be used with large fish also. Well executed, this layer should hardly be perceptible — its purpose is only as a shield and protector, and the skin should be crisp, but without any feel of a thick crust. A flour-only coating is common not only in Western cuisine, but is used regularly for deep-frying whole large fish in Chinese cuisine.

Another common coating is breadcrumb, more often used on shrimp, scallops and seafood than fish. To coat with breadcrumbs is easy for the home cook — dry the chosen ingredient with paper towelling, dip it in flour, a little beaten egg, and finally a plate of seasoned breadcrumbs. A touch of cayenne or paprika, along with more salt and pepper, gives a flavour lift.

Then there are the true batters — leavened (with yeast) and unleavened. It is easier for the home cook to coat with unleavened batter than leavened, so it often ends up the preferred method. However, the batter rarely retains its crispness for any length of time, and the dish is best eaten just as it is lifted from the frying basket.

To coat with a leavened batter is the bane of the home cook's life because, to many people, dried yeast seems difficult to reconstitute, and bakers' yeast (although readily available in health shops) can't be kept on hand as easily. Yeast batters also take time to rise.

There is a general suspicion that working with yeast is difficult, but it really only takes some understanding of technique to make it simple. Ten to one if you have eaten a brilliant piece of battered fish, it is this type of batter that has pleased you. And if you have eaten tempura in a good Japanese restaurant, then you've discovered who are the true masters at the game. Japanese batters are magnificent — generally acknowledged as the lightest and crispiest of all. Their control comes from two main things — a mixture of cornflour (cornstarch) and flour, and the use of ice at the last minute.

Following are recipes for several batters. Try them — they're not as hard as you may think! All these recipes will coat enough seafood or fish fillets for 6–8 people. Halve the ingredients if only coating one large fish.

ALL-PURPOSE UNLEAVENED BATTER

135 g (4¹/₂ oz) plain (all-purpose) flour
2 eggs
2 tablespoons peanut oil
200 ml (7 fl oz) beer or soda water
1 teaspoon salt
¹/₂ teaspoon black pepper
pinch of cayenne pepper

Place the flour in a bowl and make a well (hole) in the centre. Add the eggs, oil and half the beer or soda water. Blend together with a whisk, then thin with the rest of the beer. Season with salt, pepper and cayenne.

If you prefer, this batter is easily made in the blender or food processor; blend all the ingredients simultaneously.

Leave the batter to stand for 30 minutes (all batters are better rested, so the flour absorbs the liquid better). When ready, simply dip in the fish strips, whole fish fillets or pieces of seafood, shake off the excess, then drop into the hot oil.

Variation

When making this and other batters, some people prefer to separate the eggs, and beat and incorporate the egg whites separately to lighten the mixture. This will make the batter lighter, but not necessarily crisper.

LEAVENED BATTER

100 g (3¹/₂ oz) plain (all-purpose) flour
20 g (³/₄ oz) compressed yeast
2 tablespoons warm water
2 egg yolks
¹/₂ teaspoon salt
3–4 tablespoons warm milk
1 egg white

For sweet batter
25 g (1 oz) sugar
2 tablespoons brown rum (optional)

Place the flour in a bowl and make a well (hole) in the centre. Crumble in the yeast and add the warm water to help dissolve it. (The water should never be too hot; hot water will kill the yeast.) Add the yolks, salt and milk, and the sugar and rum, if using. Blend well, then cover the bowl with an upturned plate and allow the yeast to rise for about 1 hour. Just before using, beat the egg white to a firm snow and fold in carefully.

FRUIT FRITTERS

You may also choose to use this sweet version of the preceding leavened batter.

120 g (4 oz) plain (all-purpose) flour
2 tablespoons sugar
1 teaspoon baking powder
pinch of salt
1 egg plus 1 extra egg white
125 ml (4 fl oz) milk
¹/₂ teaspoon vanilla extract
2 teaspoons melted butter

Combine the flour, sugar, baking powder and salt. Separate the egg and set aside the two egg whites. Place the dry ingredients in a mixing bowl, and make a well (hole) in the centre. Add the egg yolk, milk, vanilla and butter. Stir in well, using ever-increasing circles to break down and incorporate the wall of flour. Whip the 2 egg whites to a firm snow, then fold in carefully.

Dip the chosen wedges of fruit in the batter and deep-fry at 165°C (330°F). Typically, banana, apple, pear or pineapple slices are good choices. Wet fruit must be dried on paper towelling before being dipped in the batter.

See also: Japanese Tempura Batter (page 89).

MARINATE IT!

The difference between macerating and marinating can be quite confusing. An ingredient is *macerated* in a liquid in order to soften it or infuse it with flavour — most often alcohol, but occasionally oil. However, an ingredient is *marinated* only in a marinade.

A marinade is also most often a liquid, but may be some form of paste made by combining spices. It may even contain alcohol, but it is normally understood to be soaking liquid of some thoughtfully combined ingredients. Therein lies the difference.

Both are used for flavour, and the marinades especially lend a hand in breaking down meat fibre and hence are particularly beneficial in tenderising the muscular structure of game.

In winter, season of stews and heavy casseroles, common marinades contain wine, chopped vegetables such as onion and carrot, and fresh herbs such as parsley, thyme and juniper.

In summer, the season of outdoor eating, the marinades and macerations that come to mind are those that give a lift of flavour to the barbecue or pan-fry. They often help caramelise and give a good appearance to grilled food — summer cooking the easy, flavoursome way. Try those on the following pages for some totally different effects. Most will macerate enough meat, chicken or fish for 6–8 people.

SOME LIKE IT HOT!

3 tablespoons coriander seed
2 tablespoons cumin seed
1 1/2 teaspoons salt
1 scant tablespoon red chilli flakes

Place the coriander and cumin in a dry frying pan and heat, shaking the pan to prevent scorching, until fragrant. Remove, add the salt and red chilli flakes, then grind in a coffee mill or food processor until you have a slightly textured powder (not dust). Use immediately or store in a screw-top jar for up to a month.

Uses
Pat onto chicken breasts or Marylands and barbecue over a well-oiled grill. The same mixture is the aromatic base for harissa, the Moroccan red capsicum (bell pepper) and chilli paste which traditionally accompanies couscous (page 147).

TERIYAKI — THE JAPANESE WAY

1 clove garlic, crushed
2.5 cm (1 in) piece fresh ginger, grated
2 tablespoons sake
4 tablespoons light (Japanese) soy sauce
2 tablespoons mirin (rice wine)
2–3 tablespoons peanut oil

Mix together all the ingredients except the oil. Pour into the base of a dish, add the chosen meat and stand for about 1 hour, turning occasionally. Remove the meat and beat the oil into the mixture. Brush the marinade over the meat and when frying or barbecuing, use remainder as a baste.

Uses

Teriyake is mostly used for beef steaks, lamb legs cut like thin steaks, and chicken. It can also be used for small pieces of sliver-cut meat in a stir-fry; in this case, use the oil only to fry, not stirred through the mixture. Add vegetables as for a typical stir-fry. Any remaining marinade can be added as a sauce base, if you like.

TERIYAKI — THE NON-CLASSIC WAY

75 ml (2¹/₂ fl oz) bottled teriyaki sauce or light (Japanese) soy sauce
2 cloves garlic, crushed or finely chopped
1¹/₂ tablespoons honey
2 tablespoons peanut oil
1 teaspoon sesame oil

Combine all the ingredients in a bowl. Add the meat and leave it for a minimum of 1 hour before cooking, turning occasionally.

Uses

It can be used for red meat, though it is more typically used for chicken, particularly wings. Both steaks and chicken fillets can be barbecued after marinating, but chicken wings are baked. After standing in the marinade, bake the wings in the oven at 200°C (400°F) for about 35 minutes, basting often to give the wings a brilliant sheen and a sticky glaze.

LIME AND COCONUT MILK ASIAN MARINADE

about half of a 400 ml (12 fl oz) can coconut milk
(use the top — the creamier part — of an unshaken tin)
juice of 3 green limes
2 small birds' eye hot red chillies, seeded and finely shredded
3 spring onions (scallions), finely sliced
6 sprigs coriander (cilantro), leaves only
1 thin piece of lemon grass, fleshy (white) part only, very finely chopped

Place the coconut milk in a bowl and stir in the other ingredients. If the lime juice is not enough to make it runny, blend in a little water. Brush the marinade on the chosen meat. Leave only momentarily before cooking as the lime 'cooks' the flesh of the meat with its acidity.

Uses

Mostly used with white meat such as chicken breast or fish pieces — white fleshy fish like ocean perch, blue eye and ling are ideal. Fish pieces can be barbecued, pan-fried in oil, or steamed in paper papillotes.

TANDOORI MACERATION (DRIED SPICES ONLY)

An Indian traditionalist would cook onion in oil with a group of spices
including ginger, cardamom, fennel, cloves, cumin and others.
But here we are talking of lazy summer cooking. The following are two
ways to make up good flavour in a simple way using pre-packaged
blended spices. The first is a dry spice method, and in the second the
spices are made into a paste with yoghurt.

3 tablespoons packet tandoori spices (your preferred brand)

Simply pat the spices onto the chosen pieces of meat or fish, or shake the pieces in a brown paper bag with the spices.

Uses

This is excellent for fish and almost any meat pieces — including chicken breasts or Marylands — destined for the barbecue. The barbecue must be well-oiled (or drizzle oil over the meat). It is also commonly used with lamb or beef pieces — simply pan-fry, add water and white wine, or water and chicken stock, and simmer, covered, until cooked. Most typically, tandoori sauces are finished with yoghurt.

Try turning small cubes of fleshy white fish fillet in the spices, then pan-frying in oil. Add some sultanas (golden raisins), chopped water chestnuts and diagonally sliced spring onion (scallion), sauté a moment, then toss into a mixture of salad greens. Make a nest of the salad on each plate. Tsop with some Indian-style fried garlic flakes, fresh mint and coriander (cilantro) leaves.

TANDOORI SPICES AS A MARINADE

2–3 tablespoons packet tandoori spices (your preferred brand)
juice of 1 lemon
3–4 tablespoons natural yoghurt

Mix all ingredients into a paste, adding water as necessary to obtain the desired consistency. Coat the chosen meat and leave to stand for about 1 hour before cooking. If the meat is in a large piece (e.g. a roast), it should be scored in a diamond pattern before marinating to allow better penetration.

Uses

Vegetables — particularly sliced potato, pumpkin and fennel bulb — as well as meat, can be coated in this mixture and then fried in oil. Chicken, lamb and squid rings are the best for barbecuing, but if the marinade is too pasty it makes for messy barbecuing — thin the paste down with a little water.

A whole leg of lamb should be left to stand for up to 3 hours in this marinade before roasting. The marinade can be quite pasty and will bake into a soft, flavoursome crust hugging the lamb, so serve it with saffron rice rather than roast potatoes.

See also: Roast Quail (page 124) for an excellent marinade for poultry and quail.

GLOSSARY

ASPIC Jelly, commonly of meat or fish, used to set and/or give a sheen to cold meats or pâtés.

BACKFAT (SPECK) Pork fat from the back of the pig, where it is not streaked with meat. Salted, it can be sliced to line pâtés and terrines of kaiserfleisch. Note that sometimes the words 'speck' and 'kaiserfleisch' are interchangeable, and speck may be meaty bacon rather than pure fat.

BAIN-MARIE Tray of hot water in which food moulds are placed to prevent rapid penetration of heat when baking.

BEURRE MANIE A paste of flour kneaded with butter. Used as a thickener after completion of cooking. Stores well under refrigeration for impromptu use.

BEARD (on a mussel) Hair protruding from edge of mussel shell. Removed when clean mussels are called for.

BLANCH (Fr. blanchir) To bring to the boil in cold, unsalted water. To remove bitterness (cauliflower, witlof and turnip); saltiness (bottled olives); and to firm flesh for easy skinning (brains, sweetbreads, tomatoes). Erroneously used to mean drop into boiling water for part cooking, particularly with vegetable cookery.

BOK CHOY Also known as baak choi, Chinese white cabbage and white mustard cabbage, bok choy is a mild, versatile vegetable with crunchy white stalks and tender, dark green leaves.

BOUQUET GARNI Bundle of herbs used to flavour simmered dishes. Includes at least parsley, thyme, bay leaf, with other herbs or a piece of celery. Fresh flavour is essential; prepared dried sachets are musty.

BRUNOISE Similar to mirepoix, but the vegetables are more finely diced.

CHINOIS Conical strainer, especially good to strain from a large vessel to a small one.

CLARIFY To render a liquid clear, brilliant. Stock: removes impurities left by meat, vegetables particles or blood. Butter: removes milk solids for better frying.

COMPOUND BUTTER (Fr. beurres composés) Butter softened and flavoured with chopped herbs and other ingredients, used instead of sauce for grills and some vegetables. Often serves as an enriching and flavouring ingredient when whisked into a sauce at the end of cooking.

CONFIT Meat, usually duck or goose, or gizzards of either, preserved in their own fat.

CORAL (Fr. corail) Orange part of a scallop. Sometimes detached and puréed to enrich scallop sauces.

COULIS An unthickened purée, commonly of fresh fruit or vegetables, used as a sauce. Can be hot or cold, cooked or uncooked.

COURT-BOUILLON Classic vegetable-flavoured poaching liquor for fish.

COUSCOUS The staple grain of north African cuisine, couscous is a form of semolina. Also used to describe the Moroccan dish.

DEEP FRY To cook in hot fat (most oils, shortening or lard) deep enough to completely cover the food being fried.

DEGLAZE (Fr. déglazer) To lift meat sediment from a pan by adding a small amount of liquid (usually wine or stock) and stirring to loosen browned bits of food on the bottom.

DEMI-GLACE Concentrated stock, sometimes thickened, made stronger with a reinjection of fresh vegetables and reduction, making it a good sauce base. Modern trend is towards veal stock. Sometimes referred to as sticky veal glaze.

DISGORGE (Fr. *dégorger*) To salt with the intention of eliminating indigestible juices. Common practice with eggplant and cucumber. Also renders sliced cucumber more flexible for use as decoration. Sometimes degorge.

FEUILLETES Puff pastry cases, of any shape.

FISH SAUCE The liquid extract from salted, fermented fish. It has an extremely pungent odour and is used as a condiment, sauce and seasoning ingredient.

FOND French generic word for stocks; also bouillon.

GRATINEE (Fr. *gratiner*) To pass under a griller — not necessarily with cheese.

HARISSA A fiery hot sauce of north African origin, harissa is usually made with chilli, cumin, coriander and red capsicum. Traditionally served as an accompaniment for couscous, it is also used to flavour soups, stews and other side dishes.

JULIENNE Matchstick-sized strips. Method of cutting vegetables, peel and garnishes such as ham or tongue.

KAISERFLEISCH German word for streaky continental bacon. Available cooked and uncooked in German butchers, continental delicatessens and good supermarkets. Uncooked is the best substitute for the French *lard fumée*. Sometimes known as speck; most speck is, however, straight fat, no meat.

KNOCK BACK To punch the air out of a ball of bread dough.

LARDONS Bite-sized pieces of thickly sliced bacon, used in quiches, or as a garnish in casseroles. In Australia, best made with kaiserfleisch.

LIAISON Method of binding or lightly thickening a sauce at the end of cooking without using flour. A simple liaison consists of beating butter or compound butter into the sauce. An enriching liaison mixes butter, egg yolk and cream together, then blends all three into the sauce.

MACERATE To bathe in alcohol; usually applied to fruit.

MARINADE The wine and vegetables etc, in which meat is marinated (*see also* Macerate).

MIRIN A Japanese wine made by fermenting rice. Very pale in colour and mild in flavour. Similar to sake.

MOUNT (Fr. *monter au beurre*) Literally, to mount in butter. A typical manner of finishing and enriching French sauces by beating in butter at the last moment.

NAM PLA (*see* Fish Sauce)

NAP To give a light coating to food, usually with a sauce or aspic.

PARE To remove the thin outer layer of foods like fruits and vegetables with a small short-bladed (paring) knife. (A vegetable peeler can also be used.)

PASSATA DI POMMODERO Italian term for puréed, fresh tomatoes, sometimes seasoned and spiced and used as a base for many Italian sauces.

PAUPIETTES Rolled meat or fish fillets, usually stuffed.

PILAF A rice- or bulghur-based dish made by tossing rice and flavouring agents such as onion and herbs in butter or oil before cooking it in stock.

PILAU   An Indian term for rice cooked using the absorption method (*see also* Pilaf).

POACH   To cook gently at a temperature under boiling point to avoid damaging delicate foods, e.g. eggs, fish, fruit. Optimum temperature is around 90°C (200°F).

POLENTA   Made from cornmeal, this northern Italian staple can be eaten hot in soft form or dried in the oven, cut into squares and fried.

PROVE   Term used to describe the action of the yeast in bread dough causing the bread to rise.

QUENELLE   A sausage-shaped dumpling, usually of fish, but also of chicken or veal. Quenelles of the Lyonnaise are choux-pastry based; modern recipes require only puréed fish, egg white and cream.

REDUCE   To boil down a mixture to concentrate the flavours.

REFRESH   To toss in cool water to stop the cooking process, a method used to keep colour in vegetable cooking.

ROUX   Combination of butter and flour basic to most sauces. Traditional recipes use equal quantities of butter and flour, the modern trend slightly undercuts the flour, thus rendering slightly thinner sauces. *Roux* can be white, straw-coloured or browned, depending on the sauce required.

SAKE   A Japanese wine made from fermented rice, sake is yellowish in colour and slightly sweet with an alcoholic content of 12 to 15 per cent.

SAUTE (Fr. *sauter*)   Literally, to make jump — the action of tossing in a hot frying medium, e.g. butter/oil.

SCALD   To heat to just below boiling point. The term is most often applied to milk.

SCORE   To make shallow incisions to aid penetration of heat or liquid.

SHUCK   To remove from shell; term usually applied to seafood.

SPECK   German word for lean pork fat, usually salted or preserved in brine to firm it so it can be cut in cubes or sliced in fine sheets (*see also* Backfat, Kaiserfleisch).

STOCK   Flavoured water made by cooking meat, poultry or fish with vegetables and other seasoning ingredients. Used as the basis for most soups and in reduced form for many sauces.

SWEAT   Waterless cooking whereby diced or sliced vegetables are tossed in butter and the saucepan covered to steam them until softened.

VINAIGRETTE   Mixture of oil, vinegar and flavourings, also known as French dressing.

ZEST   Orange or lemon peel, or oil squeezed from it, used as flavouring.

INDEX